ENTRANCE1

Entrancement

*The consciousness of dreaming, music,
and the world*

edited by

Ruth Finnegan

University of Wales Press
2017

www.uwp.co.uk

British Library CIP Data
A catalogue record for this book is available from the British Library

ISBN   978-1-78683-000-5 (hardback)
          978-1-78683-076-0 (paperback)
eISBN   978-1-78683-001-2

The rights of the Contributors to be identified as authors of this work has been asserted in accordance with sections 77 and 79 of the Copyright, Designs and Patents Act 1988.

Typeset by Eira Fenn Gaunt, Cardiff
Printed by CPI Antony Rowe, Melksham

Remembering
Alan Sell

that wise human spirit who takes us, still,
into and beyond all things earthly

Contents

Contents

PREFACE

Until I somehow found myself in the middle of this book I hadn't known that I was interested in what I call (for the moment) the experience of entrancement – extra-sensory perception, separate-togetherness. Nor did I realise that the same is probably true of countless others. Far less did I think it was, or could be, a subject of study. With a wild story-telling and 'spooky' mother from the magical land of Ireland, I should have known better – and perhaps in some reaches of the self I did.

At any rate I began at last to look more directly into the literature, and, equally, into myself. I was increasingly intrigued. I saw that in many ways it was a natural extension of my earlier interests as an anthropologist, historian and (up to a point) classical scholar: in modes of thinking, memory, multi-sensory experiencing, and, perhaps above all, in things that are known, humanly experienced, but somehow, though in plain view, *hidden*. For me these all emerged as obvious links to my earlier work. More surprisingly but even more profound, it dug deep into my interest in the human-divine arts of quoting and of communicating through allusion, myth and metaphor. This led almost imperceptibly to a more conscious exploration of the significance of dreaming – where most people first find themselves entering this mysterious realm – and of what I might call (again for the moment) the ethereal, noetic and psychic dimensions of human experience. This in turn complements my earlier discussion of quoting, that profound human mechanism for extending memory and contact across time, by some consideration of communicating – communion – across space, or, better put, beyond spatial limitations. It takes us, in some kind of Einsteinian myth, *outside* time and space into a hidden but fully existent dimension of experience.

The subject is now in many (but far from all) circles accepted as worthy of serious study. But how to pursue it, or the terminology to articulate it, is far from easy (an issue to return to in the final chapter). One way in however is, as here, to draw extensively on the findings and insights of cultural anthropology and related studies. Here, essentially from an interdisciplinary perspective, we can find ourselves in close contact with the detailed, carefully observed and unquestionably *real* experiences of ordinary people on the ground, allied – this too is needed – with the theoretical insights that link these to the more far-reaching contemporary studies of the mind and the imagination.

The volume also touches, as is necessary, on the burgeoning current research, in this area, especially that on consciousness and mental processes, research that sometimes challenges the very roots of our inbuilt preconceptions. Here we encounter thinking at the interface between neuroscience, anthropology, musicology, scientific theory, psychology and cognitive studies. And if this sounds over-ambitious, I can only say that any exploration of the core topics of the human mind, experience and imagination, and how we make contact with one another, separate but together – all that must necessarily draw something from a wide range of perspectives, inevitably transdisciplinary.

Anthropology, like history, like any truly open-minded discipline, allows, indeed encourages, its readers to treat seriously, and learn something from, unfamiliar beliefs and actions which they would normally dismiss as nonsense or at any rate to which they would attach little or no credence, whether within their own time and culture or elsewhere. Dear reader, I ask you to follow this suspension of belief and pay attention to many things strange and wonderful as you peruse this volume; and to follow the authors here in learning from these creatures and creations of, perhaps, another world.

Old Bletchley,
May 2016

ACKNOWLEDGEMENTS

I have many thanks to offer, above all to the imaginative University of Wales Press for their preparedness to take on a topic which other established presses shunned. I thank especially their truly wonderful and thoughtful reader who radically (and I *mean* radically), improved this volume, sticking with it through successive, slowly improving, versions, most significantly of all insisting on the need for a concluding chapter. I salute also all those, past and present, who have worked in this area, including those with whom I disagree (much to learn from them too), as also the many, named and unnamed, from whom I have gained in informal discussion – the Platonic dialogue lives on.

Throughout the years I have had great support from my wonderful institution, the Open University, its library and, specially, from open-minded and friendly colleagues in sociology. I must also mention, with joy, David, my husband of over fifty years, and my sceptical but ever-loving daughters. I think too that our pair of cairn terriers may have had something to do with it – who can tell?

1

'There'

Ruth Finnegan
Department of Sociology,
The Open University

Everywhere there is enchantment, it seems, everywhere the rational. In the modern West we have the achievements of science. We also have shamanic trancing, zodiac-inspired name changes, healing workshops, web prophecies of the future, birthdate predictions, all widely advertised and paid for on the internet. We have offers of help with ethereal communicating, swathes of high-selling books on dreaming, returns from death and telepathy, and wide popular interest manifested in everyday conversations once people let their guard down, and by the candid reports from the hundreds-strong Mass Observation panel.[1] There is immense interest, not always openly declared, in the nature and experience of entrancement and of entranced, altered, shared consciousness.

The normality of 'queer' experiences is reinforced when we look at current approaches to human – and other – consciousness described more directly in the concluding chapter of this volume. To some these ideas are blind alleys, misleading. To many, including myself, they are advances in insight, linking the topics of this volume and in doing so bringing new understanding of the ether, the noosphere, the beyond – call it what you will (an issue to return to in the final chapter). So much is now becoming common knowledge for those prepared to open their minds to new understandings and have the perseverance to look.

This chapter, however, shorn of documentary references, is different. As in some other chapters of this book it digs into a single case to move close and deep. The case is my own, and not easy to enunciate.[2] Like many who have tried to speak of their own unusual (but perhaps not so unusual) experience I struggle to communicate it. For a number of reasons I cannot recount all my own experiences or frame them with complete detail. But what I do say is, I promise you, fully candid. Having led, I believe, a truthful life as scholar, as human, why would I now take the trouble to lie?

The first thing to say is that I do not have the vocabulary to describe what I mean by 'there' or my experience of it. It seems to draw on some 'other' sense(s) beyond our usually recognised 'five': on dreams, visions, perhaps prophecies and certainly telepathy (what some would rather call 'extra sensory perception', 'psychic', or 'the third sense' – I myself prefer the term 'shared minds'). In discussing such phenomena we do indeed seem to reach the limits of our currently agreed linguistic resources. So to describe what to me have by now become somewhat familiar experiences, if still mysterious and not as yet understood even though they are known through my own senses, I have to go a kind of roundabout route. 'On wings of song I'll bear you', or maybe *Stille Nacht*, or in the imagery of the medieval mystical poet from Persia, Rumi:

> Out beyond ideas of wrongdoing and rightdoing
> There is a field.
> I'll meet you there.
> When the soul lies down in that grass
> The world is too full to talk about.

I struggle to express myself, but know I should do so, endeavouring through overt or, more often, implicit metaphors.

This is not because I think of these experiences as necessarily especially 'mystic' or 'exotic', closed to all but a select few. Some are, in a way. Others most certainly are not, or not anyway in my reaction to them. While to me precious, they feel to be an everyday part of the normal world. It is just that our established language does not provide us with an obvious resource for dealing with it and has not yet developed an agreed poetics for trying to capture it.

Still, I will try. And in doing so I will for the most part do my best to avoid grand-sounding abstractions and stick to what I know from my own experience. So this chapter will, unavoidably, be an informal and personal offering, doing my best.

Me

I live a very ordinary life. Typical 'retired academic', I continue to research and write; accumulate too many books; walk in the woods with my husband and dogs when my only too ordinary knee allows; chat with friends, listen to music and sometimes sing; love visiting my daughters and grandchildren. Recently I have taken up knitting again; it progresses rather slowly but is very peace-making.

Several of my academic books – my favourite ones to be honest – have, in the way of anthropology, taken something so common, so obvious, that no one has noticed it. First (1967, 1970/2012) it was the literary art of the then widely ignored, even scorned, African stories and song; then (1989/2007) the quality and ubiquity of the 'hidden' amateur musicians in my home town of Milton Keynes, that supposed 'cultural desert', soon followed (1998) by some account of the contradictory stories told about it and about cities generally (deep ingrained, seldom admitted) and by some of its amazing dwellers; next, still on the way, the never-before-told tales of taxi drivers and their lives. These books served to reveal truths that were – and are – always there; but it needed attention, insight, sympathy and a measure of committed research to notice them properly. But also – here, dear reader, is the point – they helped others to see the 'obvious', the depths that are for the moment under covers, the extraordinary in so many people's lives: hidden but always there for the looking by those prepared to see.

I hope that the same may be so of this account, incomplete as it is. Hopefully it will add a clearly first-hand set of conventionally hidden examples to those others included in a volume that consists not just of analysis and reflection but of personal, individual cases.

So, as one with some close contact, unexpected, with the liminal, the ethereal, the beyond, but without quite understanding the process, let me try. Despite my doubts (after all I am trained as a sceptical social scientist) I am in the end, I must be, a truster of evidence (that is social science too), and as a consequence am forced to take seriously what I see and hear with my own senses.

It started before I had any idea that my experiences had any parallels, except perhaps for dreams and oracles away back in classical times – but those were nothing, I thought, to do with *me* or with the here and now of the modern world! It was also before I had begun looking at the relevant literature: that was the *result*, not in any way, as might be assumed, the *cause* of what happened. And in the relatively few cases when, as you will see, my experiences were to any extent intermixed with what I had learned from others (notably my 'thatcher' dream) they invariably worked out in a different, and unexpected, way from what, from my reading, I might have expected.

That indeed has been one of the most striking features of these last three years, the one thing that I can perhaps generalise about: the constant *unexpectedness*. I have learned to (try to) resist the temptation to speculate about what will happen knowing that *that* surmise is the one thing that will *not* happen.

So I have concluded that, in spite of everything, I must take the evidence of my own senses seriously. It has not just been one occurrence, which I might dismiss, but an accumulation of happenings. At the end – I *know*.

Starting

For me the first (semi-)conscious half-awareness, not knowing what it was I could be feeling, was in New Zealand. Staying yearly with my daughter and granddaughter as I do, that land has become for me a liminal and sacred space: home but not quite home, both under and over, at once day and night, the new world of opportunity and technology that is at the same time a land of ancient magic and wisdom.

It began a few months after my recovery from a brain disturbance – an event I now think of as a kind of rebirth. Declared 'normal' again by my physicians and with no possibility, they said, of a relapse, my mind's brainwaves seemed – somehow – to be starting to grow in new directions. My first intimation, as I recall it, was faint and I was hardly aware of what was happening. But yet I somehow knew – felt – that there was something there, out there . . .

It came as I saw from my bed the sun rise over the lovely Hauraki Gulf in New Zealand's North Island, neither night nor day, when faint through the just-glimpsed or perhaps only felt and known air, I saw a dim hill far beyond (others could too, but to them it did not mean anything special). It was new to me but I knew that I had been there, or was, or would be. Or that one I loved had or would be. It came to me with great emotion, enough to break through the veil that would normally have hidden its effect on me.

Next was a dream – or was it? A poem that was suddenly, unbidden, standing in my mind when I woke in the morning. It was already complete, there, with all its sonic assonances, rhythm, rhymes, meaning, no need to change or revise it. It seemed to me, despite its 16 lines, to be a sonnet. It was about someone, beloved, travelling to me, welcome, across space. It was not until my husband pointed it out some weeks later that I recognised that the poem-song had come on the very night that he was flying across half the world to join me.

How did, do, these poems and, later, a full novel arrive in this half-dream, half-waking borderland? I do not know. It is still for me an en-tranced mysterious process. The nearest I can get to it is when you forget a word or a name and cannot, try as you will, recall it – so, sensibly, you just leave it for the unconscious or whatever to get to work. Then suddenly – there it is, standing in your mind. You know it had always been there, just something had concealed it from your conscious grasp. So it is, it seems to me, with that inexplicable forever there-ness if I could but see it when I wanted.

The next was another dream, the third event as I recall it of that momentous New Zealand borderland. This time it was self-contained and did not demand any following action – easy as that had been – of the kind I had had to undertake in transcribing my husband's poem. In the down-under world of New Zealand I sleep very sound. One night I felt a dream – or something: at any rate I was asleep. Someone was whispering a short three-word message in my right ear; then there was a time (long, short, eternal? who can tell?) of staying, then the same quiet words in my other ear, and departure. Though it was a message that pleased me I didn't feel any particular emotion when I awoke, from the – was it a dream? A moment of deep truth? I wasn't 'uplifted' or extra happy, I just went on with my usual round. But it was not something to forget.

Reflecting on those first experiences I now recognise them as the first of my knowing journey into and in the noosphere, the 'other realm', 'there', call it what you will, I had no handy name to capture it with. I say *knowing* journey . . . for of course I had, like many people I guess, experienced moments of awe at particular places, at encounters with art and poetry and, especially, music (the classic oratorios above all and singing in them – once heard who can recall without a throb the last chorus of Bach's *St John Passion*; Peter hearing the cock crow; Mendelsshon's magical 'still small voice'; or the trancing tenor opening of *Messiah*?). I had had bad dreams too, like everyone else, from which I would awake terrified, greeting with immense relief the familiar reality of the day.

Here I need to take a step backwards. For there had been one striking event about twenty years ago, a one-off I'd thought at the time, that now (not then) I recall with great emotion. I can but link it with my later experiences, its precursor in the journey between life and death, a bond of love. It concerned my mother, her known to us all as the one of the 'spooky' awareness. She had always loved butterflies, especially the humble but beautiful tortoiseshell of the woods, and several of the numinous events she wrote of in her memoirs concerned butterflies. As a child she had shunned butterfly collecting, then a common girls' pursuit, because, as she explained to us, you had to kill them first.

She died after a long illness on a Monday in August 1995, my sister wonderfully tending her to the end. On the day before, I learned later (I did not know at the time nor was I then specially thinking of her), her spirit was already leaving as her body closed down and her limbs grew cold. That morning in church I saw a huge, a colossal, tortoiseshell butterfly high in the dome. The windows up there were shut, no way in or out for a butterfly; nor, later, was there any sign of it. It was not there for long and no one else saw it.

I knew it was my mother, come to see me and give me her love.

Then, much later, it was Sally, my oldest friend. We learned Greek from scratch together, and fast (in classical languages girls always started behind); shared the same study in the sixth form; were together in the classes we attended in the boys' school preparing for Oxford entrance – an emotive time for me and perhaps her, a time for growing up and realising we were girls. After we left school she spent many months with me in my family home, studying more Greek, walking, cycling, talking, growing. My father became very fond of her, and one of my best recollections is of the three of us sitting in his sacred study in front of the cosy stove, her on the left, me centre, my father on the right beneath the lovely Holbein portrait of his revered Erasmus that now hangs in my own study. He was sharing with us his favourite Greek poem, a lovely lyric by the anciet Greek poet Callimachus, one that, unlike most, grows rather than suffers in translation:

> They told me, Heraclitus, they told me you were dead,
> They brought me bitter news to hear and bitter tears to shed.
> I wept as I remembered how often you and I
> Had tired the sun with talking and sent him down the sky.
>
> And now that thou art lying, my dear old Carian guest,
> A handful of grey ashes, long, long ago at rest,
> Still are thy pleasant voices, thy nightingales, awake;
> For death, he taketh all away, but them he cannot take.
>
> William (Johnson) Cory (Quiller-Couch 1919, no. 759)

I have loved it ever since, enjoyed the original Greek version (it has 'nightingales' too), relished the inspired translation, and from time to time look it up. But I have never been able to remember it whole. Sometimes one line, sometimes another is missing, I don't know why, as usually I am not bad at memorising.

After that I saw Sally only once before her death, in her late seventies, at a school reunion. She was still just the same – eccentric, engaging, one-of-a-kind. But we kept more or less in touch with Christmas cards, even, up to point, after her mind was clouded by dementia, always tenderly and lovingly cared for by her dear and much fitter husband. She always, I think, felt close and, though meeting so seldom, we were indeed best and oldest friends.

One Wednesday night the poem suddenly and unexpectedly stood there clearly in my mind, for the first time whole. Then I forgot about it.

On the Saturday following a phone call came through with a name I did not know. 'Are you sitting down?' 'It's Sally . . .' (I knew). 'Yes – her son. She died three days ago. In her care home, just slipped away. We went to tell our father. No answer. We broke in, we found him dead too.'

So – they waited for each other so that they could enter heaven's gate together (I still cry when I think of it, but not from sorrow: joy more like, and thankful emotion). And – how else can I see it? – my friend came to say farewell on her way there.[3]

Dreaming

Dreams again . . . like music they are everywhere, our en-trancing opening to another world.

First was the dream that is still the strongest and strangest of them all, one that I have reproduced as a turning point in my later novel. For me it had dire or miraculous results depending how you look at it, and kept coming.

I was entering a great archway with an old, trusted, friend, a great soaring dome full of awe. We were alone there, the people who had previously thronged it had by now all left. Then, the last thing I expected, I found the friend's hand on my arm transforming into something else, something ethereal, something more than just friendship. Then it ended and I woke. It was, and is, by far the most powerful dream I have ever had, more even than the dreams that later came with my novel. When it started I do not know – many years before maybe, perhaps twenty, perhaps inspired by the great dome of the then British Library. But it was long before I allowed myself to see it. I suppose I was not yet ready.

Gradually within the dream itself, perhaps only in its recurrences years later, I came to know that I was not experiencing it for the first time. After some time (how long? I do not know) I came to remember the dream in my waking life. But I was still unwilling to ponder its meaning – or meanings (for sure dreams can have many meanings): perhaps it was about someone else, the gender was the other way round, it was a sign of enmity not friendship? But then a friend's chance – chance? – remark gave me a clue and threw me into the greatest turmoil of my life, reflected, though with different outcomes, in the Africa chapter of my subsequent novel (surely no one can write a novel or, indeed, dream a dream, that is not in some way intertwined with the reality of their life).

Later, there was another dream, not recurrent but very clear in my mind. It had an unusual prelude (my dreams mostly just arrive, with no apparent root in preceding events). I was due to deliver a paper at an international conference, in Finland. An old hand by now, I generally take these things pretty well in my stride. But this was an emotive occasion for me. Not only was I standing in for a very dear friend who had just died, so wished to speak, as it were, for him, with his presence all around, but it was the first time I had spoken in public about my 'strange' personal experiences. I did cope and was kindly received, but was left exhausted and emotionally wrought. Most of all I was shattered that the friend whose unseen presence I had felt so intensely as I had been preparing myself had somehow abandoned me during my presentation. I was not only disappointed, I was *angry*!

At that point I remembered an account of telepathy that I had seen on the web. Authentic or not, it was interesting. It pronounced that sometimes someone participating from the other end, as it were, had it too easy. They thought they could just lie back, receive the other's telepathic contact, and not bother further, knowing that the other person would just hang in there regardless. Selfish! A challenge was called for! The only way to deal with it, it went on, was to cut them off. Build a barrier in your mind, they said, that very night. Picture a gate, a padlock, a locked door and *lean* on it, refusing all pleas to open. In the morning you will be exhausted, as if battered all night. But just wait. Soon you will receive a real-life contact – an email, letter, phone call, asking to meet.

As often, I was sceptical. But I had nothing to lose, so I tried. And yes, it was hard. And no, I did *not* get any earthly message in response to my demand. Clearly it was all nonsense!

But the next night or the following one I had a strong and clear dream, one of my vividest ever. The part I recall most clearly is of being with that same person, lying side by side asleep, when I was wakened by a huge wind. I asked him, as was reasonable – he was a sailor and a thatcher – to climb up and repair the thatched roof, or perhaps it was the sails of a great windmill flailing above us, surely as a sailor used to climbing the rigging in great storms he could do that . . . He refused. Very firm. 'I am not here to do your bidding, stop asking.' I knew that he was telling me – it was in character, something I should have known – 'Don't seek to control me, I make my own decisions, independently of you, of everyone.'

And then I remembered the fainter but still clear dream that had come just before on that same night. The same two of us were working together in a team, as often at the Open University where our task was to mutually criticise each other's work. In my dream he was giving me some suggestions for improving my piece, but at the same time conveying that he appreciated what I had done and that I should, fundamentally, carry on doing it my way. I knew that he too (I think it was 'he' – but in dream who can tell?) was saying, but less incisively, 'I am not seeking to control you, continue independent.'

Needless to say I was both astonished and comforted. I have tried a couple of times since when similarly angry or bereft. I have sometimes had some response, but never of that vividness or in the form of a dream – or if I have I have forgotten it (by now I have become convinced that if it is important for me to remember a dream I will do so, otherwise not; so I no longer worry or struggle to retrieve it when the fleeting dream shreds fly away from me in the morning).

Reflecting on this and other communications later, I have realised something important about what might be called telepathic communication: that it does not go beyond a person's own nature. It cannot be something that the other would not have willed in 'real life'. Or would wish you to know. However united with another, however 'en-tranced', you are still you. Also that this kind of communicating is not some once-and-for-all discrete 'message' but rather a sharing, often a kind of reinforcement, of something already there and in some measure already known.

In the last three years I have had many more dreams. I especially recall two sets, coming night after night, different but clearly part of a sequence, each going on (probably) for several weeks. These dreams were highly disturbing.

The first sequence was of dreams full of dirt – sins, faults, dire misdeeds, filthifying for both myself and others, horrifying, disgusting. I woke each time revolted. My first feeling was of relief – only a dream! My second? No, it was real. But then! Utter relief – not about *me* after all, but rooted in someone else's fear and guilt. It took a bit of time each morning to turn the personas round in my mind and to remember that gender can be changeable in dreams (I revised my recollections of some earlier ones).

I had not heard before of people sharing dreams. Looking through the literature I found occasional mentions of joint dreams by long-married couples (and have checked this from my own small investigations), but I have found nothing about having someone else's dreams. But *I* had. I knew.

This series of dreams continued for many months, and each time I woke up shaking, believing it was, as indeed in the dream it was, my own self, before again realising better. Gradually they changed. At first they were about soaking murky dirt (I wish I had made notes at the time but they were too full of disgusting filth to verbalise). As they improved they became not utter filth but dirty misplaced blood; once, I recall, it was red strawberry jam soaking into my clean white top where I had spilt it. Then in time dry dirt. Finally it was just dust in smaller and smaller amounts that I was thankfully sweeping up with a small brush into a little child-sized dustpan. And that was the end of that.

A second set followed, not this time full of horror but to me infinitely sorrowful. Again, as I woke, I knew after a few grievous moments that they were not, as in the dream, about my own actions but someone else's. He (when I awoke it seemed to be 'he'), that is, my dream self, wanted passionately to engage with life. I would go to the fair, I would enjoy myself. But in a long series of sequels, night after night, I was first (typically) unable to find the bus stop, then not the right bus stop, then it was going in the opposite direction (I'd been waiting – me again! – on the wrong side of the road), then, having at last got the right bus, I got off at the wrong place, then it was the right one – but it wasn't a fair at all. Failure again.

The following sequence started the same, but this time it was a market I was planning to visit. I got there, triumph! But I couldn't speak the language. Then when in the next dream I was able to communicate I didn't have the right currency to buy anything. Fruitless journey. In the last of that series I was going, full of anticipation, to a feast that I knew would be lovely. I got there. But the food looked unappetising, I didn't want any of it. There *was* one lovely-looking dish laid out on the buffet. Mine! But then I saw it was all messed up, someone else had already eaten part of it.

Each time when I woke I saw after a moment that it was not me after all (though I have since pondered the symbolism, for me, of that part-taken dish). And I recalled an old friend (though was the gender, the timing right?) bereaved twenty years ago who must have wished to engage once again in life – but so hard, so many aborted attempts. I was so very glad that at last those dreams had died down. Had they helped? Had 'my' disappointments led some-how to freeing the chains? Even to a life reclaimed?

Unlike some, I do not normally have the kind of prophetic pre-view dreams described in a later chapter. But I did have just one, so ordinary that it somehow carried extra credence for me, encouraging me not to be too sceptical about other strange happen-ings. One early afternoon during the sleep I now usually take at that time (but during which I seldom dream), I had a vivid picture – just a glimpse but (like the pre-dreamers I later read of) in full colourful detail. I saw a sandy path by a stream lit by bright sunlight under a gleaming blue sky. The path curved gently to the right, with trees curving beautifully over it in a distinctive pattern. I remembered it when I woke.

Later that afternoon my husband and I went for our usual walk but, unusually, went not on our normal dark-surfaced path but on a route we had never been before. He went on further while I, the slower walker, cut back by a shorter route, one I did not know. And there it was: the sandy path, the stream, sun, sky, curve, the trees' shape. It was exact, every detail.

Besides the ordinary dreams that many people have, of no particular interest (I think), I have constant dreams about getting lost. I have always had a poor sense of direction – my husband despairs – but by now have found strategies to cope, so am surprised that in the last three years I have so often had these dreams: not identical but with recurring motifs.

Sometimes it is coming out of a different exit in a large building from the one I went in, thus no longer knowing where I am. More often I am on a country walk and I find myself taking longer and longer circuits hoping to get home. Sometimes I have to cross a difficult chasm-like gulf of foaming sea or find myself on a shore about to be cut off by the rising tide. I am not too panicky for myself but worry about those at home wondering why I am so late. At last I come to a hill, not a steep one but rising gently up to an as yet unseen summit. Up there I will find my bearings. But before I get there, I wake, relieved, and then, till next time, forget. There seems little effect otherwise on my life (though perhaps it was that chasm that inspired a crucial episode in my later novel?).

One version was different, and, unlike the others, had a major impact on my thinking It was soon after my brother-in-law, very dear to me, had been encouraged, with the early signs of dementia, to go, unwilling, to a care home, a lovely one. In dream I was him. I was walking in the calm early evening by a gentle sea which I knew, somehow (why?), was in Wales. The way seemed to get longer and longer and I began to be a little anxious, not about myself, for I was loving the walk and the quiet evening air, but that those in the home would be worrying about me – people with dementia are known to get lost and need finding. I began to hasten my steps, perturbed.

Ah, there was the hill, this time with a kind of open tunnel leading upwards in the grass, uphill but not too steep. I began to scramble up it (in my waking life I know the exact spot, just above the strand where my heroine Kate fled at the start of the *Black Inked Pearl* novel). But before I could reach the top, two-thirds of the way up (dreams are so exact), I was not with myself or in myself at all but somehow in the presence of two becloaked figures (or was it wings they were wearing? angels? – even at the time I wondered). I saw them looking down at a figure lying on the ground between them at the top of the rise. They were–looking so lovingly at it (me – yes I knew it was me they were looking at and that the tunnel was the way to heaven). I heard them saying to each other with the uttermost tenderness something like

> What matter if she loses her way
> We will always be there to bring her home
> We will carry her on our shoulder
> And let her feed by the bright waters.

When I woke I had several reactions. First, immense reassurance that this compassionate message actually applied to me: it was all right to get lost, as I so often did; it was all right to be me. I was cherished, however lost (metaphorically, religiously, physically, spiritually . . .), wherever, in sin or in confusion, I found myself wandering. And from this, second, I saw that human free will was the one thing that even the Creator could not control: he had perforce (I don't quite know why) to allow his creatures freedom to go astray (later, in another short but unspeakably sorrowful dream, I felt, really *felt*, God weep for that impotence),

That dream of the hill with its summit message was immensely powerful for me, the breakthrough into my never-before-thought-of fiction writing. It gave me the final scene of my novella, *The Little Angel and the Three Wisdoms*, my first dream-inspired short story. This was the first tableau to grow in my mind and become flesh: that is, for me, to become words, my craft. There was one other intense scene in that story (that was what, in dream again, came next) but those final words were the climax. Along with Kate's self discovery at the end of *Black Inked Pearl*, they are still among the great revelations in my life.

Dreams and . . .

But I have got ahead of myself for I have not yet properly explained about my novel or the poems that after a short interval followed that first one.

First, the poems. Over a couple of years a scurry of these started arriving in dreams, often one a night, occasionally coming when I was walking alone through some en-tranced liminal space during the day – through a park, waiting for the doctor, on the stairs. They arrived complete, standing ready in their own (varied) genres with their appropriate styles and subjects.

These poems mostly seem to come into my dreaming senses first as a single word, one that is not seen, heard or spelled, just somehow *felt*, on its own. Then as I lie half awake, usually at the dead hour around two in the morning, sometimes later, I feel words grow round the edges of my mind, in my head, I can sense them there as I somehow draw them down from the ether. It feels as if there are innumerable words out there, countless like the stars (perhaps they *are* stars, for I have to wait for the right ones to fall). And then, there they are in my conscious mind: the verse divisions, the sounds, the line-end rhymes (if there are such, but not always; it may rather be internal or cross-rhymes, or assonances and alliterations scattered through the whole). Sometimes too there is a paradox or resolution for the closing cadence, and that too comes to me in the same way.

So the next morning, or later if that isn't practical, I write them down, as if from dictation. Having done so I forget them. Now, two or three years later, there are only a small handful of which I recall even the titles, and I am amazed and surprised when I read them. Though I sometimes play a little with the wording to smooth the rhythm, change a word or two to improve how it sounds, or experiment a little with the order of the lines or verses (reasonable with lyric poems as these just about all are), I otherwise make no changes. The poems are there already, not to be fiddled with, scores of them.

Apart from revisiting and occasionally slightly revising those that, I realised later, were really part of the novel, I have not kept up much contact with them recently. I know, uncomfortably, that other poems are waiting (from time to time I feel them in the night); they are *there* if I choose to capture them. But for now I am engaged with other things, so, even when I feel a complete one during the night, I refuse to pause to write it next day. In time I will return to them. I know they will still be there, and in profusion.

Then it was short stories (*The Little Angel and the Three Wisdoms*, *Wild thorn rose*), all, again, arriving unexpectedly from 'somewhere'. Though they are not in any normal sense directly by 'myself' they do reflect many of my preoccupations: my love of the Irish mountains and seaboard, my interest in the spiritual, in wisdom (the 'three wisdoms' in 'the little angel' were all, I found later, called by versions of 'Sophia', the Greek 'wisdom' – Athene, the Greek goddess of wisdom was, with my father's prompting, my favourite deity, and, at a young age, aspiration). Mine too, I think, was the perseverance against the odds that revealed the little angel's compassion and understanding in the stories (I am 'Ruth' after all), and the need, like the fieldworking anthropologist that I was and am, to accomplish the impossible of at once standing back *and* being fully involved. It was something that the angel, still at the start of his career, found hard but, like me, he did his best.

Then came several sequels, making up a little-angel series, which, as it turned out, became the story of the long quest for the self and the need to find and become at last reconciled with her – not yet quite my heroine Kate's black-inked search, but now, I see, its precursor.[4]

The stories, like the poems, also came first in dreams, but in a different way from the poems. This time it was not as a word, but as a kind of static seen tableau, perhaps better described as a somehow intensely *felt* node of knowing emotion that became the heart of each narrative. Then that started to clothe itself with words, sometimes the same night, sometimes over several, again somehow gathering from the edges of my mind. At times there was music. This took the form of hymns or carols, always with words as well as melody. The tune came first, then I struggled to unwind it to find the often startlingly fitting familiar words. On successive nights more image-feelings appeared, grew, and became transformed into that other rich medium, words. I cannot now tell how fast or slow each stage was, but certainly each story was complete within a few weeks,

Then came a momentous conversation. It was in 2014, early one May morning in New Zealand. I spent an hour on the telephone with Mark Malatesta, an American creative writing coach, or rather, to be precise, a selling-yourself-and-your-work adviser. I'm not sure what made me sign up for this one – there are so many offers – but it seems, looking back, no random chance. He liked my poetic allusive writing style, advised me on many things, but, most important of all, explained that publishers never looked at novels under 60,000 words (my longest novella so far was 3,000) and that anyway – memorable saying – 'behind every novella is a novel.'

Well, mine *was* a novel. Decided! So much for 'mystical' communication. Plenty of that, but the eventual push was that single piece of practical worldly advice.

Then and there it happened. It was as if a plug had been unstoppered by the decision, releasing into free flight a novel that was already there but I had tethered down. It was no great effort after all, or, after that single deliberate decision, any conscious act of will at all.

The dreams came thick and fast. First it was in New Zealand ('down under', how fitting), then, finishing, back in England, a chapter a night for about seven weeks in the early summer of 2014. It was not that I ever went to sleep planning or anticipating the next episode – it was always somehow, just there. But I suppose that, as with other creative projects, my unconscious was keeping at it. Neither was I feeling tired or stressed from the process but *was* frantically keeping up. It was fortunate – somehow fortuitously 'planned' yet again? – that I had had experience of, and reflected on, the process of transcribing and translating African stories during and after fieldwork. It was just like that. It was a matter of intense concentration as I wrote the transcribed words, this time by computer not hand, finding them twisting and turning in unusal spellings and collocations. Then, as with transcribing the African stories, I would forget the details as I moved on to the next one, changing nothing but hesitating occasionally for a better format in the written-down words or, as again from my field texts, for a more accurate translation.

Seven weeks – it was done, a chapter a night. forty-nine of them. I felt that for symmetry it should be fifty and looked for which chapter I could, if somewhat artificially, divide in two to achieve that. But then I saw that the fiftieth was already there. It was a short one but just what was needed, I had just been too busy to pick it up.

So there it was, a novel, *Black Inked Pearl,* 62,000 words

I am still amazed by the process. Though I had of course read about Coleridge's Kubla Khan and of dream-inspired discoveries, I had never at that point heard of such a long, sustained, process as my own.[5] And when I reread it now I am equally amazed. It does not feel like mine and, having forgotten most of it, I only recognise it in part.

Away

A year later I was walking by the sea in New Zealand. In the last few days I had been thinking, as I so often have in the last three years but now with extra intensity, of a deep hurt I had once, or so I felt, dealt a very dear friend. It was a kind of promise broken – unintentionally, unknowing. That utter grief, expressed so movingly in the song 'Greensleeves', I knew that no remorse of mine, or scarring over of the tissue, or even forgiveness, could ever wash away. It had happened. That was that. But we seemed to be drawing into a kind of shared mind, or rather, feeling ('mind' after a while becomes too intellectual a concept) and I was drawn to say something.

So a few days before, I had sent not so much an apology as an explanation of how a letter I had once written had, in my impatience for what I wanted and lack of proper care, expressed, or anyhow been read as, the exact opposite of what I intended. As a kind of validation I added a reference to a setting only one other would know. Having done so I felt emotionally wrung out – no wonder after twenty years' silence, fifty years of wounding.

No reply, nor had I expected one. How could I deserve, even need, one? My saying what I had was enough in itself.

About thirty-six hours later I was wandering through the grass beside the southern sea, thinking of other things or perhaps not thinking at all. Peaceful. The air was still and balmy. Suddenly – from nowhere – came the strong vibrating perfume of wild thyme, a scent already special to me. It surrounded me. *There.* I was immersed in it. It lasted for two of my paces, then ceased, not gradually as a scent would, but suddenly, in a flash. There was no sign of thyme around, nor could there have been on that terrain, no hint of any perfume like it. But it had happened. I knew – *knew* – then that my message had not just been heard but in its way accepted. It had meant something colossal, heaven-like in its acceptance at the other end, a revolution in a life of hurt.

It was some months later, but in my mind connected, that the number 'thirty-four' came to me as, at home now, I put one step on the stairs: up but not up, liminal. Thirty-three was there too, more faintly, but I knew it was thirty-four that was meant. Shakespeare, it must be Shakespeare. Had not the number of one of his other sonnets come to console me a few years before, almost my first message, a poem with a lovely and relevant meaning? [6] That one had proved its worth, why not now too?

I looked it up. Sonnet 34, 'Why didst thou promise . . .?' It recalled a broken commitment. I knew what that meant. The promise was an unspoken one, it is true, looked and felt, never uttered. But it was one that I felt I had broken. Forgotten. And here was a poem about one who, untypically, had trusted in a promise and ventured out uncloaked – the very metaphor, cloak, that I had previously used in thinking of it; the cross too, already in my mind. Alas to be female (and, at one point, a girl, much sought):

Why didst thou promise such a beauteous day,
And make me travel forth without my cloak,
To let base clouds o'ertake me in my way,
Hiding thy bravery in their rotten smoke?
'Tis not enough that through the cloud thou break,
To dry the rain on my storm-beaten face,
For no man well of such a salve can speak,
That heals the wound, and cures not the disgrace:
Nor can thy shame give physic to my grief;
Though thou repent, yet I have still the loss:
The offender's sorrow lends but weak relief
To him that bears the strong offence's cross.
Ah! but those tears are pearl which thy love sheds,
And they are rich and ransom all ill deeds.

And there, in it, were all those references to inner experience
and to hurts that none but two ever knew: the betrayal of a promise;
rash uncloaking of a hidden self; dark, anguished clouds. And
the everlasting scar which, even after my remorse had tried to heal
the hurt, over which so many tears had been shed, was one that
could never vanish. Not redeemed either, even by the purging in
my novel (Shakespeare surely knew of that, for was my book
not named for another of his sonnets: '. . . in black ink my love
shall still shine bright'?). And then, again, the ending, in a kind
of earned ransom in the words as I (slightly) changed them to
myself:

Ah, but thy tears are pearl that thy love sheds
And they are rich and ransom all ill deeds.

I was convinced already that the poem was uniquely borne through
the ether directly to me, only me, Perhaps it was written in the first
place for just this moment (what need of time or place or first cause
'there'?). Had I read it before? I knew I had not, I could not have
forgotten that symbolism, those sonic associations (my memory,
built up from school and university and oral story-telling, seems
to be largely auditory).

But perhaps, I thought, sceptic ever, 'thirty-four' was just a random number. Anyone could have come up with it by chance, one in one hundred and fifty-four. Unlikely perhaps, but possible. But when I thought further I remembered the fainter 'thiry-three' that had also come to me. I looked it up.

Sonnet 33, often seen as a kind of companion to no. 34, is by far the more famous, unforgettable with its echoing throbbing words:

> Full many a glorious morning have I seen
> Flatter the mountain tops with sovereign eye . . .

I had indeed read that sonnet before, even declaimed it aloud, though if asked I would have had no idea what number that or any other Shakespeare sonnet was. The accompanying notes on the web explained that Sonnets 33 and 34 are linked by the same thought, the same image. Similar indeed, I saw, though with a less resounding final couplet and, to me, infinitely less moving. I found no. 34 the more intimate, the more lovely, it was written for me. And now I knew why they came linked in my mind. Not chance.

Paths

And how, for me specifically, do I find the process of *getting* there in the here and now? Before trying to explain what 'being there' is like, let me first say something about the rather easier subject of the paths for getting there.

What I have experienced about getting there is, up to a point, common to the ways well used by many others. The practices of meditation, silence, prayer: all these seem to prepare the way; maybe to *be* themselves the way, the experience of thereness. I have never quite known what 'prayer' is, but perhaps my pleas for others or my longing for union and the end of separation, or my feeling that I can have equal, even teasing, conversations with God just like with anyone else are all part of it. It is only recently that I have thought much about 'meditation' or that fashionable term 'mindfulness', but I have now begun to read a bit about them and find that I have, perhaps because of my Quaker school experience, had a touch at practising them all along.

Then listening to great music or making it – enchanted human states – and, surely allied to these, 'trance', 'entrance-ment'. This can either be unintended or, in various human ways, induced through, for example, particular fragrances, potions, drugs, rituals – or, in my own experience, perhaps others' too, the self-forgetting focusing-down that in some mysterious way alters consciousness when making or hearing music or in the course of making a public presentation or performance. Or the undeviating concentration I sometimes know when writing or, less often, while reading (most recently parts of Andre Agassi's incredibly moving *Open*). And then for me (and for many it seems) dreams, along with music the most powerful of all, even if – no, *because* they can be at the same time a place of suffering, of remorse, perhaps eventually, as in Shakespeare's wisdom, of ransom.

And the contexts? Liminality seems to be the key here – settings that are in some way double, turning points between two states or places, in one way not quite either but at the same time partaking of both. For me it is often at home that I find myself stepping into the liminal. Almost all the specific experiences I have mentioned have come near the turning point between night and morning, three of them when I was entering or just outside one of our toilets (part but not quite a full part of the house), another as I had my foot on the bottom stair. Others have been in the familiar but always changing woods, or when travelling: ships on the sea are always special, airports too, sometimes too with their own chapels full of enchanted quietness and the signatures of passing voyagers. Many, as I say, were in New Zealand. One sweet one, of touch not words, was in a dream, sitting on a seat just off a familiar path looking down onto a (wet-dry) dried up swamp.

Sometimes, as I have said, something has just arrived with no connivance from me, like the brief stand-alone messages that I somehow just knew (don't ask me how) came from God; unexpected all, never more than seven words, most recently just one. There was nothing for me to do but hear them, seemingly no effort required on my part, not even an acknowledgement: presumably God has no doubts about his messages getting through! And then there was the unsought dreamed whisper described earlier (that one was not from God – strange that on certain things I, the doubter, am so sure).

Well, I say 'hear' because that is the nearest I can get. But actually 'hearing' would be too literal a word. It was more a matter of feeling, of knowing that I then translated into verbal language. I just *knew* what was being 'said', or rather, conveyed to me

The first occasion I was fully aware of some kind of message transfer was rather different and came early. From somewhere I would receive a vision – no, not a picture, nor a word or sound, more like a non-verbal material concept of some object that I wanted to share. Later it might become a poem but for now it was just the object: a bird, a fountain, a seashell. Gradually it emerged and took form in my mind. Then I found that I wanted and was able, somehow, to send it – to hurl it like a skimming frisbee – through space. Slowly I felt it take shape on the other side: the shell building up, ring by ring, from its outer rim; the bird flying and alighting; the water seeping, then bubbling up. I could sense it (it was not seeing, hearing or touching, just being aware) as it gathered in that other mind, no longer in my own. That ability was short-lived. I have concluded that though everyone has the potential fot some such ability, some tend more towards being senders, others receivers. In the main, I feel I am predominantly the latter, or at any rate am learning to be (perhaps in whichever case learning, as with any skill, is necessary).

Dreaming has for me been a major channel for this receiving. It is something very different from the delimited crisp messages I mentioned above. For me and, I suppose, up to a point for most people, dreams have been felt, however difficult to read or even recall, as a kind of immersing in another realm. Some of mine have in a way been simple in the sense of being single-purpose and in that sense uncomplex. These were the experiences that quickly transformed into, and emerged as, verbalised expression in the everyday light of the morning. First, as I have described earlier, poems, then, concurrently, short stories, and finally the process that for the moment took over from the others, the full novel.

None of these dreams or messages, strange as they were in some senses, did actually *feel* strange to me. I was surprised, but once I woke I felt just as normal, getting on with my usual day's work, in this case transcribing the dreams. Writing is in any case my normal pursuit, so I just carried on, the difference from my usual drafts-upon-drafts in academic writing being the relative rarity of any alterations.

But dreams and verbal messages have not been the only medium. It could be in daylight, just some ordinary thing that only I knew ('knew' again) was, like my mother's butterfly, also *extra*-ordinary. On the other hand things that to other people seemed strange, like a pigeon inexplicably appearing in our ship's drawing room in mid-ocean, I knew were in fact just ordinary, coincidental.

Often it was through something perfectly normal – but that I myself could see was extra-ordinary. Sometimes, but not always, it was something out of its usual setting and behaviour, certainly unexpected and with no explanation as to why it should suddenly appear – or perhaps why I should suddenly notice it. But at the same time I would know that it was un-ordinary because it meant something. It could be a bird in flight by the road, or flying across my bedroom window, maybe hopping past me by the Savage memorial in Auckland or on a treetop where it could show off its cocky stance. Once it was a butterfly at a time and place quite out of season, seen by another while I was out, a verification (but I knew it was for me); or a beetle or the sudden sight (but of course in the sun it had always, like the noosphere, been there) of the shadow of a beautiful piece of intricate ironwork at the foot of the steps I had struggled down below a medieval Spanish castle; or the way the strap of my daily-carried bag had somehow twisted into a cipher on the chair.

The signs manifest themselves in several senses, not just the somehow enhanced, entranced, visual and material (though they have been the commonest). Twice it was a touch on the lips (in church and in a dream), once a soft pull on my hair from some unknown hand as I lay on my front for a massage. I have often, when in distress, felt a comforting touch on my shoulders. At the launch of my novel I was sad to miss one friend's presence; but as, later in the evening, I sat waiting for my train I felt a light touch on my shoulder: three times I turned to find no one, nothing, there, no touch even of wind; so then I knew that that friend was and had been with me (time was irrelevant), supporting me all through. Another – lovely – occasion it was a soft fingertip touch on the back of both my shoulder blades, so light that it was like a spider's feet, so softly set that I did not feel it until months afterwards: and yet knew that it had been there.[7]

In these and similar cases I am pleased, and feel that I know what is happening. But I do not have any particular emotion or feeling of aura or similar 'queer' emotiveness.

Somewhat different is when in some strange way I feel a sense of another presence with me, something that I now, thinking about it, recall having encountered in several accounts of perilous journeys. I know it behind me as I walk – no perilous venture – on the moors or in the woods, so palpably close that I turn round to look or to say something. Or when my breath hastens as I lie in bed – I know someone is there, is with me.

There was a period about eighteen months ago when this feeling would hit me, shocking in its import, jerking me out of my concentration at times that were both unwelcome and totally unexpected (perhaps at the (irregular) end of someone else's working day?). For some reason that no longer happens. But there are still times that I feel some kind of call – a touch of greater or lesser force at different times. One regular occurrence, still, is when I enter my username and password on a particular computer site – *something* still happens, and not just when I'm thinking of the possibility (I sometimes am, but mostly not). I picture it as something like a bell with my name on it sounding in heaven in the way those old-fashioned Victorian bells used to ring down in the servants' quarters. Other times are unique and totally unexpected, but I know that someone is thinking of me, even if only fleetingly, unwillingly; at other times it feels more sustained and deliberate, especially when waking in the morning, I find my breath has shortend: someone is thinking of me or perhaps praying for me.

Like others I have often been moved into a feeling of the infinite through the awe of places. Who could be impervious to the sight of mountains, of a great peak in the clear sky, a flaming sunset? Or of buildings and places of ancient magic and worship – the legend-laden medieval rings on the peak of Greenan (Grianan of Aileach), a heathery walk from my native Derry; of Newgrange (Bru na Boinne), parallel to Stonehenge; of Istanbul's Hagia Sophia, greatest of human-made erections. But my recent experiences have felt to have a different quality from before (perhaps it was I who have been more open), and to partake of something wider, more permanent. Perhaps most moving, most surprising of all – but this time surely shared with many others – was visiting the soaring transitional cathedral in Christchurch hastily constructed from cardboard after the earthquake: just built but you feel the place has been sacred for ever.

Sometimes, then, attaining this touch of the infinite has been through the aura, the *mana*, of a place. This is something for which, as I now remember (but had not before taken seriously), there are many parallels, and I had of course, without really reflecting on it at the time, been moved by the mystique of particular places. In New Zealand I had what I think of as that first intimation, barely recognised at the time, of the emotive far-off hills at dawn. It happened other times that first year, and at dusk too – but, strangely, no longer. Then there were the unexpected vibes from a spot, unknown, that I passed on an Auckland train, both ways (from a place where I would one day stay?) – but only on that one train journey. That reminded me of feeling a friend's home from a train in England, not knowing exactly where it was or how it looked; then, strange again, seeing its street view on the web, just the tip of its roof, and twice, only twice, the gateway to its drive and the ancient postbox set into the grey stone wall outside: why only twice when the other showed itself so often? (I tell myself that that might just be one of the well-known idiosyncrasies of Google mapping.)

I am touched by memories of other places in New Zealand too, ones that have become highly emotional for me. There is one especially where I have often walked, unthinking then but now full of resonances: what can have happened to me there or would happen, that made it full of emotion? There are similar memories (if that is what they are perhaps they are rather anticipations, forward memories of some searing emotion there?) of places in Ireland – not, intriguingly, from the Clonmass estuary where I spent so many intense years of my childhood and after but from the strand over the hill, the vivid (to me) site of my novel's opening (I know the exact spot from which the heroine fled and the long strand she raced across). In England too, there is one place, a medieval, tree-shaded church walk near my home, just wide enough for a horse-drawn hearse. Regularly forgetting what to expect, I pass it on my evening walk to t'ai chi. But, strange, I do not feel anything as I walk back; then it is the blackbird singing from the tree as I enter our drive.

Fragrance has occasionally been the medium taking me to 'there', either in actuality, as it were, or in my memory. This surprises me for, unlike insects, we humans are not good on smells. But it was just the once, that time in a New Zealand meadow; but perhaps also, subliminally, from the thyme growing by our front door, home but not quite in, and my childhood memories of lying on wild thyme on a sea cliff in Ireland.

Most of all, though, it is through that deepest path of them all, the first and last sense known by us humans, the way of sound. It comes to me every night in classical music on the radio. Regularly I find that I have slept through the loud jangly pieces that would wake others (I can check the programme next day), but that I have wakened, however soft the music, for my loved pieces: anything by Bach, specially keyboard; slow piano by Beethoven, even more by Mozart; Schubert's 'Ave Maria' in its many versions; Mozart's 'Laudate Dominum', most beautiful tune ever; John Rutter's 'Blessings' . . . oh and much else: Handel, Purcell, Byrd, 'Greensleeves' (and I have loved you so long), and Bach, Bach, Bach.

At other times I myself seem to be the one to initiate things. Often this isn't anything like a deliberately planned session, just as if in my mind, lying in bed, I am saying a kind of 'By the way I was just thinking that . . .', reaching out to someone off-handedly ('just a chat . . .'). It's something for everyday with little that you could call mystical about it, just a conversation, a chatty interchange.

It's not spoken aloud or deeply felt, just a throwing back and forth of views or witticisms or (often) mock-insults between two friends, sometimes serious but always with a touch of humour and teasing about it – light-hearted banter you could call it.

Thinking about it I have noticed two characteristics of these relatively frequent conversations (perhaps, though irregular, an average of three or four times a week). First, they are just what they seem – everyday conversations. In this context I have learned from long experience (and I am after all also an ethnographer of language) that they have rules that lie below the level of consciousness but are for that reason all the more obligatory: about turn-taking, about avoiding offence. Those rules apply there too. If I want to barge in when the other is speaking, I am not allowed to (I know it). I must wait my turn even when the words are already clear and known in my mind (I did not know before that there were so many layers in which we can hold words; for me a new perception of language). Even when it comes to my turn, I sometimes find that there are a couple of words that would finish off my sentence, necessary to its meaning, that I hesitate over – potentially embarrassing perhaps, or too emotionally fraught. However clear in my own mind I cannot, even in this silent exchange, utter them. I usually try two or three times – I am determined, they are needed – but then have to give up. If I do force myself (an immense effort) to speak them aloud I end up truly uncomfortable.

I have stressed that these are normal conversations, free exchanges between two (or more?) people. That is true. But exactly the opposite is true too. Or so it seems. For in another way these are not really independent exchanges between two separate people at all, just a bit of fancied interchange, as anyone might do. The words, on both sides, are there in my mind or in both minds, not because he/she utters the words at the other end but because in minds with the same background, education, professional predilections, vision; we know already what the other will say. Or rather the kind of thing they *would* say, are at some time or place saying. In this sense there is no need for a conversation. And yet there it is – reinforcing and manifesting that shared mind. Though ordinary, though in general unemotional and everyday, it is still, in some way, to engage in the en-trance-ment of there.

Other times are different, intense. Achieving this second kind of togetherness is harder. But when I try I know I am at least embarking on the way and, having decided, I mostly do not give up (I'm a Capricorn after all: persevering). I call again and again, three times, more, again, again, repeating the same words. And again, intensely, emotionally, sorrowfully, it is hard to persuade myself that it is not fruitless, though often and often it feels that way. But then I recall Rumi's poem where a man, calling again and again, in despair, learns that it is not the reply from God that he should look for: the calling is the reply. Mostly after my intense effort it resolves, I am outside myself yet never more intensely myself. Not with an answer, just floating in that 'there no-where'.

How is 'There'?

How then does it feel, there? What can it be? This is so hard to describe – or even, for myself, to really know how it feels. But I will try. A long-time anthropologist and writer, I know it is good to reflect on one's experience, critically and with imagination (I love Joan's young-girl reply to her hostile interlocutors in Shaw's play: 'It's only your imagination!' Of course. That is how God speaks to us). It is in part the process itself of getting there, or trying to: the senses and routes described in the last section were indeed a necessary preliminary. 'There' seems to be the becoming, the journeying, as much as the *being* in a particular state or place. But still I will try to say a little more, and, for me but not necessarily for others, tackle this more directly.

The experiences I have tried to describe – separate, different, and yet cumulative – have for me joined to make up some kind of integrated, if not yet fully known, time-place-outside-the-spatial-and-the-temporal: 'there'. Like the light clouds wisping past, seen yet not seen but always in our sure knowledge *there*; like the separate-together notes of the quartet I heard on a ship in the Mediterranean, mid-earth sea, near the ancient middle city of

Mdina, notes that I heard at once separate and united; like the Michelangelo bronzes, always existent but only now, it seems, discovered and known – so too with the existence that I find there. Un-speak-able in easy words, by me at least, it exists beyond time and space, infinitely present. Everyone knows something of that somewhere-no-where there. For me it is standing on a mountain or a clifftop at sunset looking to the sea, the sky at sunrise as the dawn star shines and fades; moved by the intense emotion of a poem by Rumi or Blake; gazing into the heights of York Minster; seeing the innumerable Milky Way, knowing it to be made from innumerable separate: stars, suns-not-suns in clouded togetherness; feeling breath quicken at night in a mysterious presence; or, for me above all, hearing great music that moves to the depths. There. Without words . . .

In the end I suppose there can be any space that is felt by anyone (no doubt different for each) to be liminal, borderland, at once birth-and-death. In a parallel way I envisage it as a kind of place, though not a physical one – a kind of attained level of wisdom, of insight, even perhaps of dementia, struggle, breakdown, dying – and equally as a gateway between knowing and unknowing leading to somewhere beyond. The earthly settings that to me feel most like there can be a building – overtly religious or not – that has taken on something of sanctity; a gathered group that is somehow of one mind; a time of repeated chanting; a work of healing, a sacred space, a place of silence – all are gateways that we can imagine being opened for us by the Greek Hermes, messenger between gods and men, with his entrancing intertwining snakes, the double-helix sign of life and staff of en-tranced in-trance-ing healing, a making whole.

I think that all this is not a matter of getting or sending 'messages', as people tend to imagine when 'telepathy' is mentioned, but of somehow being in a somewhere-nowhere sometime-no-time that is heightned from the normal. Of being together with those with whom I commune, living or dead, in a domain that is outside time and space, suffused with souls, with music, spirituality, with what is at once sensory and cognitive, human and beyond-human. It seems a realm where I am myself, fully individual, more fully than in any other place; but at the same time feeling, knowing, that I am wholly united with others in a fusion that is greater than the sum of all those parts that make it up. What can I say about it but that this is the impossible 'there'?

In a way it is ordinary, human. Part of the time it is, necessarily, a process, a journey rather than an arrival, but still a journey to, through, in, there. It sometimes begins, as I said, with my starting things off myself: reaching out, calling. After a time – sometimes long, more often quite short (but what is time?), sometimes never – the other seems to come on the line as it were, connected as if by a kind of telephone. Good but not yet fully there. Then the line broadens, now it is a wide road, a kind of swathe through the ether. It vibrates like a violin string. And now it is the vibrations, the music of the once-narrow string, now it is wide like the sky, the heavens, embracing the universe.

And now it is no longer a connecting band, we are on it, in it, part of it, making it. And not just a two-in-one but all the souls of heaven and earth, now, before and to come, created and yet to be: more a cloud (computer-speak) of being than a one-dimensional once-at-time email link. Separate (we never lose our own selves) yet moving and still, singing and silent as one immersed (as so well comes through in a later chapter) in the flock, the swarm, the choir. It is, yes indeed, to be fully part of a wonder-realm in a sphere that is somehow beyond space and time that for want of another word we might call 'heaven'.

The band is like when, in a more moderate, less extended setting, often when half asleep, I seem to feel the wind, the earth, moving past me. It is in motion, sometimes whirling fast, more often slow and stately, passing me as I lie still. Or I am moving past *it* in motion from the other direction (but in an Einsteinian universe what is direction, what motion?), I am now the one travelling past a stationary world. I know that it is the atmosphere going past, either way, the earth and sun in mutual circling, the sun round the galaxy (in space and no-time which goes round which?), and that too round the cosmos, past me, with me. I could step off into that no-where some-where eternal ether. But for now I am content to be where I am.

Sometimes the ethereal experience comes instantaneously or unexpectedly with no apparent input from myself – other than, as a poet's or painter's experience, my whole life. It can be while reading (hearing) a poem or some lovely quotation that I have met hundreds of times but never before noticed; or a parable with a simple, familiar, ending that suddenly brings tears. Above all, as I keep saying – for it is true – it is immersion (immersion – what other word can be right?) in music.

Strangely, though all this must in some sense constitute mystical experiences, they are, as I say, everyday too. I am not out of the body or wondrously 'uplifted', and my engagement is not interrupted by small distractions. As with meditating, it is not ultimately interfered with by the wandering mind, by turning over in bed for greater comfort, even by responding to an everyday voice. I just bring my mind, my self, back again. There are no magic rituals. Just – come back and not mourn that it is too late. For it is not too late, and there will be other times. As with any other dimension of life, being there is sometimes light-hearted, joyful, sometimes sorrowful, grievous, full of remorse. Often deeply intense. Its quality is indeed greater than in other parts of life – it must be that very intensity that brings us there. But otherwise the principle is the same as in other spheres of life: are we not, wherever we are, human as well as divine, en-trance-d in the ether whether we know it or not?

So?

How could these things have happened to me? That I should sometimes rest in that mysterious field beyond time, in a way outside myself? A social scientist, a child of western culture, I must believe that these can only be coincidences, wishful thinking.

But then, student too of the insights of antiquity, I remember the Greek version, Jung's synergy, of that dismissive, Latinate word, coincidence. So I think again. And what is wishful thinking but the yearning of the soul? Is that not something to which we beings are drawn to respond? Can we be misguided to search, to feel for the wisdom of the ancients?

One of the things that draws my credence amidst my ingrained incredulity is, as I said earlier, the unexpected nature of my – let me call them – visitations. So let me return to that.

Sometimes it is the total unexpectedness of some message or appearance and what it has to tell me: words in my mind, a thought, an insight, feeling. Mostly, however, it is less the *content* of what I learn, but the unexpected *medium* of the response when I try to initiate things. I look for an email or phone call – the answer is a dream; for a dream, as when I attempted to call to my (dead) parents – the answer (and there was one – two in fact), came in music; for an object like a bird or butterfly – instead a sudden insight threw itself up in my mind; for a reinforcing, second dream or perhaps a written message – and it is a passage from the Old Testmanet that, unanticipated, I am asked to read aloud in church; for a dream or, again, an object or verbal message, intensely sought – I get an unnecessary and irrelevant email out of the blue about (what?) – apostrophes! Another time, looking for comfort in dire distress of mind, it was an unspoken, unseen, one-word explanation that I had not seen before but was now standing there before me: jealousy. On my silent cry for comfort on hearing of a dear relation's death – instantly the radio was playing the beautiful 'In paradisum' from Fauré's Requiem. Once, when rather downcast, though not deliberately seeking a response, it was a small book of short quotations that I suppose I must have bought many months before and never looked at, forgotten – and there, first thing one morning, it was lying on my desk: it had not been there the night before. And so on. How could I not be affected by the accumulation of these unexpects?

It is also the unexpected and, one might say, *unnecessary* nature of many communications (how could I not have noticed till now the origin, the literal meaning, of that word commune-ication?). Many of them came in twos. Sometimes it was through employing two different mediums, one followed by another, usually on the same day: a dream followed by an object, music by an email or a bird's flight. More often it was twice in the same medium. There were the double thatcher-teamwork dreams, the pair of comple-mentary sonnets, of vibes from different places (or sometimes the same place on a return journey), of communications in music one night from *each* of my parents in turn. In each case one experience might not have been convincing on its own, but it seemed validated by the second. Often the second was fainter or not of quite such immediate importance, a kind fail-safe mechanism perhaps if the first did not get through, or a hint to notice the first and take it seriously?

Sometimes it was both same and different. With dreams in particular I now try to work over their disparity in the mornings to see what they have In common. Oh, so *that* was the point, I might conclude. Perhaps the common theme is a journey even where the actors are totally different in the two dreams, or a failure of control, ranging in the dream, amidst a thicket of distracting details which I had to see my way through, from losing my way (again!) to driving a runaway car – in both cases *just* saved by some miraculous-seeming intervention (that perhaps being the point rather than the uncontrol?). Interpreting dreams is certainly no conclusive process. Not all have been like this: the two most powerful dream-messages have been single – though now that I consider them again, there was much *internal* repetition within them. Perhaps it is because I feel that a real effort is being put in to ensure it really reaches me and that, again, I treat it seriously..

So there you have it. Reality? the demented wanderings of an octogenarian? illusion? story-making (I'm good at that)? self-deceiving fabrication? insight? contact with a mysterious there?

Living in this world I lead a very ordinary life. Yet in its ordinariness I have encountered some of that world's, and another's, depths, its infinities, the hidden extraordinary.

Notes

[1] To be elaborated in Finnegan, forthcoming.
[2] I have, naturally, hesitated to pen this chapter, delving as it does into experiences that are both personal and sometimes deeply emotional. I fear too that some may feel that it also smacks somewhat of the narcissistic. However, in light both of the current interest in reflexive anthropology and of the volume's focus on first-hand evidence, I felt

it was insufficient to expect *others* to open up their inner experiences but refuse to do so myself. In any case what could be more primary, more close to the experienced facts, here and now, than things I had experienced in my own self? So, though not easily, I finally decided to go ahead (though how to interpret and evaluate the evidence, here and elsewhere, must in the last instance of course be left to others).

3 For a sequel and further examples see Finnegan, forthcoming.

4 I was to publish the stories, mostly under the pen name of Catherine Farrar (the name arising from part of my maternal family's history) with Callender Press, the press I founded with my mother, Agnes Finnegan, in 1992 to publish her memoirs, *Reaching for the Fruit*, which also includes the journal of her solo visit in 1929 to a Germany already showing signs of the coming Nazi rule – yet another serendipitous step in my strange journey which, unforeseen, came into its own twenty years after its first beginning.

5 Some further discussion and examples are given in the final chapter below.

6 To be detailed in Finnegan, forthcoming.

7 I have since discovered from my reading – not that these points are very widely or fully described in the literature – that all these experiences are not uncommon (further discussion and referenes in Finnegan forthcoming).

References

Farrar, Catherine (2013a) *The Little Angel and the Three Wisdoms* (Milton Keynes: Callender Press).

Farrar, Catherine (2013b) *The Wild Thorn Rose* (Milton Keynes: Callender Press).

Finnegan, Agnes (1992) *Reaching for the Fruit: Growing up in Ulster* (Milton Keynes: Callender Press).

Finnegan, Ruth (1967) *Limba Stories and Story-Telling* (Oxford: Clarendon Press).

Finnegan, Ruth (1970/2012) *Oral Literature in Africa* (Oxford: Clarendon Press; Cambridge: Open Book).

Finnegan, Ruth (1989/2007) *The Hidden Musicians*, Lives of Milton Keynes, 1 (Cambridge: Cambridge University Press; Middletown, CT: Wesleyan University Press).

Finnegan, Ruth (1998) *Tales of the City*, Lives of Milton Keynes, 2 (Cambridge: Cambridge University Press.

Finnegan, Ruth (2015) *Black Inked Pearl: A Girl's Quest* (New York: Garn Press).

Finnegan, Ruth (forthcoming) *The Shared Mind: Living in Dream, Experience, and Knowledge.*

Quiller-Couch, Arthur (ed.) (1919) *The Oxford Book of English Verse* (Oxford: Clarendon Press).

2

Walking with Dragons[1]

Tim Ingold
Department of Social Anthropology,
University of Aberdeen

Facing the Facts

In the year 1620, the English philosopher-statesman Francis Bacon set out a plan for what was to be a massive work of science, entitled *The Great Instauration*. Dedicated to King James I, who had recently appointed Bacon as his Lord Chancellor, the work was never completed. In his prolegomenon, however, Bacon railed against traditional ways of knowing that continually mixed up the reality of the world with its configurations in the minds of men. If only the mind were as clear and even as a perfect mirror, then – said Bacon – it would 'reflect the genuine rays of things'.

But it is not. Cracked and deformed by flaws both innate and acquired, by instinct and indoctrination, the mind distorts the images that are cast upon its surface, by way of the senses, and cannot – if left to its own devices – be relied upon to deliver a true account of things as they are. There is but one way out of this predicament, Bacon argued, and that is by appeal to the facts. 'Those', he wrote, 'who aspire not to guess and divine, but to discover and know, who propose not to devise mimic and fabulous worlds of their own, but to examine and dissect the nature of this very world itself, must go to the facts themselves for everything.'[2]

Bacon's words have an unmistakable contemporary ring. Today's science continues to found its legitimacy upon its recourse to the data, which are repeatedly checked and rechecked in a never-ending search for truth through the elimination of error.[3] And for the most part the sciences of mind and culture, psychology and anthropology, have ridden on the back of the same enterprise.

That is to say, they have colluded in the division between what Bacon called the 'world itself', the reality of nature that can be discovered only through systematic scientific investigation, and the various imaginary worlds that people in different times and places have conjured up and which – in their ignorance of science and its methods – they have taken for reality. Where anthropologists busy themselves with the comparative analysis of these imaginary worlds, psychologists purport to study the mechanisms, presumed to be universal, that govern their construction. All agree that the realms of reality and the imagination should on no account be confused. For the very authority of science rests upon its claim to disclose, behind the home-made 'figments' that the imagination paints before our eyes, the facts of what is really there. One can of course study figment as well as fact, so as to deliver what many anthropologists still call 'emic' rather than 'etic' accounts, but to mix the two is to allow our judgement to be clouded by error and illusion. 'For God forbid', as Bacon put it, 'that we should give out a dream of our imagination for a pattern of the world' (Bacon 1858: 32–3).

I want to argue in this chapter that Bacon's injunction, which modern science has taken to its heart, has had fateful consequences for human life and habitation, cutting the imagination adrift from its earthly moorings and leaving it to float like a mirage above the road we tread in our material life.[4] With our hopes and dreams suffused in the ether of illusion, life itself appears diminished. Reduced to biochemical function, it no longer gives cause for wonder or astonishment. Indeed, for those of us educated into the values of a society in which the authority of scientific knowledge reigns supreme, the division of real life and the imagination into the two mutually exclusive realms of fact and fable has become so ingrained as to be self-evident.

The problem, in our estimation, has been one of how to reach some kind of accommodation between the two. How can we make a space for art and literature, for religion, or for the beliefs and practices of indigenous peoples, in an economy of knowledge in which the search for the true nature of things has become the exclusive prerogative of rational science? Do we suffer the imagination to persist in our midst, or tolerate its penchant for fantasy, out of a compensatory wish for enchantment in a world that has otherwise ceased to enthral? Do we keep it as a sign of creativity, as a badge of civilisation, out of respect for cultural diversity, or merely for our own entertainment?[5] Such questions are endemic, yet the one thing we forget in posing them is how hard it is, in our experience, to split the reality of our life in the world, and of the world in which we live, from the meditative currents of our imagination. Indeed the problem is the very opposite of what we take it to be: not of how to reconcile the dreams of our imagination with patterns in the world, but of how to separate them in the first place.

Historically, this separation was but slowly and painfully achieved, in the religious upheavals of the Reformation and the turbulent beginnings of early modern science, in which Bacon – along with his exact contemporary, Galileo – played a pivotal part. But the historical process is recapitulated today in the education of every schoolchild who is taught, on pain of failure in his or her examinations, to distrust the sensuous, to prize intellect over intuition, and to regard the imagination as an escape from real life rather than its impulse.

Almost by definition, it seems, the imaginary is unreal: it is our word for what does not exist. As every modern parent knows, for example, there is no such thing as a dragon. We grown-ups are convinced that dragons are creatures of the imagination. Yet most of us would have no difficulty in describing one. Having seen pictures of dragons in the books we read when we were children, and that we in turn read to our own offspring, we are familiar with their general appearance: green scaly bodies, long forked tails, flared nostrils, sabre-like teeth and flaming mouths. These monsters roam the virtual terrain of children's literature alongside a host of other creatures of similarly fictive provenance. Some of them, of course, have real zoological counterparts. While the ever-popular Tyrannosaurus rex, perhaps the nearest thing to a dragon that ever lived, is conveniently extinct, other animals – from cobras to crocodiles and from bears to lions – are still around and occasionally claim human lives.[6] Encountered in the flesh, we do well to fear them.

Their fictive cousins, however, give no cause for alarm, for the only people they can eat are as imaginary as themselves. Along with the stuff of nightmares, these creatures are sequestered in a zone of apparitions and illusions that is rigorously distinguished from the domain of real life. We calm the sleeper who wakes in terror, at the point of being consumed by a monster, with the reassuring words, 'Don't worry, it was only a dream.' Thus the boundary between fact and phantasm, which had seemed moment-arily in doubt at the point of waking, is immediately restored.

What, then, are we to make of the following story, which comes from the Life of St Benedict of Nursia, composed by Gregory the Great in the year AD 594? The story tells of a monk who encountered a dragon. This monk was restless: his mind was given to wandering and he was itching to escape from the cloistered confines of monastic life. Eventually the venerable Father Benedict, having had enough of the monk's whinging, ordered him to leave. No sooner had he stepped outside the precincts of the monastery, however, than the monk was horrified to find his path blocked by a dragon with gaping jaws. Convinced that the dragon was about to eat him up, and trembling with fear, he shouted to his brothers for help. They came running. Not one of them, however, could see any dragon. They nevertheless led their renegade colleague – still shaking from his experience – back inside the monastery.

From that day on he never again went astray, or even thought of doing so. It was thanks to Benedict's prayers, the story concludes, that the monk 'had seen, standing in his path, the dragon that previously he had followed without seeing it'.[7]

The Shape of Fear

Perhaps the monk of this cautionary tale was merely suffering from nightmares. Medieval people, however, would not have been so readily reassured as their modern counterparts by the realisation that, in their encounters with dragons and other monsters, what they had seen was but a dream. They were not, of course, so gullible as to suppose that dragons exist, in the specific sense of existence invoked by modern people when they assert, to the contrary, that dragons do not exist. It is not as though the monk, in our story, came face to face with some other creature that, with the benefit of scientifically informed hindsight, we moderns can recognise, say, as a species of reptile.

Remember that the brothers who came to his rescue saw no dragon. They saw nothing there at all. What they did see however, as Gregory's account repeatedly testifies, was that the monk was trembling. No doubt they saw the look of terror etched in his face. And yet when the monk cried out to be saved from the jaws of the dragon, his brothers understood his predicament at once. They did not react to his outburst – as the modern psychiatrist might react to the ravings of a lunatic escaped from the asylum – as the idio-syncratic, possibly drug-induced hallucinations of a fevered and unsettled mind that would be best recaptured and shut away, in solitary confinement, to avoid further contagion. Rather, they immediately recognised, in the vision of the dragon, the form of the monk's otherwise inarticulable agitation, and imperilled themselves in responding, affectively and effectively, to his distress.[8] The monk was on the point of being consumed by fear, and already felt the accompanying symptoms of personal disintegration. The dragon was not the objective cause of fear; it was the shape of fear itself.

For the brethren of monastic communities, this shape would have been entirely conventional and well known to all, drummed in through rigorous discipline of mind and body. In this training, stories and pictures of dragons and of other equally terrifying monsters were used not, as we would today, to create a comfort zone of safety and security by consigning everything that might be frightening to the realms of make-believe, but to instil fear in novices, so that they might experience it, recognise its manifestations and – through a stern regime of mental and bodily exercise – overcome it. As the manifest form of a fundamental human feeling, the dragon was the palpable incarnation of what it meant to 'know' fear. Thus in medieval ontology, the dragon existed as fear exists, not as an exterior threat but as an affliction instilled at the core of the sufferer's very being. As such, it was as real as his facial expression and the urgency in his voice. But unlike the latter, it could be neither seen nor heard save by the one who was himself afeared. That is why the monk's rescuers saw no dragon themselves. They were most likely motivated by a feeling of compassion, which may for them – in the idiom of the time – have called to mind the image of a saintly figure, radiating light. Both saints and dragons, in the monastic imagination, were concocted from fragments of text and pictures shown to novices in the course of their instruction. In that sense, to adopt the apt term of the historian Mary Carruthers (1998: 187), they were 'figmented'. But these figments of the imagination, far from being cordoned off in a domain separate from that of 'real life', were for medieval thinkers the outward forms of embodied human experience, lived in the space of rupture between Heaven and Hell.

The monk of the story was of course torn between the two. Expelled from the monastery by the saintly Benedict, the devil – in the shape of the dragon – was waiting for him outside. Rescued in the nick of time, he was led back in. Thus the story unfolds along a path of movement, from inside to outside and then back inside again. From the very beginning, we are told, the mind of the monk was prone to wandering. Indeed in a puzzling twist at the end of his tale, Gregory recounts that for all that time, the monk was following the dragon without actually seeing it. What happened when he stepped outside was a complete loss of bearings, the kind of bodily disorientation that occurs when one is thrust into a totally unknown environment. It was as though the ground had been pulled away from under his feet. He panicked, and at that moment the dragon reared up before his eyes, blocking his path. He found he could no longer carry on. So in truth, the story concludes, Benedict did the monk a good turn by throwing him out, since it led him to see – and thus to know – the dragon that he had otherwise blindly followed. For writers in the monastic tradition, as the narrative brings out so clearly, knowing depended on seeing, and both proceeded along trajectories of movement.

To understand what they meant we have to think of cognition, as Carruthers explains, 'in terms of paths or "ways"'. The medieval thinker, in a nutshell, was a wayfarer, who would travel in his mind from place to place, composing his thoughts as he went along.[9]

Dreams and Reality

I shall return in due course to the question of wayfaring. In the meantime, let me introduce another example.

Among the Ojibwa, indigenous hunters and trappers of the Canadian North, there is said to be a bird whose sound, as it swoops across the sky, is a peal of thunder. Few have seen it, and those who have are credited with exceptional powers of revelatory vision. One such, according the ethnographer A. Irving Hallowell, was a boy of about twelve years of age. During a severe thunderstorm, Hallowell recounts, the boy ran out of his tent and saw a strange bird lying on the rocks. He ran back to call his parents, but by the time they arrived the bird had disappeared. The boy was sure it was pinési, the Thunder Bird, but his elders were unconvinced. The matter was clinched, and the boy's account accepted, only when a man who had dreamed of the Bird verified the boy's description.[10] Clearly, pinési is no ordinary bird, just as the dragon is no ordinary reptile. Like the sound of thunder itself, the Thunder Bird makes its presence felt not as an object of the natural world but, more fundamentally, as a phenomenon of experience.[11] It is the incarnate form of a sound that reverberates through the atmosphere and overwhelms the consciousness of all who hear it.

Just as the monk's brethren, as they rushed outside, saw no dragon, so the boy's parents did not themselves witness pinési. But as the conventional shape of a powerful auditory sensation, it would have been entirely familiar to them. The Thunder Bird may be a figment of the imagination, but it is an imagination that has saturated the fullness of phenomenal experience.

Recall that the boy's observation, in this case, was confirmed by a dream. Bacon would have been mortified. For us moderns it is more usual, and certainly more acceptable, for dreams to be confirmed by observation. A well-known instance is the story of how the chemist Friedrich August Kekulé discovered the structure of the benzene molecule, comprised of a ring of six carbon atoms. According to Kekulé's own, admittedly retrospective and possibly embellished account – in a speech delivered during a celebration held in Berlin City Hall in 1890 to mark the twenty-fifth anniversary of his discovery – it happened one night in 1865, while he was staying in the Belgian city of Ghent. He had been up late in his study, at work on a textbook. Making little progress, he had turned his chair towards the fire and dozed off. In his reverie, atoms gambolled before his eyes, twining and twisting in snake-like motion. 'But look! What was that? One of the snakes had seized hold of its own tail, and the form whirled mockingly before my eyes. As if by a flash of lightning I awoke . . . I spent the rest of the night in working out the consequences of the hypothesis' (Benfey 1958: 22). Whatever Kekulé might have felt at the moment of waking, we can be sure that once the flash that shook him from his slumber was extinguished, the gyrating serpent of his dream was no longer an affectation of vision but an abstract figure of thought – a snake 'good to think with' – that was peculiarly apt for deciphering the structure of a given reality. Thus the serpent and the benzene ring fall unequivocally on either side of an impermeable ontological division between imagination and reality. It is this that allows the one to stand metaphorically for the other. The congruity between serpent and ring reinforces the division rather than breaking it down.

The dream-induced conjecture, however, is but a chimera until subjected to empirical test. It was in precisely this vein that Kekulé went on to advise his audience. 'Let us learn to dream, gentlemen, then perhaps we shall find the truth . . . But let us beware of publishing our dreams till they have been tested by waking understanding.'[12] Indeed, subsequent experimental work in the laboratory proved Kekulé's hypothesis to be substantially correct, and it went on to become a cornerstone of the emerging field of organic chemistry. The dream itself, however, did not. In the harsh light of day, the dream vanished into oblivion.

Thus science concedes to the imagination the power of conjecture – or, as we say, to think 'outside the box' – but only by banishing imagination from the very reality to which it affords insight. For the Ojibwa, by contrast, it would have been quite the other way around. For them, the truth of things is not only found but also tested by personal oneiric experience, which is why the boy's sighting of pinési could be corroborated by his elder's dream. In this quest for knowledge through experience, the powerful more-than-human beings that inhabit the Ojibwa cosmos, including Thunder Birds, are not analogical resources but vital interlocutors. This cosmos is polyglot, a medley of voices by which different beings, in their several tongues, announce their presence, make themselves felt, and have effects. To carry on your life as an Ojibwa person you have to tune into these voices, and to listen and respond to what they are telling you.

Another Thunder Bird story from Hallowell – admittedly one told to him by an informant – perfectly illustrates the point. Hallowell's informant was sitting in a tent, one stormy afternoon, with an old man and his wife. The thunder rolled and clapped. At once, the old man turned to his wife. 'Did you hear what was said?' he asked. 'No,' came the reply, 'I didn't quite catch it.' Commenting on the exchange, Hallowell remarks that the old man 'was reacting to this sound in the same way as he would respond to a human being whose words he did not understand' (Hallowell 1960: 34).

This was not, however, a simple failure of translation. It was not as though the Thunder Bird had a message for the old man that he failed to grasp because of his imperfect command of Bird language. 'By and large', Hallowell observes, 'the Ojibwa do not attune themselves to receiving messages every time a thunderstorm occurs.' It transpires that this particular man had, in his youth, become acquainted with the Thunder Bird through the dreams of his puberty fast, and had gone on to develop a close relationship of tutelage with pinési.[13] In the context of this relationship, listening and responding to thunder was a matter not of translation but of empathy, of establishing a communion of feeling and affect or, in short, of opening oneself up to the being of another.[14]

And it is above all in dreaming, where the boundaries that surround the self in waking life are dissolved, that this opening up occurs.

Such exposure, however, was not something that a sober scientist like Kekulé could even contemplate. For him, the path to true knowledge lay not in opening up a dialogue with beings of the more-than-human world, but in an exact and literal reading of the facts already deposited there. The investigator who would 'follow the paths of the Pathfinders', Kekulé advised, 'must note every footprint, every bent twig, every fallen leaf. Then, standing at the extreme point reached by his predecessors, it will be easy for him to perceive where the foot of a further pioneer may find solid ground' (Benfey 1958: 23). The object, as Bacon had put it, was to write a 'true vision of the footsteps of the Creator', inscribed in the works of His creation (Bacon, 1858:33). It was a matter of unlocking the secrets of nature. For that you need a key or rather several keys, to unlock door after door. Kekulé's serpent offered one such key, in the figure of a ring. In his book *The Assayer*, dating from 1623, Galileo found his keys in the characters of mathematics, in the 'triangles, circles and other geometric figures' which comprise its special language: 'Philosophy is written in this grand book, the universe which stands continually open to our gaze. But the book cannot be understood unless one first learns to comprehend the language and read the letters in which it is composed' (Galilei 1957: 237).

Of Words and Works

The idea of the book of the universe, or of nature, is of considerable antiquity, and was as current among medieval scholars as it was subsequently to become in the rise of modern science. It rested, at root, on a homology between the word of God (*verbum Dei*), in the composition of the scriptures, and the works of God, in the creation of the world and its creatures. The question was: 'how could humans read those twin books?' (Bono 1995: 11). With this, we can return to the monks of the medieval era, for whom – as I have already observed – the meditative practice of reading liturgical texts was a process of wayfaring.

Over and over again, they would compare their texts to a terrain through which they would make their way like hunters on the trail, drawing on, or 'pulling in', the things they encountered, or the events to which they bore witness, along the paths they travelled.

The word in Latin for this drawing or pulling in was *tractare*, from which is derived the English 'treatise' in the sense of a written composition. As they proceeded, the various personages whom they would meet on the way, and whose stories were inscribed on the pages, would speak to them, with words of wisdom and guidance, to which they would listen and from which they would learn. These were known as the *voces paginarum*, 'voices of the pages'.[15] Indeed, reading was itself a vocal practice: typically, monastic libraries were abuzz with the sounds of reading as the monks, murmuring the voices of the pages, would engage with them as though they were present and audible. To read, in its original medieval sense, was to be advised by these voices, or to take counsel, much as the old Ojibwa man would have been advised by the voice of his mentor the Thunder Bird – if only he had heard what it said![16]

Surrounded by the voices of the pages as the hunter is surrounded by the voices of the land, the medieval reader was a follower of tradition. In his encyclopedic survey of animals in myth, legend and literature, Boria Sax points out that the word 'tradition' comes from 'trade', which originally meant 'track'. 'To study a tradition', Sax writes, 'is to track a creature, as though one were a hunter, back through time.'[17] Each creature is its story, its tradition, and to follow it is at once to perform an act of remembrance and to move on, in continuity with the values of the past. Often, the name of the creature is itself a condensed story, so that in its very utterance, the story is carried on. But it is carried on, too, in the calls or vocalisations of the creatures themselves – if they have a voice – as well as in their manifest, visible presence and activity.[18] As a node or knot in a skein of interwoven depictions, stories, calls, sightings and observations, none of which is ontologically prior to, or in any sense more 'real' than, any other, every creature – we could say – is not so much a living thing as the instantiation of a certain way of being alive, each of which, to the medieval mind, would open up a pathway to the experience of God. And so it was, too, with the letters and figures of the manuscript which, according to Isidore of Seville, writing in the seventh century, enable readers to hear again and retain in memory the voices of those not actually present (Carruthers 1990: 106). Thus was the book of nature mirrored in the nature of the book: a second nature comprised not of works but of words (Clingerman 2009).

For Isidore, reading should be done quietly, but it could not be altogether silent since it depended on gestures of the throat and mouth (Saenger 1982: 384). This was because, at that time, there were no spaces between the words of a manuscript. The only way to read, then, was to read out, following the line of letters much as one would follow a line of musical notation, allowing the words to emerge or 'fall out' from the performance itself.

In the twelfth and early thirteenth centuries, however, there gradually came about a shift towards reading with the eyes alone, unaccompanied by voice or gesture. What made this possible was the division of the line of text into word-length segments, each of which could be taken in at a glance, with spaces in between. The medievalist and palaeographer Paul Saenger has shown how, with such visual reading, the voices of the pages were effectively silenced (1982: 378, 397). As long as everyone in a monastic library was reading aloud, the sound of one's own voice would have sufficed to screen out the voices of others. But as every modern student knows, when one is trying to read silently, the slightest sound can be a source of distraction. So it was that silence came to reign within the cloistered confines of the monastery. In the world outside the monastery, however, in lay society, oral reading continued to predominate well into the fourteenth and fifteenth centuries. As the historian of cognition David Olson has pointed out, it was the Reformation that heralded the key transition in ways of reading, from reading between the lines to reading what was on them, or from the search for revelations or 'epiphanies' to the discovery of the one literal meaning lodged in the text, and available to anyone with the necessary key to extract it (Olson 1994: 143ff.).

Reading the New Book of Nature

In the early sixteenth century, Martin Luther urged readers to abandon the dreams and fantasies that their predecessors had found in their attunements to voices that they felt were speaking to them through the pages of the manuscript, and to draw a line in the sand between the given meanings of words and their subsequent interpretations (Olson 1994: 153–4). And from there it was but a short step to extend the same reasoning from words to works, that is, to the reading of the book of nature.

Thus did Bacon, a century later, insist on an absolute distinction between dreams of the imagination and patterns of the world. I would like to draw attention, in particular, to three corollaries of this transition in ways of reading the natural world. The first has to do with the imagination of what is yet to come. Reading the voices of nature, of the more-than-human world, medieval people were advised by them, and would follow this advice, in parallel with their own experience, in laying a path into the future. With a sensibility attuned by an intimate perceptual engagement with their surroundings, they could tell, not only of what has been, but also of what will come to pass. But such foretelling, as Olson shows, has to be clearly distinguished from the kind of prediction to which a scientific reading of the book of nature aspires (Olson 1994: 174–5). For to predict is not to open up a path through the world but to fix an end-point in advance. Where foretelling is guided by a dialogue with nature, prediction extrapolates from observable facts. Drawing on these facts, it is to speculate about the future rather than to see into it.

The second corollary concerns performance. I have shown how for medieval readers, meaning was generated in the vocal-gestural activity of reading out. Doing and knowing, here, were as clearly coupled as chewing and digestion – an analogy explicitly drawn in the ancient characterisation of thinking as a process of rumination. To ruminate, we still say, is to chew things over – as cattle chew the cud – and to digest their meanings.[19]

Moreover medieval people, as we have seen, would have read the book of nature in the same manner, through their practices of wayfaring. Thus, knowledge of nature was forged in movement, in the course of going about in it. This knowledge was performative in the strict sense that it was formed through the comings and goings of inhabitants. Reading as performance, in short, was both word-forming and world-forming. As the case of the Ojibwa and the Thunder Bird clearly demonstrates, in a way of knowing that is performative – that goes along – any boundaries between self and other or between mind and world, far from being set in stone, are provisional and fundamentally insecure.

In a science constructed in the spirit of Bacon, however, to know is no longer to join with the world in performance but to be informed by what is already set down there. Rather than seeking to follow the trails of a familiar terrain that is continually unfolding, the scientist sets out to map a terra incognita that is ready-made – that is to discover, through some process of decoding or deciphering, what exists in fact. The book of nature having been in-scribed by the Creator in the language of things, the task of the scientist – for Bacon, as indeed for Galileo – was to de-in-scribe, or in a word, to 'describe' what was written there.[20] This is to obtain knowledge not by reading out but by reading off. And from the moment when reading out gave way to reading off, the world ceased to offer counsel or advice and became instead a repository of data that, in themselves, afforded no guidance on what should be done with them. The facts are one thing, values quite another, and the latter had their source not in nature but in human society. Thenceforth, wisdom took second place to information.

The third corollary takes us back to the idea that animals and other beings of the more-than-human world were known in medieval times by their traditions, as skeins of stories, depictions and observations. To track an animal in the book of nature was like following a line of text. But just as the introduction of word-spacing broke the line into segments, so also – in the book of nature – creatures began to appear as discrete, bounded entities rather than as ever-extending lines of becoming.

Nature thus became amenable to the project not of trail-following but of classification. The lines were broken, but the resulting objects could be sorted and arranged, on the basis of perceived likeness or difference, into the compartments of a taxonomy. One could speak, for the first time, of the building blocks of nature, rather than its weave, and of its architectonics. Nature, in short, was perceived to be built up from elements rather than woven from lines. And the creatures of this natural world were no longer known as traditions but as species.

Those creatures, however, that were known only by their traditions, and for which no corroborating evidence could be found in the facts of nature, fell through the cracks. There are no dragons or Thunder Birds in scientific taxonomies. It is not just that they do not exist in the new book of nature; they cannot, since their story-bound constitution is fundamentally at odds with the project of classification. Dragons, along with other beings that rear up or make their presence felt along the ways of the world, can be told but they cannot be categorised. Nor, of course, can they be precisely located, as on a cartographic map. Just as they fell through the cracks of taxonomy, so also they were 'pushed into the wings', as Michel de Certeau put it, of a scientific cartography that had no place for the movements and itineraries of life (1984: 120–1). The same, of course, is true of experiences of fear, and of the sounds of thunder. They, too, can be neither classified nor mapped. But this does not make them any less real for a person who is frightened or caught in the eye of a storm.

Science and Silence

It seems, then, that as the pages lost their voice with the onset of the modern era, so the book of nature was also silenced. No longer does it speak to us, or tell us things. And yet this allegedly silent nature can be, and often is, a deafeningly noisy place. As the philosopher Stephen Vogel observes (2006: 145–71), the world of nature abounds in movement and gesture, and much of this movement is manifested as sound: think of the clap of thunder and the howling of the wind, the cracking of ice and the roar of the waterfall, the rustling of trees and the calls of birds. We may also admit that at one level, human talk may also be understood as vocal gesture, and that the voice manifests human presence in the world just as the call manifests the presence of the bird and the clap the presence of thunder. On this level, voice, call and thunder are ontologically equivalent: as the voice is human being in its sonic manifestation, so the call is the bird and the clap is thunder.

Yet none of this, Vogel maintains, warrants the conclusion that natural entities actually converse with human beings, let alone with one another. This is for two principal reasons. Firstly, conversation requires participants to attend and respond, in turn, to one another. Humans do indeed attend and respond to the sounds of nature: they listen out for bird-calls and are moved, even terrified, by thunder. But does nature, Vogel asks, respond to us? 'Do the self-speaking entities we attend and respond to in nature ever give us their full attention . . ., engage us, respond to our claims?' (Vogel 2006: 148). The answer, he is convinced, is 'no'. The sounds of nature, he suggests, are more like the commands of a monarch who is deaf to his subjects but compels their obedience. Secondly, a conversation is necessarily about something (Vogel 2006: 147). It enables participants to compare each other's perceptions of the world in the common task of figuring out how it actually is. Human interlocutors do this, but birds, trees, rivers, thunder and the winds do not. It is not that they are irresponsible interlocutors; rather, they are not interlocutors at all (Vogel 2006: 157).

For Vogel, then, the silence of nature means that however much noise it makes, it takes no part in the conversations we hold about it. It might sound to us as if nature is speaking, but that is a delusion. 'I have listened carefully', writes Vogel, 'and I hear nothing' (Vogel 2006: 167).

Recall the old Ojibwa man and the Thunder Bird. He thought the thunder was speaking to him, but could not comprehend what it said. Was this a failure of translation, as Hallowell seems to suggest? I have argued that it was rather a failure of empathy. For Vogel, however, had the old man comprehended thunder's speech, he would have succeeded neither in translating it nor in empathising with it. He would rather have performed an act of ventriloquism. For whereas the translator speaks for another but in his own tongue, the ventriloquist projects his own words onto a mute object while creating the illusion that it is the object speaking for itself. (Vogel 2006: 162).

This charge of ventriloquism is of course the foundation for the scientific abhorrence of anthropomorphism, where those who claim empathy with non-human creatures, or to know what they are feeling, stand accused of merely projecting their own thoughts and sentiments onto their unwitting subjects. It is an accusation, however, that has not gone unchallenged. In an important debate conducted in the pages of the journal *Environmental Values*, Nicole Klenk (2008) has entered on the other side. She replies that non-humans can and do respond to human voice, gesture and presence in ways that are meaningful both to them and to us.

It is true that non-humans may not compare their perceptions of the environment with humans in a collaborative effort to establish the truth of what is actually 'out there'. But to insist that conversations can only take this form, Klenk argues, is to take such a narrow view of conversation that it would exclude most of what we commonly call conversation in the human world. For most people, most of the time, conversation is a matter of understanding what others are telling us – of 'getting the story right', not of verifying the rightness of the story (Klenk 2008: 333). Thus human beings who take it upon themselves to render in words what nature is saying are indeed translators and not ventriloquists.

For Klenk, this is precisely what happens in scientific work. Were this not the case, she concludes, scientific interpretations would be mere fictions created through dialogue among humans, rather than the results of careful interaction with – and observation of – components of the natural world. But in this, I believe Klenk is mistaken. Or more to the point, she is mistaken so long as we remain bound by the methodological protocols of normal science. For the claim of science is that, as a specialised knowledge practice, it does seek to verify the rightness of the story, rather than merely getting the story right. Ever since Bacon, science has insisted on discovering the literal truth of what is there, and thus on the strict separation of fact and interpretation. Reading what is on the lines of the book of nature, rather than between them, the one thing that scientists insist they do not do is what Klenk takes to be their number-one priority: 'to listen to the voices of those beings they interact with' (Klenk 2008: 334).[21] Arguably, indeed, scientists do all they can to avoid listening, for fear that it would interfere with or compromise the objectivity of their results.

Knowing in Being

So there is, I contend, a real parallel in the modern constitution between the book of nature and the nature of the book, as a completed work whose contents can be read by those with the keys to decipher it. The parallel lies in the idea that both are to be read in silence: not in the course of an ongoing conversation whose manifold participants open up to one another and whose stories intertwine, but as a record of results that – rendered inert and impassive, in objective and objectified forms – have turned their back on us, presenting to our inspection only what Mae-Wan Ho has called an 'opaque, flat, frozen surface of literalness' (Ho 1991: 348).

To science, the facts are given; they comprise what are called the 'data'. But the world does not ostensibly give of itself to science as part of any offering or commitment. What is 'given', in science, is precisely that which has fallen out of circulation and has settled as a kind of residue, cast off from the give and take of life. It is this residue – dredged, sampled and purified – that is then subjected to a process of analysis, the end-results of which appear on the written page in the forms of words, figures and diagrams. Thus the knowledge so constituted is created as an overlay or wrap-around, on the outside of being. Having silenced the world, we find knowledge in the silence of the book. Indeed the very concept of the human, in its modern incarnation, expresses the dilemma of a creature that can know the world, of which it is existentially a part, only by leaving it. Yet in our experience as inhabitants, moving through the world rather than roaming its outer surface, our knowledge is not built up as an external accretion but rather grows and unfolds from the very inside of our earthly being. We grow into the world, as the world grows in us. Perhaps this grounding of knowing in being lies at the heart of the kind of sensibility we are apt to call 'religious'.

But was it not in the name of religion that leaders of the Reformation insisted on turning the relation between knowing and being inside out? In its stress on the literal truth of words and works, the religion of the Reformists was trumped by the very science it unloosed. For in any contest over the facts, science is bound to win, and religion to lose, leaving the puzzle of why people – including, it must be said, many scientists – tenaciously adhere to representations of reality that are demonstrably false.[22] Yet questions about which can better represent the world, religion or science, are wrongly posed, for the real contest lies elsewhere. It turns on the question of whether or not our ways of knowing and imagining are enshrined within an existential commitment to the world in which we find ourselves.

To compare religion and science in terms of their respective purchase on a reality from which we ourselves are fully disengaged is to assume that they are not – in other words, that in our conscious deliberations, whether scientific or spiritual, the world owes nothing to us, nor we to the world. But if, on the other hand, we owe our very existence to the world, and if the world, at least in some measure, owes its existence to us, then we need to ask instead: what is the nature of these owings, these commitments? How can knowing and imagining let us, and the creatures around us, be? For it is surely in their discharge into being – that is in the recognition, as the anthropologist Stuart McLean puts it, of an essential continuity between 'human acts of imagining' and 'the processes shaping and transforming the material universe' – that the common ground between religion and science is to be found (McLean 2009).

This is where Klenk might be right after all. All science depends on observation, and observation depends in turn on a close and immediate coupling, in perception and action, between the observer and those aspects of the world that are the focus of attention (Ingold 2011: 75). Perhaps the most striking characteristic of modern science lies in the lengths to which it has gone to deny or cover up the practical, observational commitments on which it depends. To highlight these commitments – to attend to the practices of science rather than its formal prescriptions – means recovering those very experiential and performative engagements which, unwritten and unsung, have fallen through the cracks or been pushed into the wings of scientific conceptualisations.

Let us not forget the advice of August Kekulé, that to 'follow the paths of the Pathfinders [one] must note every footprint, every bent twig, every fallen leaf'. Scientists in practice are as much wayfarers as are people of faith, and must perforce tread where others have gone before, ever attentive and responsive to the rustlings and whisperings of their surroundings. Joining with things in the processes of their formation, rather than merely being informed by what has already precipitated out, practising scientists do not just collect but accept what the world has to offer them. They may, in deference to official protocols, feign not to listen to the voices of beings around them, but listen they must, if they are to advance beyond the bare pick-up of information towards real understanding. Like it or not, they too are beholden to the world. And it is in this more humble profession, rather than in arrogating to itself the exclusive authority to represent a given reality, that scientific inquiry converges with religious sensibility as a way of knowing-in-being. This is the way of imagination.

The Bible and the Land

Let me conclude with one further example from the ethnography of the circumpolar North. It comes from a recent study by Peter Loovers, carried out among Teetl'it Gwich'in people living in and around Fort McPherson, in the Northwest Territories of Canada.[23] The study is exceptional in combining a sensitive account of the ways in which people relate to their environment as they hunt, trap and move around on land and water, with a detailed history of Gwich'in engagements with the written word – above all in the translation and reception of the Christian Bible.

The immense work of translation was undertaken by Archdeacon Robert McDonald. Born in 1829 of a Scottish father – an employee of the Hudson's Bay Company – and an Ojibwa mother, McDonald was educated at the Anglican mission school at the Red River settlement and spent a decade serving with the Ojibwa people before embarking, in 1862, on a mission to bring the Anglican faith to the people of the Mackenzie River district. Over the ensuing decades, McDonald worked tirelessly to introduce Christian teachings to native Gwich'in communities and many of the men and women whom he encountered on his travels became key advisers in helping him to transcribe liturgical texts into their own language, known at the time as Tadukh. For McDonald, the translation of the entire Bible into Tadukh was a lifelong endeavour, and the work was not completed until 1898.

Though the Tadukh Bible was warmly received by the Gwich'in, this reception was not quite as McDonald intended. Unlike his rivals from the Catholic mission, who took a rather more relaxed attitude, McDonald was steeped in the traditions of the Reformed Church, and believed that the text of the Bible was to be read literally, as the unalterable record of a singular truth that is not open to negotiation. Much to his discomfort, however, many people, including several of McDonald's own pupils, began to experience dreams and visions in which, it seemed, the pages of the Bible were talking to them, issuing instructions and revealing prophecies. These pages spoke with the voices of their elders, the people with whom McDonald had been working in transcribing the text (and whose particular dialectal idiosyncrasies had become incorporated into it), and even with the voice of McDonald himself. Thus for the Gwich'in, to read the Bible was to open up a conversation with these elders, to listen to their voices, to be taught by them, and to learn. For his part, McDonald was mightily displeased, and felt compelled to denounce the 'false prophecies' that were being mouthed by the people (Loovers 2010: 117).

The mismatch between these ways of reading was not, however, confined to the Bible. It has continued to surface in other contexts, most notably in the interpretation of treaties and land claims agreements drawn up with officials of the Canadian government. In these cases the dismay was on the side of the Gwich'in, who were surprised to discover that documents which they had thought to open up to ongoing dialogue with those whose voices were incorporated therein, were treated by officialdom as set in stone, silent and unyielding (Loovers 2010: 138).

Exactly the same mismatch, as Loovers elegantly shows, can be found in ways of reading the land. For colonisers, explorers, scientists and others who have come to the land from outside, whether on a mission to civilise it, to develop it, to research it or to appreciate its natural beauty, there is no disputing that what is there is already fixed, awaiting discovery, explanation and possibly transformation by the hands and minds of men. For the Gwich'in, however, it is quite different. To read the land, for them, is to attend to the multiple clues that reveal the activities and intentions of its manifold human and more-than-human inhabitants. These clues, Loovers tells us, 'include animal movements, trails, old and new camps and cabins, marks on the land, wood, snow and ice conditions in winter, river-banks in summer, and places where events have unfolded' (Loovers 2010: 300). Wherever they go, Gwich'in are listening, remembering, learning, taking counsel from the land. It is their teacher, not just a repository from which can be extracted materials for the construction of propositional knowledge. Thus the land speaks to people with many voices, just as the Bible does.

Should we then go along with Archdeacon McDonald and conclude that such a way of reading the land is equally false, or that it rests on the kinds of delusions to which in western colonial eyes, allegedly primitive native peoples have always been supposed to be prone? Even McDonald, with his Ojibwa upbringing, would have known that there is more to indigenous understandings than this. And so, in light of what I have argued in this chapter, do we.

Epilogue

There's no such thing as a dragon. That's the title of one of the great classics of children's literature, authored by Jack Kent.[24] It tells the story of a little boy, Billy Bixbee, who wakes one morning to find a dragon in his bedroom. It is pretty small, and wags its tail in a friendly way. Billy takes the dragon down to breakfast, and introduces it to his mother. 'There's no such thing as a dragon,' she declares firmly, and carries on preparing pancakes for break-fast. Billy sits at the breakfast table; the dragon sits on it. Sitting on the table is not normally permitted in the Bixbee household, but there was nothing to be done, since if a dragon does not exist, you can't tell it to get down from the table. The dragon is hungry and eats most of the pancakes, though Billy doesn't mind.

As his mother continues to ignore the new arrival, the dragon begins to swell. It swells and swells. Soon it occupies most of the hallway, and Billy's mother has difficulties cleaning the house as she can only get from one room to another by way of the windows. All the doors are blocked. The dragon swells and swells – now it is as big as the whole house. Then the house is lifted off its foun-dations and careers off down the street on the dragon's back. Billy's father, home from work, is surprised to find that his house has vanished. But a helpful neighbour points in the direction it went. Eventually the family is reunited, and by this time Billy's mother has reluctantly acknowledged that perhaps the dragon does exist after all. Immediately, the dragon begins to shrink, until it is once again of a manageable size. 'I don't mind dragons when they're this size,' Mrs Bixbee admits, as she sits comfortably in an armchair giving the dragon a good stroke.

The moral of this story, of course, is that initially small problems – if we are afraid to recognise them or to speak their name, for fear of infringing the norms of rational conduct – can grow and grow to the point at which ordinary social life can no longer be sustained. I think, in the present day, that there is a dragon in our midst, and that it is growing to the point at which it is becoming increasingly difficult to lead sustainable lives.

This dragon inhabits the rupture we have created between the world and our imagination of it. We know from experience that the rupture is unsustainable, and yet we are reluctant to acknowledge its existence since to do so would fly in the face of accepted scientific rationality. I believe such acknowledgement is long overdue.

In this chapter I have suggested how studies of medieval monasti-cism and of so-called indigenous ontologies could suggest alter-native ways of reading, and of writing, which might allow us once again to take counsel from both the voices of the pages and the world around us, to listen and be advised by what they are telling us, and to heal the rupture between being and knowing.

This healing must be a first step towards establishing a more open-ended and sustainable way to live. Perhaps, then, the dragon will subside.

Notes

[1] An earlier version of this chapter appeared in *Animals as Religious Subjects*, ed. C. Deane- Drummond, R. Artinian-Kaiser and D. I. Clough (London: T. & T. Clark, 2013). I make grateful acknowledgement to T. & T. Clark.

[2] Citations from Bacon's *The Great Instauration: The Plan of the Work* are drawn from Bacon 1858: 22–33, at pp. 27–8. The text is also available at *http://www.constitution.org/bacon/instauration.htm* (accessed 4 November 2011).

[3] At the time of writing, a team of scientists led by Professor Antonio Ereditato has just reported that the neutrinos they have been blasting through a tunnel under the Alps have reached speeds faster than that of light. The team's findings, based on some 15,0000 separate observations, have caused consternation in the world of particle physics. Commenting on the furore, the leader writer in *The Guardian* (24 September 2011) opined that 'the first thing in science is to face the facts; making sense of them has to come second.'

[4] Here, I am developing an argument initially sketched out in Ingold 1997: 231–52 (see p. 238).

[5] This latter view is exemplified in the pronouncements of science policy-makers who support public funding for scholarship in the arts and humanities on the grounds of its direct or indirect contribution to the 'creative industries'.

[6] To this list could be added the *komodo dragon*, the largest extant species of lizard in the world, which inhabits the islands of south-eastern Indonesia. Though rare, these animals are extremely dangerous, and attacks on humans have increased in recent years.

[7] From Carruthers1998: 185 (author's translation).

[8] I am grateful to Godelieve Orye for this insight.

[9] Carruthers 1998: 70; see also Ingold 2007: 15–16, 95.

[10] The story is told in Hallowell 1960: 32.

[11] On this distinction, see Ingold 2000: 278–9.

[12] Benfey 1958. See also Roberts (1989), pp. 75–81.

[13] This crucial qualification appears in one of Hallowell's last papers on the Ojibwa (Hallowell 1966).

[14] I have discussed the distinction between translation and empathy, drawing on Hallowell's example, in Ingold 2000: 106. For an exploration of the significance of empathy within relations of tutelage, see Gieser 2008.

[15] See Leclercq 1961: 19; Olson, 1994: 184–5; Ingold 2007: 14–15.

[16] On the early medieval sense of reading, see Howe 1992.

[17] Sax 2001: x. I am grateful to Maan Barua for bringing this work to my attention.

[18] I have discussed the ways in which the naming and vocalisations of animals enact their own stories in Ingold 2011.

[19] Carruthers 1990: 164–5; see also Ingold 2007: 17.

[20] On Bacon and the 'new *de-in-scriptive* hermeneutics of nature', see Bono 1995: 244.

[21] Klenk 2008: 334. The exception to this are advocates of Goethean science for whom to engage in scientific study is to 'enter into a conversation with nature [and] listen to what nature has to say' (Holdrege 2005). The contempt in which the Goethean approach is held by mainstream science reveals it, however, to be an exception that proves the rule.

[22] There is an ever-growing literature devoted to this puzzle, which frames the problem in exactly these terms: why is the human imagination primed to come up with representations of entities, such as spirits, which – if they existed in fact – would violate obvious principles of physical or biological causation? See, for example, Boyer 2000. From the perspective advanced here, this literature, which treats religion as a domain of cognitive illusion, completely misses the point.

[23] Loovers, 2010. It was my privilege to supervise Peter's work, alongside my colleague David Anderson, and it was my experience of helping him pull together the sections of his thesis on literacy and living on the land that first planted the idea for this chapter in my mind.

[24] Kent 2009.

References

Bacon, Francis (1858) *The Great Instauration*, tr. James Spedding, Robert Leslie Ellisand Douglas Denon Heath, in *Works of Francis Bacon, Baron of Verulam, Viscount St. Alban and Lord High Chancellor of England*, vol. IV (London: Spottiswoode).

Benfey, Theodore (1958) 'August Kekulé and the birth of the structural theory of organic chemistry in 1858', *Journal of Chemical Education*, 35/1: 21–3.

Bono, James J. (1995) *The Word of God and the Languages of Man: Interpreting Nature in Early Modern Science and Medicine* (Madison: University of Wisconsin Press).

Boyer, Pascal (2000) 'Functional origins of religious concepts: ontological and strategic selection in evolved minds', *Journal of the Royal Anthropological Institute*, 6/2: 195– 214.

Carruthers, Mary (1990) *The Book of Memory: A Study of Memory in Medieval Culture* (Cambridge: Cambridge University Press).

Carruthers, Mary (1998) *The Craft of Thought: Meditation, Rhetoric and the Making of Images, 400–1200* (Cambridge: Cambridge University Press).

Clingerman, Forrest (2009) 'Reading the book of nature: a hermeneutical account of nature for philosophical theology', *Worldviews: Global Religions, Culture, Ecology*, 13/1: 72–91.

De Certeau, Michel (1984) *The Practice of Everyday Life*, Berkeley: University of California Press.

Galilei, Galileo (1957) *Discoveries and Opinions of Galileo* (Garden City, NY: Doubleday Anchor).

Gieser, Thorsten (2008) 'Embodiment, emotion and empathy: a phenomenological approach to apprenticeship learning', *Anthropological Theory*, 8/3: 299–318.

Hallowell, A. I. (1960) 'Ojibwa ontology, behavior and world view', in *Culture in History: Essays in Honor of Paul Radin*, ed. S. Diamond (New York: Columbia University Press).

Hallowell, A. I. (1966) 'The role of dreams in Ojibwa culture', in *Contributions to Anthropology: Selected Papers of A. Irving Hallowell*, ed. R. D. Fogelson, F. Eggan, M. E. Spiro, G. W. Stocking, A. F. C. Wallace and W. E. Washburn (Chicago: University of Chicago Press).

Ho, Mae-Wan (1991) 'The role of action in evolution: evolution by process and the ecological approach to perception', *Cultural Dynamics*, 4/3: 336–54.

Holdrege, Craig (2005) 'Doing Goethean science', *Janus Head*, 8/1: 27–52.

Howe, Nicholas (1992) 'The cultural construction of reading in Anglo-Saxon England', in J. Boyarin (ed.), *The Ethnography of Reading* (Berkeley: University of California Press).

Ingold, Tim (1997) 'Life beyond the edge of nature? Or, the mirage of society', in J. B. Greenwood (ed.), *The Mark of the Social* (Lanham, MD: Rowman and Littlefield).

Ingold, Tim (2000) *The Perception of the Environment: Essays on Livelihood, Dwelling and Skill* (London: Routledge).

Ingold, Tim (2007) *Lines: A Brief History* (London: Routledge).

Ingold, Tim (2011) *Being Alive: Essays on Movement, Knowledge and Description* (London: Routledge).

Kent, Jack (2009) *There's No Such Thing as a Dragon* (New York: Random House Children's Books).

Klenk, Nicole (2008) 'Listening to the birds: a pragmatic proposal for forestry', *Environmental Values*, 17/3: 331–51.

Leclercq, Dom Jean (1961) *The Love of Learning and the Desire for God* (New York: Fordham University Press).

Loovers, Jan Peter Laurens (2010) '"You have to live it": pedagogy and literacy with Tweetl'it Gwich'in' (unpublished Ph.D. thesis, University of Aberdeen).

McLean, Stuart (2009) 'Stories and cosmogonies: imagining creativity beyond "nature" and "culture"', *Cultural Anthropology*, 24/2: 213–45.

Olson, David R. (1994) *The World on Paper: The Conceptual and Cognitive Implications of Writing and Reading* (Cambridge: Cambridge University Press).

Roberts, Royston M. (1989) *Serendipity: Accidental Discoveries in Science* (New York: Wiley).

Saenger, Paul (1982) 'Silent reading: its impact on late medieval script and society', *Viator*, 13: 367–414.

Sax, Boria (2001) *The Mythical Zoo: An Encyclopaedia of Animals in World Myth, Legend and Literature* (Santa Barbara: ABC-CLIO)

3

The Double Language of Dreaming

Barbara Tedlock
Department of Anthropology,
State University of New York at Buffalo

Following the post-colonial critique (Asad 1973; Said 1978, 1981), many ethnographers changed from the quantitative analysis of dreams to qualitative studies of the social and discursive conventions, or the etiquette of dreaming. They observed that the manifest content of dreams reveals a dreamer's life circumstances as well as conscious and unconscious state of mind, body, spirit and self, including all aspects of subjectivity, identity and personhood (Hollan 2003; Mageo 2003). By updating our relationships with internal and external worlds, dreams offer us the nightly news of the self and in so doing help to fashion models of ourselves.

The imaginal world of dreaming is located halfway between the external reality of sensual knowing and the interior reality of intuitive understanding. Whenever energy flows inward towards the spiritual and intellectual senses, rather than outward towards the worldly and perceptual senses, one enters an imaginal space. The images in this enchanted land, like those reflected in a mirror, are both there and not there. Rather than 'mirroring' the everyday face of ego-consciousness, dreams reflect the shadowy face of the Other within the self.

Dreams display an empathetic understanding of spiritual phenomena which occupy a paradoxical space located neither within our bodies or minds nor outside in the natural or social worlds. Rather, they exist in a sacred space located between the tangible and the intangible; the visible and the invisible; the audible and the inaudible. The reality of this sanctuary, that mystics perceive, is created through the process of living in and dialoguing with the world. In Native North American cultures the conversation rapidly moves from the dream as a personal entity to dreaming as an interactive social process. And such enhanced experiences, as my Dine friend Gloria Emerson has noted, 'can open cosmic doorways' (Emerson 2003: xiv). This is an enactive theory of dreaming, one that insists on moving beyond being into the richness of becoming (Tedlock 2004).

Engaged Participation and Self-disclosure

Dream exchanges between self and other, involving the braiding of narration and performance with interpretation, reveal an I–thou relationship of mutual communion and self-disclosure. Many ethnographers today practise dream sharing as a way of interacting with other subjects, a self dwelling among other self-disclosing selves. The Canadian anthropologist Jean-Guy Goulet (1993) reported that knowing how to dream appropriately and how to share his dreams was essential to his research among the Guajiro of Colombia and the Dene-Tha of Canada. In northern Alberta he observed that after he had shared intimate details of his own dreams with his subjects, they began to communicate with him at ever deeper levels and to trust him as a friend and potential relative.

Shortly after the funeral of a young woman who was accidentally shot and killed, she unexpectedly appeared before the ethnographer during an academic conference in an auditorium in Ottawa. She looked at him and extended open hands towards him. 'I looked at Nancy and turned my eyes towards the podium. Yes, the speaker was still there. I looked at my hands and at the paper on which I had been taking notes. Yes, I was wide awake. I looked back up and to my right. Yes, Nancy was still there' (Goulet 1998: 179). Moments later the vision subsided and everything returned to 'normal'. Nancy's mother interpreted the dream as saying that her daughter had returned to say goodbye. A month later Nancy's grandmother reported that her brother had a dream announcing that his daughter Roberta was now pregnant with Nancy; in other words, a family reincarnation was on the way. Dene, like other Native Americans, West Africans and South Asians, share a broad sense of self that includes family members, spirits, and past lives (Young 1999: 158; Obeyesekere 2002: 19–71).

Similar shifts in identity are revealed in Marie-Françoise Guédon's research among the Inuit of Quebec, the Gitksan and Tlingit of the north-west coast of Canada and the United States, and the Dene of Alaska and north-western Canada (Guédon 2005). She found that by participating in dream sharing she gained social acceptance; over time she noticed that her dreams became clearer and stronger, and began using them as starting points in conversations. Since Native Americans greatly value dream learning, the topic of shamanic spirituality was no longer taboo for her, and she was told that 'everybody who dreams is some kind of sleep-doctor, everybody has power' (Guédon 1994: 53).

One night she dreamt she was a falcon flying upriver and shared this dream with her Dene hostess. 'I told her that at the end of the dream, I saw myself piercing the sky with my beak and I emerged right in front of the cabin.' Her friend shyly replied, 'I dreamt I was an otter, and I swam down into the water, into the mud at the bottom. And when I got out, I too found myself in front of the cabin.' The ethnographer reported that 'we marveled together at the coincidence, speculating at the nature of a world where many paths lead home' (Guédon 1994: 56–7). Here we see that self and other are not so different after all and that they can co-create a deeply participatory reality.

Glenn Shepard, a medical anthropologist, published a sensitive discussion of his own and another's dream sharing during his field research in Peru:

I awoke from a long night of disturbing dreams to the heat and humidity of the tropical morning . . . my head was throbbing, a hangover from several consecutive days consuming liter after liter of manioc beer.
'Are you well?'
'No, I had bad dreams.'

'Demons. Dead people . . . The wife of my father-in-law, the one who died long ago
. . . I was hunting in the forest, on the path that goes out to the hilly country. It was daytime, here where I was sleeping it was night, but there it was like day. I came to a clearing I hadn't seen before. "Whose garden is this?" I wondered. There was a house. She was sitting outside the kitchen door, straining manioc beer when she called to me, "Son-in-law! Come! Have some manioc beer with me." I got very mad at her. I knew she was a ghost. She called again, "Don't you recognise me, Son-in-law, why won't you drink my manioc beer?" So I ran out of the clearing the way I had come. I ran fast . . . I knew I was in the Land of the Dead. It was a very bad dream. I just woke up. Now I am sick, I have a headache.'

'Me, too,' replied the ethnographer, and then described his own nightmares and pounding headache.

'Brother-in-law, get out your tobacco! Let's snuff some tobacco and burn off these bad dreams.' We sat face to face and took turns blasting the pungent green power up one another's nostrils. The throbbing pain in my temples and behind my eyes was supplanted by the stinging of strong tobacco in my nose. (Shepard 2002: 223–4)

This is a classic description of the type of engaged participation which has been labelled 'going native'. Thomas Csordas (2007) noted there are moments during the course of fieldwork that lie along the continuum between the engaged participation, called 'going native', and the disengaged boredom of egocentricity. One night, during his Navajo fieldwork with members of the Native American Church he took part in an all-night peyote healing ceremony. At dawn the following morning, as the effects of the peyote slowly receded he talked with fellow participants; then suddenly remembered that his rental car was low on petrol and left for a service station. While filling the tank he noticed a pay telephone and phoned home.

The first thing his wife said was that their nine-year-old son had shared a remarkable dream from the previous evening. A group of people got into the family car and he drove them across a body of water in the direction of a place of freedom. When he noticed they were low on fuel, his son replied, 'Here, Dad, I have a gallon of gas, you can use this.' He checked the container to make sure there really was gas inside, then put it in the tank saying, 'Now we can really travel!'

Csordas returned to the tepee and described his son's dream to the other participants. As he spoke he realised that not only did his son's dream petrol allow him to make it to the petrol station, but the water he drove across emphasised the central role of water in the peyote religion. The ceremonial leader replied that he should include this story in his book. Another participant added; 'Now you know for yourself how this medicine works. This is your story that you can tell' (Csordas 2007: 114). His narration of his son's dream revealed an appropriate inter-subjective self which his Navajo friends clearly recognised and approved of.

Karla Poewe in her fieldwork memoir, *Reflections of a Woman Anthropologist: No Hiding Place* (1982), explored her own self within the culture of the Other. This Canadian ethnographer of German extraction reported a dream from the early days of her fieldwork in Zambia (Cesara 1982: 22). She saw a group of Africans waiting in a long line to do the bidding of a fascistic government, and an official approached her saying that an important person wished to see her. He took her to a room off to one side where she glanced out of the window and saw a child playing with an animal that suddenly bounded off into the bushes. Looking around furtively, the girl slipped through the shrubbery to freedom. A gorgeously dressed elderly woman appeared and stood before a mirror remarking how absurd it was to emphasise clothing. She awoke realising that freedom lay neither in the line of waiting people nor in the body of an overdressed woman; it was instead with the child who escaped beyond the shrubs. Then she realised that the dream child was in reality herself.

Vulnerability in the Dream Space

Ethnographic work may entail a painful human linkage that amplifies the vulnerability between all involved. In a sensitive study of slavery amongst modern Ethiopian immigrants to Israel Hagar Salamon listened to the dreams of Ethiopians and shared her own dreams with them. In what she felt was her most important dream, she found herself standing in front of a house across from a black cat which was climbing up a rainspout. She picked up a stone to scare it away; but as the cat tried again and again to climb the rainspout, she began to feel respect for it. Suddenly the cat stood up and spoke to her in Hebrew: 'Very well, if you don't approve of this way of going in I shall use my key' (Salamon 2002: 256). With that the cat nonchalantly entered the apartment and helped itself to some meat. At this point the ethnographer decided that they take a bus and gave the cat a fifty-shekel bill to cover its fare. They got on the bus and her companion, now even more humanlike in appearance, handed the ticket collector the fifty-shekel bill for both of them; the man returned eighty shekels change. This caused her extreme discomfort since she realised he would have to pay for his error. But since she did not want to call attention to the cat, she decided to return the money to him indirectly by way of her computer. When she turned it on, a message flashed on the screen. It was the email address of the director of the university press where she had accepted an advance contract for her book about modern-day Ethiopian slavery.

In a flash Hagar realised that the black cat represented her Ethiopian key informant who had found various ways to keep her life story out of reach. The black cat invoked the metaphor of Africa as the 'dark continent', and the dual catlike and humanlike form of her partner combined associations of the instinctive with the more humane qualities of reason and morality. When the cat stood upright, stared at her intently and opened its mouth to speak, she experienced an epiphany, suddenly realising the deep feelings aroused by her research: dependency, compensation, exploitation, power and control, together with warmth, empathy, encouragement, cooperation and hope. Her dreaming memory was an attempt to defuse the tension surrounding the asymmetrical research situation filled with exploitation and evasiveness.

A year after she recorded her black-cat dream, she met Almaz, an educated Ethiopian woman who showed an interest in her interviews about slavery and offered to help her transcribe them. The ethnographer impulsively gave the woman her tape recorder, the symbol of her professional identity and tool with which she planned to work on the story of Ethiopian slavery. Almaz was pleased and said:

> Hagar! A few days ago I had a dream. I was in a car being driven by an Ethiopian friend. Suddenly, a woman stopped us. She had light skin and short hair, but she was Ethiopian. The woman said to the driver: 'You owe me ten shekels.' He gave her a fifty-shekel bill, but she did not give him any change. So I went up to her and took the bill back. Just then, the woman touched my hand and I felt her warm hand. She looked at me and said softly, 'Almaz, when you turn 28, you're going to lead a revolution.'

Later, while recording the warm-hand dream in her fieldnotes, Hagar reached the words 'fifty shekels', and her black-cat dream returned to her consciousness. Both dreams introduced similar tensions regarding possession, ownership and dependence. They were also filled with warmth, empathy, gentleness and mutuality revealing the nature of the subconscious level that enabled the co-participants to navigate the ethnographic space together.

The In-betweenness of Dreaming

The Moroccan scholar Abdelkebir Khatibi chronicled in his auto-biographical writing – a memoir (1971) and three novels (1976, 1983, 1990) – the impact of unequal power relations and colonisation on his consciousness. He grew up in Morocco speaking a Berber language, then learned Arabic in a local Koranic school, followed by French in a government school. Finally, as a young adult, he left Morocco for the Université Paris-Sorbonne. There he received his doctorate in the School of Civilisations, Cultures, Literature and Societies.

In his first published book, *La Mémoire tatouée: Autobiographie d'un décolonisé* (*Tattooed Memory: An Autobiography of a Decolonized Man*, 1971) he suggests that his memories are corporeal rather than cognitive. The tattoo, a symbol of writing and of magic in

Morocco, is a sign of the sacred and the sensual, which he associated with Berber women's henna-colored hands. His love affair with French culture and language inverted this relation of writing to the body, and he found himself captivated by the evocative power of words rather than by their semantic meanings. 'L'autre soir j'ai rêvé que mon corps était des mots' (1971: 89) ('The other evening I dreamt that my body was words'). This dream revealed his seduction by the French language into an abstracted state fore-shadowed by his family name. Khatibi is closely related to *khitaba* meaning 'orator', 'rhetoric', and contains the root *kateb* meaning 'word' and 'writer'. The narrator explained that he was born on the opening day of the Great Feast (Aïd el Kebir) and that his parents chose his given name, Abdelkebir, to commemorate his birth on that day.

His novel, *Amour bilingue* (1983) (*Love in Two Languages*) centres on his love affair, imbued with all the problems of a bilingual, intercultural, long-distance relationship between a North African Arab man, himself, and a European French woman, his alter ego. He portrays himself existing between superimposed dream and waking languages overlaid one on top of the other at the threshold of the untranslatable. He reported that his fleeting dreams – frag-ments revealing sleeping but not sleeping, dreaming but not dreaming – enabled him to get nearer and nearer to the unsayable.

To evoke his linguistic and cultural in-betweenness where his mother tongue, Tamazight (a Berber language), remained functional but repressed within his childhood Arabic and scholarly French, he developed the metaphor of the *bi-langue* meaning 'double tongue', or 'double language'. The narrator of *Un Eté à Stockholm* (1990) (*A Summer in Stockholm*), tormented by the question of the Other, is a translator who admits, 'Je suis successivement moi-même, l'autre, et de nouveau moi-même' (49) ('I am alter-nately myself, the other, and then myself again'). He is a foreign self living in a field of constant initiation suspended within an interlanguage.

Throughout Khatibi's work translation functions as an allegory for love, and love is a metaphor for translation. In *A Summer in Stockholm* he placed himself in front of a simultaneous translation booth and remarks to his feminine alter ego, 'Shall we lock ourselves inside to translate each other?' Then he directly addresses her: 'La bi-langue! La bi-langue! Herself, a character in this story, on her intercontinental quest, beyond my translations' (Khatibi 1990: 98). Here stands a trilingual translator tormented by the question of the Other deep within his Self. His condition resembles that of a Sufi who describes his or her dreams as not their own but messages from the *barzakh*, that intermediate imaginal realm located between spiritual and bodily existence, the unconscious and consciousness, self and other, male and female, the living and the dead.

During an ethnographic inquiry into the lives of Morocccan Berbers an Italian ethnographer by the name of Stefania Pandolfo (1997) reported conversations in which her dreams were filled with characters that looked and sounded like her Italian aunts speaking with her Berber interlocutors.

In an important dream she found herself in a large house after a death; it was a woman, the *rûh* (soul) of the house, who had died.

> I think in the dream, the life breath of the textile – the woman who held the house together. No one in the house makes any mention of the event. Have they forgotten? If the walls of this old building have been shattered by the laments of the women, no trace is left of all that. It is silence heaving with waiting . . . an empty room, like all the rooms of the old houses in this village.

She describes this dreamscape, which she shares with three other people: an old man, a middle-aged woman, and a child. Suddenly, a voice from the roof warns her to watch her head:

> I raise my eyes and see the corner of the ceiling falling in. This house, I think, is collapsing. Then the house transforms, dissolving and expanding it becomes a landscape of rocky red soil at the edge of a palm grove. The inside becomes the outside. A young man I don't know is telling me, 'Watch your step, don't walk, don't sweep there, you are standing on a graveyard. Everything is disintegrating – the ground is sinking. If you step on it you'll find yourself inside a grave.' Corpses are coming out in the open. (Pandolfo 1997: 166)

In the second scene she climbs the exterior stairs of a new house with an exposed staircase.

> It doesn't look at all like the staircases I know. I notice the smooth, freshly made earth walls. I say to myself, 'This is one of the houses of the outside, of the New Village. But unlike those houses, which are flat, one-story buildings, this house is elevated – as if suspended in air.' I climb the staircase [and] stop halfway, look up, and see the corner of the house . . . I think, unlike the staircases I know this one is exposed and disengages itself from its base. A man comes, the same man who had warned me not to walk in the graveyard. I recognize him [and] say, 'Your house is suspended in air.' He answers, 'Of course! Here everything is sinking; it is a world in ruin.' (Pandolfo 1997: 170)

Even though she experienced this dream in the United States rather than in Morocco, she realised that it was not totally her own, so when she returned to Morocco she recounted it. The villagers felt it was a moral commentary on recent events in the community which led to their resettlement in a new village far from the gardens and forgotten graveyards. Her dreaming encompassed the dialogical after-effects of her Moroccan encounter and its mechanisms were comparable to the grammatical words of a *bi-langue* of the sort described by Khatib. Like him her dreams revealed herself as living between languages and cultures; the traditional house, like her own self-concept, was expanding and collapsing with Arabic, Berber, French, English and Italian languages and cultures. She explains that this occurs because dreams are never one's own but rather sendings from elsewhere (the *barzakh*), the region of death and the beyond which all human beings share.

Going Native Then Coming Home

I have experienced this type of self-understanding and freedom as well as the problem of the Other within the self during my own ethnographic research. During my 1991–2 sabbatical, which I spent in Santa Fe, New Mexico, I became ill. After two weeks of constant coughing I spontaneously received a healing dream. Tola, a Zuni friend of mine, appeared in my dream wearing a traditional black woven-wool blanket dress. She smiled and rubbed cornmeal into my cheeks, wrapped my legs and feet in doeskin leggings, and covered my head with a flowered silk shawl. She took me to a mirror and as I stared at myself, dressed in traditional Zuni women's clothing, I caught a glimpse of my deceased mother standing directly behind me. She was dressed as a *femme fatale* in a hot-pink pants suit, high-heeled shoes and spun silver dream-catcher earrings. As I gazed in disbelief I became aware I was dreaming, but decided to stay inside the dream to see what might happen.

In the next scene Tola and I are in a home at the centre of the village. It is past midnight and a Zuni medicine society is singing, dancing, drumming and healing. Tola reaches under her shawl, pulls out a ceremonial wand, wrapped in long macaw tail feathers, and hands it to me. I realise that it must be her *mi'le* ('breath-heart' in the Zuni language), and am terrified at being in the presence of this powerful icon. Once again, I realised that I was within a dream, and chose to remain inside my dreaming.

Tola sits me down on the linoleum-covered earthen floor before a wooden-slat altar, she takes the two-foot-long wand into her hands and, while speaking rapidly in the Zuni language, rubs the feathers across my neck. Then, holding it perpendicularly towards me, she shoots her healing energy down the feathers into my throat. I see orange, blue and purple sparks, hear a bang and feel multi-coloured lightning ripping into my neck. I die in my dream, but then suddenly awaken to discover myself face down on wet wrinkled sheets.

When I sat up and wrote down and dated the dream (11 March 2002) I thought the clothes and jewellery represented my cultural conditioning and attachments. Then I meditated on my deceased mother's dream-catcher earrings. These woven circular nets strung with tiny gem stones and feathers, originated long ago among the Anishnaabe people. They were tied to the top of an infant's cradle-board to allow good dreams to flow through the opening at the centre into the baby's fontanelle. In recent years dream-catchers became symbols of Pan-Indian cultural identity. Today, they are made in many forms and sizes: small silver earrings as in my dream, medium-sized fishing line and feather dangles for rear-view car mirrors, and large willow, deer sinew, feather, shell, and gemstone for home decorations.

I interpreted the dream-catchers and the healing medicine wand as metaphors for my hybrid cultural identity: First Nations Anashinaabe Canadian and Irish-American ethnographic researcher. Because my initial interpretation centred only on a set of symbols, it failed to uncover the grammar, or composite whole, of the dream with its rich contextual features. It appeared six months after three hijacked commercial jetliners crashed into the World Trade Center Towers and the Pentagon. This disaster occurred during the first week of my residency at the School of American Research, and for several weeks all of us living on site experienced waking and sleeping nightmares. My nightmares subsided, six months to the day after the disaster of 9/11 when my Zuni 'healing dream' appeared. Since it involved moments of dream awareness, or lucidity, and a powerful kinaesthetic sensation of lightning shooting into my throat, it might be described as an archetypal or titanic dream (Hunt 1989: 132). As I continued to contemplate my dream I read an essay in the *Santa Fe New Mexican,* reporting that Governor Gary Johnson had purchased nearly 10,000 dream-catchers, made by indigenous craftsmen, and placed them in the capital building, where Pueblo, Navajo and Apache healers blessed them. Then they were flown in a private jet to New York City where they were handed out to surviving family members.

Even after contemplating the dream for several more days I remained uneasy, so I shared it with a Zuni elder. She replied, 'Dreaming is good medicine all right. I'll bet your grandmother healed you when you were a child with her good dreams. But this dream is *pocha* [bad]. It's lucky you told it right away so that it could not *yuk'iis mowa'u* [complete itself] or continue dreaming itself inside your body. Eventually you might die.' She was right about my grandmother healing me by means of dreaming, but why did she think my dream was 'bad'? Was it because among Zuni one tells a recent dream only if one feels it is 'bad' (Tedlock

1992: 117); or was the dream 'bad' because of so many innocent deaths on 11 September 2001?

Two weeks later when I told Tola's eldest son the dream, he replied: 'Tsilu [aunty] dreaming about your deceased mother and my mother's medicine society healing is *attanni* [dangerous, taboo]. It's good you told Mother so she could dream with you and send you good dreams for your dream-catcher and save you from death.'

By sharing my dream with Zuni elders I changed it from an inner psychological possession to an outer inter-subjective social process and moved beyond being into becoming. In so doing I put into practice the Native American enactive theory of dreaming (Tedlock 2004). According to this understanding, dreams that begin as personal entities shift during telling providing a doorway into another dimension. The anomalous image of my deceased mother in a hot-pink pants suit, and silver dream-catcher earrings, opened into a paradoxical dreamscape in which I experienced a form of doubling, or conscious awareness of both being in a dream and being sound asleep. This moment of lucidity appeared a second time when Tola's energy shot down her feathered wand into my throat; at this crossover point between sleeping and waking I experienced visual, auditory and tactile synaesthesias as my dream emerged from the landscape jolting me awake. Although the dream coincided with the end of illness and might be considered 'good', it was nevertheless 'bad', indicating that I needed healing to save me from an early death.

Several weeks later, I realised what my Zuni friends were advising me: I could only protect myself from death if I accepted my grandmother's Anishnaabe dream-catcher tradition as authentic and powerful. This was so, even though the tradition had been captured and transformed within the New Age Spirituality Movement. My years of searching for 'traditional', 'authentic' or 'pure' Native American spiritual traditions – including my formal training, initiation and practice of Highland Mayan spirituality (Tedlock 1982) – could not protect or heal me. I realised that instead of attempting to 'go native', I had 'to come home' in order to continue to learn, grow and live.

Barbara Tedlock

Conclusions

Ethnographers today practise dream sharing as the self-disclosure of a subject dwelling among other self-disclosing selves. In dreams the self speaks in multiple voices: those of people we appropriate from during our waking lives, who represent our own self fragments. To put it another way, the dream is the Self as Other with whom we interact. Dreams like other memories engage us in a phenomenological descent into our consciousness revealing the etiquette – or cultural, social and discursive conventions – surrounding the creation of an authentic identity. Since sensory experience is mediated by its translation into interpretable forms, dreams are culturally variable expressive representations.

Within indigenous societies worldwide, dreaming and waking reality are not compartmentalised worlds but overlapped experiences. Dreams provide an arena where human beings come into intimate contact with fused natural, social and spiritual worlds. This commonly occurs when one is fully within the landscape of dreaming but on the edge of waking consciousness. All of a sudden one realises that one is awakening to the outer world but still engaged in the inner world.

Many cultures worldwide use the cultivation of dreaming consciousness as a way to gain access to their past and autonomy for their future. Children are trained to become more self-reliant by developing a dream self. Such enhanced awareness of the self, leading to mental alertness during dreaming, produces powerful life-changing dreams. This experience, in turn, encourages dreamers to move beyond perceiving dreams as static entities, beings or mythic texts into experiencing dreaming as a process of sharing and becoming within the poetic landscape of the soul. By studying the double language of dreaming – of the Other within the Self – one learns how subjects experience cultural life and forge identities from their personal, cultural and spiritual experiences.

References

Asad, T. (1973) *Anthropology and the Colonial Encounter* (New York: Humanities Press).
Cesara, M. (1982) *Reflections of a Woman Anthropologist: No Hiding Place* (New York: Academic Press).
Csordas, T. J. (2007) 'Transmutation of sensibilities: empathy, intuition, revelation', in Athena McLean and Annette Leibing (eds), *The Shadow Side of Fieldwork: Exploring the Blurred Borders Between Ethnography and Life* (Malden, MA: Blackwell), pp. 106–16.
Emerson, G. (2003) *At the Hems of the Lowest Clouds: Meditations on Navajo Landscapes* (Santa Fe: School of American Research Press).
Goulet, J.-G. (1993) 'Dreams and visions in indigenous lifeworlds: an experiential approach', *The Canadian Journal of Native Studies*, 13: 171–98.
Goulet, J.-G. (1998) *Ways of Knowing: Experience, Knowledge, and Power among the Dene Tha* (Norman: University of Oklahoma Press).
Guédon, M-F., 1994, 'Dene ways and the ethnographer's culture', in J.-G. Goulet. and D. Young (eds), *Being Changed by Cross-Cultural Experiences* (Peterborough, ON: Broadview), pp. 79–87.
Guédon, M-F., 2005, *Le rêve et la forêt: historires de chamanes Nabesna* (Montreal: Les Presses de l'Université Laval).
Hollan, D., 2003, 'Selfscape dreams', in Jeannette Marie Mageo (ed.), *Dreaming and the Self: New Perspectives on Subjectivity, Identity, and Emotion* (Albany: State University of New York Press), pp. 61–74.
Hunt, H. T. (1989) *The Multiplicity of Dreams: Memory, Imagination and Consciousness* (New Haven: Yale University Press).
Khatibi, A. (1971) *La Mémoire tatouée: autobiographie d'un décolonisé* [*Tattooed Memory: An Autobiography of a Decolonized Man*] (Paris: Denoël).
Khatibi, A. (1976) *Le Livre du sang* (Paris: Gallimard).
Khatibi, A. (1983) *Amour bilingue* (Paris: Fata Morgana); *Love in Two Languages*, trans. R. Howard (Minneapolis: University of Minnesota Press, 1990).
Khatibi, A. (1990) *Un Eté à Stockholm* [*A Summer in Stockholm*] (Paris: Flammarion).
Mageo, J. M. (2003) 'Theorizing dreaming and the self', in Jeannette Marie Mageo (ed.), *Dreaming and the Self: New Perspectives on Subjectivity, Identity, and Emotion* (Albany: State University of New York Press), pp. 3–22.

Obeyesekere, G. (2002) *Imagining Karma: Ethical Transformation in Amerindian, Buddhist, and Greek Rebirth* (Berkeley: University of California Press).

Pandolfo, S. (1997) *Impasse of the Angels: Scenes from a Moroccan Space of Memory* (Chicago: University of Chicago Press).

Said, E. W. (1978) *Orientalism* (New York: Pantheon).

Said, E.W. (1981) *Covering Islam: How the Media and the Experts Determine How We See the Rest of the World* (New York: Pantheon).

Salamon, H. (2002) 'Between conscious and subconscious: depth-to-depth communication in the ethnographic space', *Ethos,* 30: 249–72.

Shepard, G. H. (2002) 'Three days for weeping: dreams, evocations, and death in the Peruvian Amazon', *Medical Anthropology Quarterly*, 6: 200–29.

Tedlock, B. (1982) *Time and the Highland Maya* (Albuquerque: University of New Mexico Press).

Tedlock, B. (1992) 'Zuni and Quiché dream sharing and interpreting', in Barbara Tedlock (ed.), *Dreaming: Anthropological and Psychological Interpretations* (Santa Fe: School of American Research Press), pp. 105–31.

Tedlock, B. (2004) 'The poetics and spirituality of dreaming: a Native American enactive theory', *Dreaming*, 14: 446–9.

Young, S. (1999) *Dreaming in the Lotus: Buddhist Dream Narrative, Imagery, and Practice* (Boston: Wisdom Publications).

4

In the Land of Dreams: Wives, Husbands and Dreaming

Irma-Riitta Järvinen and Senni Timonen
Finnish Literature Society, Helsinki

A journey to a new environment, stepping outside one's ordinary circles, always sets into motion and changes the order of one's mind. Would it have occurred to us earlier that burial and food, death and celebration, the male sex and God, loneliness and belonging together are concepts so tightly bound together that from a certain angle they are the same?

In summer 1992 we talked about these themes with women from the village of Yläleh, Olonets Karelia in Russia. The village is situated only about 230 km from the Finnish border to the east, but in our experience the distance is vast, frightening and charming like a dream. We drove with our van, just the two of us, for nine hours, on bumpy roads, with no signs where to go, endless distances in the forest without people. There were logs across the road, and the strong smell of the marshland in the air. At last, at midnight, the village, with its image reflected in the dark and quiet river, was in front of us. Which one was more real – the village or its image in the water?

We wanted to study the religious conceptions and traditions of the Karelian village women, who had been living in a Russian Orthodox religious culture which was kept alive in homes during the Soviet period. However, they soon showed us that there are no separate religious conceptions. Life is a unity, and the ways things are secretly connected is shown to them in an indirect but indisputable way through dreams and images.

It took some time to understand this. This field trip was our second one to the village, but there were still two more trips to come. And, thinking back to them, it is clear that each field trip had its own special theme and sub-themes according to the circumstances in the village.

Dreams and Life

This time we were driving our van, getting lost at times, and talking about the village people and our themes of research. It would be exciting to see and hear what had happened in the village during the past year. Had any newcomers moved into the village? Was the oldest inhabitant, ninety-year-old Aunt Katja still alive? During the winter we had been listening to our recordings and noticed that every once in a while, and not what we would have particularly asked, the women had started to tell about their dreams. It seemed that the dreams were important for them, and they willingly talked about them.

One of these dreams that caught our attention was told by the sixty-year-old Nina, who had offered her house for our residence. Her dream was connected to the memorial traditions of the dead; these traditions were cherished by the village women. Nina had lost her husband some time ago, and she was very careful to lock the gate and the door of the house in the evening (she was typically a very cautious woman). This is her dream: The dead husband comes to her and says: 'Why did you shut the gate and the door? I cannot come home!'

In the morning Nina tells her dream to Aunt Katja, who lives in her house. Aunt Katja tells her that Nina made a mistake: she should not lock the gate and the door during the six-week period after a death, because during that time the dead person (*pogoiniekku*, meaning 'the one who has peace') is visiting his home and sleeps in his own bed. Nina and other widows in the village always kept the bed of the deceased prepared and empty for six weeks after death.

We were thinking of dreams and death rituals when we settled down again in Nina´s house. Things were pretty much the same:

nobody had died and Aunt Katja had moved to Nina´s house. She was well, but seemed more fragile.

Still, things were not quite the same. A new and exciting series of images from the outside world had entered the women's lives: a Mexican soap opera, called *Even the Rich People Cry* was shown on television. Practically everybody was following the film. A note from Irma-Riitta´s field diary on 2 July 1992:

> Yesterday we, Senni and I, also watched the 'kino'. Anni from the neighbour and her grandchild came here to watch because Anni´s tv was broken. The blind Aunt Katja was standing on the threshold and listened. Nina explains to her what is going on in the 'kino'. She explained the plot to us, too. In the film there is the evil Ester who tricked the man Louis-Alberto to marry her – she lied that she was pregnant. But yesterday Ester suddenly died (oh God), and now the good girl Mariana has chances to get married with the unhappy Alberto. But bad luck, Mariana has an evil stepmother, who is plotting against her stepdaughter . . . she has seduced Louis-Alberto once . . .

What makes the women eagerly follow this film? It seems to have nothing to do with their everyday lives. Still, there are connections. For example, Nina told us about her loneliness now when living as a widow. She was brought up in a very large family, and now she was missing that life, because 'the evenings were like in the kino.' The women, like Jevgenia, keep thinking of the complications of the human relationships in the film, who is bad and who is good, how love affairs can be unhappy, and they reflect their own lives in it.

For Jevgenia, the 'kino' has proved her own experiences as universally true. She thinks that it is unavoidable that the world disturbs, messes up and breaks human relationships, and separates people who love each other. This happened to her: her mother forced her to marry a man she did not like and break up with her true love. The logical consequence of this state of affairs is suffering. Jevgenia sets suffering into a mythical context: 'I suffer, and you must suffer,' Christ said when he was on the cross. Jevgenia says these words to people who come to seek for her advice; the women trust her wisdom. The command to suffer sounds cruel but, according to

Jevgenia, those who have suffered understand more and are able to help other people. As she does.

When the 'kino' is over, a new flow of images is seen. The women turn to the holy corner, from where the 'gods', the holy icons, look at them. The closest holy woman for them is the Virgin Mary, God's mother, who dreamt everything in advance: the suffering and death of her son, his resurrection and the Last Judgement. The vernacular legend song 'The Dream of God's Mother' tells about it.

When the women go to bed and sleep, the images go on: the dreams. Often the main characters in their dreams are the husbands. Even before marrying the future husbands appeared in the dreams – as a bear or as a fox. Jevgenia's husband came as a bear – and he was a powerful beast.

Masha said that it is good if the future husband comes in the dream as a fox – she had seen a fox. For Masha, her daughters-in-law had appeared as animals in her dream. First, a fox jumped at her – she was the forsaken bride of her son. Then two wolves came to bite her, and one of them had a knitted woman's cap on her head! Masha was worried that her son would be divorced because the second 'wolf' had not yet appeared.

The idea that a man and a woman have been predestined by God to each other and that everybody has a fate ordered to him or her at the moment of birth, which humans may not try to change, is one of the Karelian conceptions expressed also in old archived folklore. Sacred legends and old poems carry this message, and dream narratives as well. Nina told us a dream she had heard from Anna. Anna's husband was a handsome Russian, but he had kept other women and was hitting Anna. Anna's mother had been following her daughter's unhappy marriage and had come to the conclusion that she needed to separate them by magic, which she told other women. And then Anna's mother had a dream: she was walking on a bridge, and two pictures, one of Anna, one of her husband, were lifted up to the sky. And a voice said: 'God has put them together but you want to separate them!' Anna's mother told the dream to other women, and they decided that it is a sin to try to separate a couple.

Dreams and Death

Only death can separate those who have been united by God'. This biblical statement did not fully apply in the village of Yläleh. The women of the village were not separated from their husbands by death. This fact was verified in the memorial rituals, which had their roots in the traditions of the Orthodox Church and in the old ethnic beliefs about the dead, which dreams were part of. In memorial rituals and in the dreams the husbands are alive again: they walk and sit, sleep and talk, they express their wishes, desires and disappointments, they come to help in daily work, they eat and drink, they kiss their wives and come to them at night.

The most critical time is six weeks after death. The women said that the dead person is still in the world during that time. He is 'led through his life', he is 'walking in his own steps'. He sleeps in his own bed and eats in the house in the morning. So, the gates and doors need to be open and the bed empty, and plate with food is placed in front of the man's picture, and the wife stays in the house at night. However, if she forgets to follow these rules, the husband appears to the dream. If somebody else uses his bed, like the wife herself, he comes and asks: 'Why did you roll in my bed?' Or, if the door is closed, he complains: 'I cannot come in, I need to enter my own house through the window!' If the wife goes to meet other women and stays away overnight, the husband comes to her dream to complain.

After six weeks a big memorial ritual is organised, and after this event the dead person finally goes to the other world. Although the husband now goes to his peace, he does not disappear from the dreams of his wife, but the dreams change according to his new existence. Memorial rituals are held half a year after the death, and one year after the death. It is possible to organise a ritual each year after the death. Nina's sister held a ritual for her husband for tenrecreatyears after his death.

The memorial rituals have a certain, clear structure. Attention should be paid to the invited guests: not only the relatives, neighbours and the village people are invited, but also the dead relatives of each guest. Every invited guest brings a paper on which the names of the deceased relatives are written. The paper is called 'spiiska' (from the Russian word 'spisok', meaning a list), and the names are read aloud in the beginning of the ceremony. The dead can enter the room unseen, when their names are mentioned, and share the food with the living. The women told us that sometimes children can see the dead.

The inhabitants of Yläleh were elderly, most of them were over sixty years old. Thus, people were dying all the time, not always the oldest. It was customary that men drank a lot, and the River Suoju which was flowing through was famous for being 'greedy' – people slipped from the bridge, or fell down from a boat when fishing. Burials and memorial rituals were frequent, and there were many of those who were coming to or going from a ritual party, 'even though you do not see them', as the women said. We were invited to the half-year memorial ritual of a young man. There were about 30 guests, but when the 'spiiskas' with the names of the dead had been read, there would have been 270 guests in the room!

Everybody wants his or her loved ones to be able to take part in the party. This wish is especially emphasised in the dream narratives around memorial rituals. The dreams reveal the personal level of the traditionally shared ritual: the fears and hopes, concerns and joys of an individual, lonely woman. Nina met her husband in a dream before the memorial ritual of her neighbour's wife. The husband was walking in the sunshine, in a long line of people, wearing the suit he was buried in. Nina embraced him, but her husband did not say anything; the line just went on. In the morning Nina thought that her husband wanted to go to this memorial ritual, even though Nina was not planning to. She changed her mind and went, inviting her husband to join by saying his name. Nina said to us, 'Before the memorial festivals I always see the dead in my dreams.' There was another dream she told: There was a big table, lots of people seated, but Nina''s husband was standing alone at the side. People kept coming and going, and new people sat down – and now Nina's husband was also sitting. She interpreted her dream: Nina had not been invited to the first memorial party of the deceased, and thus her husband could not join, but she was invited to the second memorial party, which meant that her husband was invited through her and could sit in the table and get food. 'They eat what we eat.' The dead husbands make it clear in the dreams that they want to be present, and it is the wife´s duty to organise this.

The dreams were shared by these women, and interpreted together. Anna had a dream in the autumn when it was raining all the time and the roads were flooded and muddy. She dreamt that she was walking on the road and met her dead husband, who looked tired and thin. He said to Anna: 'I got no food!' In the morning Anna was thinking of her dream. Later on that day a woman from the village entered her house and came to apologise, in great distress: on the day before there was a memorial ritual in village, and she had promised to go to Anna´s house and invite her (she lived four kilometres from the village). However, because of the rain and the muddy road she could not come. Anna's husband's name had anyhow been mentioned there, because she had forgotten her 'spiiska' paper in the house earlier. Anna told her dream right away, and together they concluded that the fatal mistake was that Anna was not in the party herself. That is why the husband could eat in the party. Anna's dream was told all over in the village, because it had an important message that supported the women's ideas about their obligations.

The next year we heard about a dream that was socially more important than any other told in the region. It was a very powerful dream, knowing the strong concerns of the women about the well-being of their loved ones 'in the other air', beyond death. We were told that in the neighbouring village of Liete there lived a woman called Pastjoi who had been sleeping for three days. Not just sleeping – she had been walking in the other world! She had had a guide who had shown her the life beyond, how the dead were living, and she had met many people she knew and seen what their place and position was there. However, her guide had forbidden her to tell anybody of what she saw; if she told she would die herself. Just tiny bits of information had come from her lips, fortunately nothing negative. We tried to interview her, but in vain, because she was ill and in pain, and could not talk about anything. Anyhow, she seemed to be respected and not bothered by the other women. For us, the dream experience of Pastjoi was another proof of the wide scale and of the importance of dream narration in this area.

Dreams and Interpretations

Husbands appear in the dreams also outside ritual connections. In Aunt Katja´s dream her husband, who had died thirty years ago, gave her a kiss. For her this dream means that she will die very soon (we know now that she died two years after). Messages from her husband were powerful for her, because she said that 'for a wife, the husband is God.' Not all women saw husband and God in this way. Instead, some of them tried to interpret the meaning of dreams on a general level, understanding that in some way the husbands and other dear deceased people and God somehow, in some inexplicable way, belong together, and to the same unseen world. After talking about dreams Jevgenia said with emphasis: 'See, there is God, there is, God, God is!' We asked why she speaks about God here, women's husbands appear in the dreams, not God! She insisted. Meeting dead people in the dreams are signs for the women of Yläleh of the existence of God (of a sacred world?), and of its functioning in the world we live in.

And what about us? What kind of signs are the dreams of the women in Yläleh for us? Narratives about dreams are an essential part of the traditional oral communication of the village women. They are by no means just little 'traditional omens' or private psychological documents, or representative series of images of universal archetypes. They do not belong to the past or reflect the future, but belong very intensely to the present which combines the past and the future. Through their dreams the women do not as such remember their dead husbands or think of meeting them in the future, after death, but they meet them here and now.

The ways the women tell each other about dreams – and to us, outsiders – reveal the subtle, changing meanings of their dreams, the whole ethos of the dream world. If one read only the texts, dream narratives in writing, one might say: 'These poor women live, still as widows, under the command of their husbands. They keep thinking if they have fed and given drink and taken care of their husbands well enough. Even after death their husbands come to them with their demands and reproaches!'

Or the dreams could be seen, according to the functionalist interpretation of death rituals, as a result of fear of the dead – that the dead must be well taken care of, so that they would not become angry and do harm to the living. Thus, in order to secure one's own well-being and prosperity, one needs to take care of the needs of the dead.

We think, however, that the way these women talk about their dreams, and interpret them, and tell them each other, does not point to those attitudes. Much more essential than anxiety or fear are presence and being in contact. The dreams bring those who are away – the dead, and God – close to the dreamer, and when the women share their dreams, they feel closeness, seeking to understand their own lives through dreams.

References

Apo, Satu, Nenola, Aili, Stark-Arola, Laura (eds) (1998), 'Gender and folklore. Perspectives on Finnish and Karelian culture', *Studia Fennica Folkloristica*, 4: 305–14.

Järvinen, Irma-Riitta (1998) 'Wives, husbands and dreams. Family relations in Olonets Karelian narratives', *Gender and Folklore*, 4: 305–14.

Järvinen, Irma-Riitta (2004) *Karjalan pyhät kertomukset. Tutkimus livvinkielisen alueen legendaperinteestä ja kansanuskon muutoksista* (*Karelian Sacred Narratives: A Study of Orthodox Religious Legends and Changes in Folk Belief in the Livvian-Speaking Area of Karelia*). Helsinki: Suomalaisen Kirjallisuuden Seura.

Järvinen, Irma-Riitta and Timonen, Senni (1992) 'Memorial rituals and dreams in a Karelian village, *Byzantium and the North*, *Acta Byzantina Fennica*, 6: 51–71.

5

Home as Dream Space

Kate Pahl[1]
Literacies in Education, University of Sheffield

My father, Ray Pahl, died in 2011. He was a sociologist and an art collector. In one dream I had about him, about a year after he died, he came to visit me in my house. He liked it but wondered why all the pictures in my house actually belonged to him. He politely said they looked nice, but would have liked to have them back. My father's house was peopled with objects – stones from beaches he visited, art he collected, books everywhere, glass, china, found objects, old tools, things of beauty, chosen carefully and displayed with pride. When we came to clear the house the job took two years. Each object had to be let go with care, given to the right person, as every thing mattered.

My father died on my birthday. I was on the Scottish island of Jura, and that afternoon was impelled to go and sit on a Neolithic burial cairn, and I watched his passing from between the two rocks that signalled the line between life and death. The next day I drove straight to his house, and took up residence among his stuff, garnering it to myself to make sense of what had happened. I wanted to reassure him and his 'stuff' (Miller 2010) that there was still someone who cared. Houses are holding spaces for memories and within houses lie objects, which themselves contribute to the making of memory and construction of stories (Hurdley 2007, 2013). The process of dying destabilises matter and objects, and things become 'matter out of place' (Douglas 2002); no longer settled, they are set adrift by death. The minute the person dies they become travelling objects, and embark on a long path of re-settlement and re-appropriation into new homes and new stories. I am sure this process caused anxiety for my father after he died, a feeling I shared and understood.

Because my father's anxiety about his objects continued after his death I initially hired house sitters to keep his objects safe and loved. Objects 'close the space between living and dying' (Hurdley 2013: 219), and this process feels very powerful just after someone has died. The objects echo with the shock of what has happened, and can jump around or move, or acquire different significance in a new and altered state of being. I found some lost objects in dreams. In dreams, nothing is lost. Childhood homes, the dead, lost toys all appear with a vividness your waking mind would not achieve (Solnit 2010).

Dreaming creates a possibility of other spaces. I recall from last night's dream a smooth attic floor, unfamiliar in my waking life. I have walked through Devon long houses and low floored Tudor barns without ever having visited them, or only in dreams. Dreaming begins to knit together some of the conundrums of loss, death, unhappiness and sentimentality, a longing for the past. By seeing the home as dream space, Bachelard (1994 [1958]) created a space to recognise the space of dreams, peopled as they are by objects, memories, stories and desire.

Inhabiting a Dream Space

In one of my dreams I return to my grandparents' house. Sometimes, after a night spent dreaming of their house, and wandering around there at night on my travels, I wonder if I disturbed the current residents of the house who, by day, regard me without emotion if they meet me at all. Confessing this to my uncle, he too suspected he haunted the same house by night, and we wondered if we would meet at all in our dream worlds, slipping up the heavy stairs to remembered rooms full of old memories. Houses shelter the souls of the living as well as the dead and in those night-time spaces, these souls can mingle, sometimes comfortably in the same space, as I and my uncle think we do, sometimes not so much, and causing sleeping house guests to toss and turn. Where do our dream souls go to at night and how do they link to the souls of the dead?

Houses are spaces to dream in but are also places where we go in dreams in order to recover our past selves and childhoods (Bachelard 1994). In my dreams of my grandparents' house, some rooms are also still too haunted to visit, even in dreams. Bachelard talks of, 'the real houses of memory, the houses to which we return in dreams, the houses that are rich in unalterable oneirism [that] do not readily lend themselves to description' (1994 [1958]): 13). These houses can remain solid but can also be discovered anew, softly unfurling under our dreaming touch, or creating portals to walk through to where we can mingle with the dead, treading old haunts in secret spaces.

I am also haunted by others' dreams. In the cottage where I spend summer holidays, I used to be woken regularly about midnight by a person calling me or somehow trying to wake me. I wondered if someone was dreaming about the room I slept in, but the feeling was not of a living person. I complained about the lack of sleep to my friend Christian, repeatedly, and wondered what I should do about it. I came to the cottage to rest and have a holiday, and was woken night after night. Christian was sympathetic, but she said the problem would pass. Christian knew she would die soon – when she died, the hauntings stopped. 'We cover the universe with drawings we have lived' (Bachelard 1994 [1958]:12).

Dreamers do however haunt houses. I wondered if the person who left the house was a living person who was falling asleep and dreaming of that room, and coming back into my dreams. He lived locally. When I met him in the country lanes around the cottage he smiled and said nothing. Perhaps he too haunted my house, living up the road as he did? The person who comes into other people's dreams at night may or may not have died, but existed in a liminal space; around midnight, the soul of the person was awoken. I found this regularity both helpful and maddening. I realised that I had lived, for a while, inside someone else's household patterns, their internal time clocks. We are crossed with the dreams of others, and dead souls' clocks and everyday rhythms haunt our days. The traces of the dead pattern the spaces of the living, and nowhere is this more evident than in homes, and in dreams.

The souls of the dead wander back into houses as ghosts and wake us up. The living also have a tendency to wander about houses they have lived in and wake other living people when they bump into furniture. I quite often will wake and wander around a strange room, in a different world from the room I am currently in, and, thinking I am somewhere else, open doors and go into corridors. I become ghostly, trance-like, I step in and out of rooms only coming to when I stumble into some furniture. In that altered state I am not myself, neither is the room I am in. My mind, dreaming, made a different room happen.

Reflecting on homes, dreaming and dead people creates a space that is in-between, crossing both sleep and wakefulness, the world of the dead and the world of the living and houses one has lived in now and in the past. These crossings can create anxiety or can be a rich source of interest, both in academic writing, from anthropology, phenomenology, literature, poetry and philosophy and in everyday experience and narratives. Writing this paper is also a kind of crossing, between the world of anthropology (Hurdley 2013; Miller 2010), phenomenology (Bachelard 1994 [1958]) and my own personal memories. These crossings create writing that is both specific and general. We can all enter the space of the dream or the space of the home, and once over the threshold, we can begin to create new dreams or homes, as we enter, imaginatively, the page of the dream. Our imagination sustains these crossings and creations.

House as Dream Space

The home provides a space from which to dream. It also inhabits our dreams. There is a dialectical relationship between the home and our dreams: as well as our occupying the home, it occupies us. The dream space is restorative, providing things that are hard to decipher but make sense years later. In my father's house, three days after he died. I dreamed that he was safe, and lived with turtles. At the time, I could not make sense of this, beyond the fact that Darwin was born near to where he lived and there seemed to be a synergy there, until I read two years later that, according to the writer Rebecca Solnit (2010), turtles are the spirits of the dead returned. I then made sense of my turtle visitation. In dreams, we look for lost significance and find links and connections that are not available when we are awake. Turtles, of course, carry their homes on their back. My father needed to re-connect with his home to be whole again.

Houses can provide restorative space, but dream houses can also leave traces within the inhabitants. They are inhabited by all the people who ever lived in them, and we can never completely own a house, which is why the people who now live in my grandparents' house find me such a difficult reminder. Moving into a new house creates disturbance, and residents might wander in to see who the new person is. When my father moved into his last house, he said that on his first night there was an immense amount of crashing and banging downstairs; it sounded as if someone was having a party or moving in. When I moved to Sheffield, the house we bought used to be rented out to young people. I got used to feeling the presence of the students who would worry me at night in my new house in Sheffield, and hoped they all had somewhere to sleep. These people are traces of belonging, but their presence keeps the houses we live in alive.

Dreams, thoughts and memories that originate in the home and the objects within it weave a single fabric which acts as a source for the imagination. Gaston Bachelard wrote about the way in which the home is the space of reverie, of 'original warmth' (1994 [1958]: 7). We particularly remember the house we were born in, which becomes the space of our dreams. Imagination is born of the process of wandering 'through the crypts of memory', in the 'animal shelter of our dreams' (ibid.: 141). By seeing the home and dreams as intimately connected, Bachelard also saw how the space of imagination and creativity could be created. Hurdley (2013) listened to people's stories as they picked up objects on their mantelpieces and told her about them, thereby recognising, 'the unusually unspoken work of small things in the making of memory' (p. 6). The home is a site for the habitus, a space of practice, generating structuring structures that make everyday practices, from Bourdieu (1977, 1990).

In my own work, I recorded how young children would play out the habitus in their text making, drawing Nanny's house in Wales or the chickens that were chased outside a grandparent's house in Turkey (Pahl 2002, 2004). These forms of meaning-making relied on lived experience, engendered in the home. The material world structures our dreams as well as our waking hours. The difference between dreams and waking life is that nothing is lost in dreams. Lost objects can also be re-created in narratives (Pahl and Pollard 2010) or memorialised in the museum as another kind of dream space (Kavanagh 2000).

The process of memorialising the home has been linked to nostalgia, which is both ideological and utopian (Stewart 1993). The sentimental memorialisation of the past has also been linked to kitsch and the space of aesthetics. Nostalgia describes that feeling of loss, 'the nostalgic is enamoured of distance' (Stewart 1993: 145), that can be conjured up by the souvenir, a trace of memory memorialised in the home, and placed on mantelpieces to record and locate past experience (Hurdley 2006). The process of remembering happens through knowledge of lived space, through bodily practices as much as through ritual and shared experience (Connerton 1989). Loss, however, makes objects and places more resonant, and these experiences can create echoes that can shatter the everyday.

Dreaming of Objects

Objects become people and people become objects in strange ways. Hoskins (1998) wrote about the concept of 'biographical objects' that grew old with the person and carried their stories. This object anchors the owner to a particular place, and they 'share their lives with us', reminding us of the process of ageing (Hoskins 1998: 8). Discarding objects when moving house or clearing after a death forces us to confront 'the detritus that is left in the wake of our passage through life' (Miller 2001: 8). Homes and their belongings occupy us as much as we occupy them, and they inhabit our souls. Marcoux writes of how 'Sorting out of things becomes a metaphor for the sorting out of relations and memories' (2001: 82). This process also re-creates the self in new ways.

One way in which the self is both created and memorialised through objects is through the process of collecting. A product of creative expression, focused on both classification and aesthetics, it can provide a safe space to inhabit the world of chosen objects as self (Stewart 1993; Hecht 2001). Particular objects haunt the present through their power. At the Jewish Museum in Berlin particular objects, everyday, not special, are memorialised and presented alongside pictures of their murdered owners. The sentimentality attached to particular objects is also a utopian vision, between the everyday and the imagined future but grounded in materialism. This concept of the 'not yet' in collecting echoes the continental philosophy of Ernst Bloch's visions (2006 [1969]) of utopia, grounded in both the everyday and the dream space, as articulated in his visions of what could be in *Spuren* (*Traces*).

When I encountered Bloch's *Traces*, I felt a shock of recognition, but also a sense of strong attachment. As I wrote this chapter, I began to feel this shock, which I identified as a sense of sentimentality, an attachment to the objects in my father's house. 'Parting is itself sentimental. But sentimental with depth, it is a tremolo hovering indistinguishably between surface and depth' (Bloch 2006 [1969]: 51). Objects within a home carry this tremolo and their resonances and echoes can shatter the self who curates them. Trivial objects, such as the beach stones in my father's house, often shaped in the form of a heart and curated, so that they formed special patterns on windowsills, were both sublime but also trivial, beautiful objects but everyday, found but also lost.

The process of creating a collection represents an attempt to create a 'new context' (Stewart 1993: 52) which involves both a process of forgetting, as old classification systems are re-thought, and new ways of constructing and categorisation. My father's art collection was both a living thing, constantly changing, and a form of imprint upon the world, a way of articulating his vision in a different kind of way from the books he was known for. The museum closes off the live collection by articulating what is important, argues Stewart (1993), instead representing certainty, not the hopefulness of the endless collector.

Contemporary museum studies acknowledges this and asks for a more open concept of the museum as dream space, where objects are unfinished, and conceptual framings disturbed (MacDonald 2003; Kavanagh 2000). These contemporary understandings of museum collections also acknowledge the importance of the dream and the reverie as a site for the museum visitor to experience and enjoy.

Objects are storied, and carry stories with them that then inhabit our dreams. Hurdley (2006, 2007) interviewed people about the objects on their mantelpieces and through this was able to listen to stories that were told and then re-told differently in relation to an object. She made visible 'the necessary inter-relatedness of the visual and the spoken, the material and the narrative' (2007: 355). The meshwork (Ingold 2011) of the visual, spoken and walking re-creates the sensory and embodied feeling of walking through a home, picking things up, touching things, telling stories about them, and memorialising them by placing them in particular sites. Re-arranging the home makes this process visible.

Material culture can be seen as a storied space of practice. When I watched children in London homes create tissue paper birds and train drawings, and then tell family stories, often with the help of their mothers, about these objects, I could see how the material and the storied were braided together. Stories can be embroidered, told and re-told and become narrative through the telling (Hymes 1996). The process of stories becoming narrative, a 'tale told by others' is one by which particular happenings become made visible and manifest. Ghost stories are a particular genre. Appearing often in association with old houses and former residents of houses, they surface also at times of turbulence and financial difficulty (Smith 2010). Smith argued that the ghost story was used by nineteenth-century writers like Dickens as a way of creating disturbance in readers as well as tracking social change.

Stories of Hauntings

'In short it is good to think in stories too' (Bloch 2006 [1969]: 6). Stories are spaces where things can be worked out, and echoes and traces of the past, sometimes long buried, become worked through and then are surfaced in new ways (Hymes 1996). As an ethnographer of literacy and language practices in Rotherham and the Dearne valley, I was struck by the number of ghost stories I heard. The story of the haunted house was particularly strong; another was the story of the abandoned haunted building. Industrial ruins were very prevalent in the areas where I was conducting the ethnography (Edensor 2005). The landscape was littered with traces of shut-down mines, steelworks and industrial buildings. Empty abandoned buildings scattered the landscape. As the UK austerity cuts became more serious, the abandoned buildings included youth centres, libraries and art centres, also lost and haunted spaces of practice.

The haunting of houses as evoked in stories became something I was interested in, and this interest translated into a focus on the everyday as strange and dreamlike, a space for daydreams and unusual happenings. I began to collect these ghost stories and make sense of them, a project that became long-term and is still continuing. I began to be interested in recurring stories that were told and re-told until 'they become a narrative told by others' (Hymes 1996: 118). I became interested in the 'underground' stories that surfaced regularly, including those involving animals, those involving death, particularly of grandparents, and those involving ghosts.

In 2012, I spent six months listening to ghost stories. I was working in an ex-mining area, Rawmarsh in Rotherham, and with a youth worker, Marcus Hurcombe, exploring the talismanic power of language in a project called 'Language as Talisman' (Pahl et al. 2013). The project was concerned with the protective power of language, its ability to confer special or magic powers upon those who inhabited this space. Marcus thought of the idea when he and I were sitting in a bandstand in the park where he was working at the time, and we were hearing stories from a group of young people. One of them, who initially said he had 'nothing' to say, then told us a story of the medal round his neck, which came from his grandfather who was killed during the Second World War. The Language as Talisman team explored the power of magic and charms, worked with a school to celebrate everyday language and dialect and developed films, poetry and special events in the park with young people (Pahl et al. 2013).

As part of the Language as Talisman project, I worked with a group of girls, aged between twelve and thirteen, called Chloe, Ella and Georgia, and together we told a ghost story. The story 'Reunion' was created with the three girls, named as authors of the story, and a fourth girl, Dina (pseudonym), who only came on the first day, together with myself, Marcus, Steve Pool, an artist, and Sam Rae, who worked with me to transcribe and analyse the stories. Sam was a second-year student in the English department at the University of Sheffield. I met weekly with the girls and we told stories. Some were recorded, some not. The girls wanted to tell ghost stories. However, real ghost stories were problematic and could not be recorded. The recorded stories were fictional, while the non-recorded stories were true stories of ghosts that had truly scared them in real life. Sometimes other people dropped in and told their ghost stories – a youth worker, Rachel, told stories of how her grandfather saw the people standing between the people who were alive, and a young father told the story of his baby's death and his experience of that. Jenna, another youth worker, told stories of real ghosts she had experienced. One particular story became told and re-told over the time of the project, and this became the story that was called 'Reunion' by the girls.

'Reunion', told over a period of time, and eventually turned into a book with illustrations by Chloe, concerned the experience of five-year-old girl twins, brought up in Sheffield in the Second World War, who loved to play outside. One day, during a bombing raid, they wandered into an abandoned warehouse. The bombs fell on the warehouse and the twins were killed. In the story, the twins continue to live inside cardboard boxes in this warehouse as ghosts. A young girl, Maria, who is interested in seeing what is inside the warehouse, finds their ghosts inside a cardboard box fifty years later. She is scared, but intrigued. The twins tell her their story and ask to be reunited with their mother. With the help of Maria's Nanan, her grandmother, and an Ouija board, this happens, and the twins and their mother are reunited in the spirit world. This excerpt from the story concerns Maria and her discovery of the twins inside cardboard boxes in the warehouse, little ghosts desperate to find their mother again:

> Little girls' laughter. She opened up a box lid; the kind that open in two ways and make a bang. She'd seen people that nobody else had seen before, because those people were ghosts. She never told anybody this because she didn't want people to think she was weird and everything, or not believe her. But looking in the boxes, she thought she might maybe see some more ghosts – if she carried on looking. Then she'd have proof and people would have to believe her.

Her Nanan believed her, about the ghosts. Nanan had actually seen a ghost – she'd seen a little girl play outside the warehouse herself. Sometimes she even saw her dead husband, on his way to the shop. Whenever Maria had bad nightmares about ghosts, her mum would simply tell her that ghosts weren't real, and to go back to bed. Nanan, though would talk to her or read her a story, and Nanan believed her about the ghosts. Her Nanan was the only one who believed her. In this excerpt the story is about the discovery of the twins in the warehouse, but also crucially is about belief – belief in ghosts and the need for Maria to be believed by her Nanan. Ghosts are important pivots between life and death and the focus of the story. The story's plot concerned the death of two girls in a bombing raid and their subsequent struggle to get back to their mother – in the story the twins are represented as spirits out of place. The people of Rawmarsh, where the girls lived, would have watched the devastating bombs as they fell upon Sheffield. Chloe mentioned previously that her grandmother had written about this experience in a publication that was shared with her family. Chloe orchestrated the story's resolution, which was to create a space for the girls, who died in the bombing, to be reunited with their mother. The young girl, called Maria, who found the ghosts in the warehouse was able to ask her Nanan (grandmother) to help the twins meet their mother, also dead, in another world. Here is Chloe, ending the story in the initial telling of it to me, Marcus and Steve:

> Chloe: And then Maria went to – uh – she saw her Nanan, like when she were cleaning
>
> Out – well her gran, when she were cleaning out the house. She saw her gran and her gran told her that where the girls' mum were,
>
> Ella: Because if she said everything were okay
>
> Chloe (overlapping): And she told her that everything were alright and everything, and that she were with – she were reunited with her husband, and so Maria told the girls where their mum were, and she saw the – and she heard like the, um, door, the warehouse doors opening and then slam shut, and she was left alone in the darkness in the girls were never heard of again. (Transcription May 2012)

The resolution of 'Reunion' took place within a female-constructed space where a grandmother told the granddaughter how to reunite two girls with their mother. Making the transition was the work of the Nanan and Maria in the story. The Nanan dies but leaves the account of where the twins' mother is in a drawer, which Maria finds. Here is the ending of the story as it was transcribed, edited and agreed upon:

> Maria went back to the warehouse, and this time, found it in herself to speak.
>
> 'What's up?' asked the twins. Now Maria wanted them to know about what had happened.
>
> 'Somebody very close to me . . . has died.' Her voice echoed a bit in the big warehouse. She hadn't really listened to the twins' story that closely before, because she'd always been scared, but she wasn't scared anymore.
>
> So she asked the twins to tell her the story again, and they did.
>
> Maria was very moved, and she was happy, because she could actually help. She calmly told the girls where their mum was; where they could be reunited with her, if they wanted. The ghosts cried, and hugged Maria, and Maria felt tears on her cheek. She suddenly

heard the warehouse doors opening, and then the wind slamming them shut. She was left alone, in the dark, but she wasn't afraid. She knew that the twins had moved on. (from 'Reunion')

The story of 'Reunion' explores the link between physical spaces, such as the warehouse, the cardboard box, the house which Maria's Nanan was cleaning when she talked to Maria about where the twins' mother was, and the graveyard where their mother, Victoria, was buried, and then the story describes the appearance and re-appearance of ghosts in those spaces. Doors open and shut, cardboard box lids open and close and people appear and disappear across the divide of life and death. Some people, like Chloe's Nanan could navigate between life and death through the Ouija board and her intuition and understanding. However, she also dies at the end of the story. The liminal space between life and death is torn down through the intervention of the Nanan and the ghosts are able to travel through. The sign that this is happening is the opening of the doors and then 'the wind slamming them shut'.

Ghosts as Dream Space

Ghosts are 'as if' people, who instantiate dead people, who also return to us in our dreams. We need to believe in ghosts as they provide us with another way of talking about the world. This confronts us with what we do not know as much as what we know. Learning to listen to ghost stories can alert us to powerful and important cultural stuff within communities that otherwise would remain unheard. Communities where things have been suppressed, such as the ex-mining communities of Barnsley, the Dearne valley and Rotherham, carry unheard stories (Bright 2010).

Houses also carry unheard stories, of lost objects and people who once lived in the nooks and crannies. Bringing these stories out into the daylight provides another way of knowing and understanding the world. I have learned to bring my ethnographic work into a more liminal space, where my own subjectivity merged with those of the people I worked with.

Fieldwork, then, is a process of inter-subjective construction of liminal modes of communication. *Inter-subjective* means literally more than one subject, but being situated neither quite here nor quite there, the subjects involved do not share a common set of assumptions, experiences or traditions . . . It is the dialectic between these poles, ever repeated, never quite the same, which constitutes fieldwork (Rabinow 1977: 155).

The ghosts that the girls in Rawmarsh told me about taught me to listen to their knowledge more deeply and to make sense of the dream space using different tools of comprehension. Weaving together the story of my experience of haunting together with my father's death, the story of 'Reunion' presents an enlarged space, where it is possible to listen to dreams, to hear the voice of grandparents and to communicate with the dead.

Conclusion

The home, as Mary Douglas says (1991), is a 'kind of space'. The space of the home can provide a source of dreams, can disturb us with its ghosts and provide a space of reflection, comfort or disturbance. Objects within the home can unsettle further the divide between life and death, and the issue of 'matter out of place' can become a site for further exploration. As an ethnographer I always want to explore the cultural framing that the people in my studies have of the world. When I was involved in Language as Talisman, that framing was often more strange and more insightful than any I could muster. Ghosts surfaced during the project and it became a comforting and special project. The metaphor of the 'talisman' accompanied us everywhere.

Writing this chapter has also been a kind of letting go, as my father's house was sold to someone who loved it, and his possessions were also dispersed. Loss is something that can be recovered in dreams, in stories and objects, and also in writing, where the experience of re-creating, becomes, like a ghost, a temporary manifestation of another reality. Houses, lives, objects, books all create traces. Like Bloch's *Traces*, these leave shocks, echoes, forms and resonances which become the ghost, the dream, the story and the written text.

Notes

[1] With help from Ray Pahl and Richard Steadman-Jones

References

Bachelard, G. (1994 [1958]) *The Poetics of Space* (Boston, MA: Beacon Press).

Bloch, E. (2006 [1969]) *Traces* (Stanford, CA: Stanford University Press).

Bright, G. (2012) 'The practice of concrete utopia: Informal youth support and the possibility of "Redemptive Remembering" in a UK coal-mining area', *Power and Education*, 43: 315–26.

Bourdieu, P. (1977) *Outline of a Theory of Practice* (Cambridge: Cambridge University Press).

Bourdieu, P. (1990) *The Logic of Practice* (Cambridge: Polity Press).

Connerton, P. (1989) *How Societies Remember* (Cambridge: Cambridge University Press).

Douglas, M. (2002 [1966]) *Purity and Danger: An Analysis of the Concepts of Pollution and Taboo* (London: Routledge and Kegan Paul).

Douglas, M. (1991) 'The idea of a home: a kind of space', *Social Research*, 58/1: 287–307.

Edensor, T. (2005) *Industrial Ruins: Space, Aesthetics and Materiality* (Oxford: Berg).

Hecht, A (2001) 'Home Sweet Home: Tangible memories of an Uprooted Childhood', in D. Miller (ed.), *Home Possessions: Material Culture Behind Closed Doors* (Oxford: Berg), pp. 123–48.

Hoskins, J. (1998) *Biographical Objects: How Things Tell the Stories of People's Lives* (London: Routledge).

Hurdley, R. (2006) 'Dismantling mantelpieces: narrating identities and materializing culture in the home', *Sociology*, 40/4: 717–33.

Hurdley, R. (2007) 'Focal points: Framing material culture and visual data', *Qualitative Research*, 7/3: 355–74.

Hurdley, R. (2013) *Home, Materiality, Memory and Belonging: Keeping Culture* (Basingstoke: Palgrave Macmillan).

Hymes, D. (ed.) (1996) *Ethnography, Linguistics, Narrative Inequality: Towards an Understanding of Voice* (London: Routledge).

Ingold, T. (2011) *Being Alive: Essays on Movement, Knowledge and Description* (London: Routledge).

Kavanagh, G (2000) *Dream Spaces: Memory and the Museum* (London: Leicester University Press).

Macdonald, S. (2003) 'Museums, national, postnational and transcultural identities', *Museum and Society*, 1/1: 1–16.

Marcoux, J. (2001) 'The refurbishment of memory', in Miller 2001.

Miller, D. (ed.) (2001) *Home Possessions: Material Culture Behind Closed Doors* (Oxford: Berg).

Miller, D. (2010) *Stuff* (Cambridge: Polity Press).

Pahl, K. (2002) 'Ephemera, mess and miscellaneous piles: texts and practices in families', *Journal of Early Childhood Literacy*, 2/2: 145–65.

Pahl, K. (2004) 'Narratives, artifacts and cultural identities: an ethnographic study of communicative practices in homes', *Linguistics and Education*, 15/4: 339–58.

Pahl, K., Bullivant, D., Escott, H., Hodson, J., Hyatt, D., Hurcombe, M., Pool, S. and Steadman-Jones, R. (2013) *Language as Talisman*, AHRC Scoping Study, *http://www.ahrc.ac.uk/Funding-Opportunities/Research-funding/Connected-Communities/Scoping-studies-and-reviews/Documents/Language%20as%20Talisman.pdf*

Pahl, K. and Pollard, A. (2010) 'The case of the disappearing object: narratives and artefacts in homes and a museum exhibition from Pakistani heritage families in South Yorkshire', *Museum and Society*, 8/1: 1–17.

Rabinow, P. (1977) *Reflections on Fieldwork in Morocco* (Berkeley: University of California Press).

Samuels, R. (1984) *Theatres of Memory* (London: Verso).

Smith, A. (2010) *The Ghost Story 1840–1920: A Cultural History* (Manchester: Manchester University Press).

Solnit, R. (2010) *A Field Guide to Getting Lost* (Edinburgh: Canongate Books).

Solnit, R. (2013) *The Faraway Nearby* (Cambridge: Granta Books).

Stewart, S. (1993) *On Longing: Narratives of the Miniature, the Gigantic, the Souvenir, the Collection* (Durham, NC: Duke University Press).

6

Pre-dreaming: Telepathy, Prophecy and Trance

Gerd Baumann with Walo Subsin
and doctoral students
Department of Anthropology, University of Amsterdam

Shortly after handing over the draft of this chapter, Gerd (Gerhardt) Baumann, a fine anthropologist and the senior author of this chapter, passed quietly away in his home in Amsterdam. In personal conversations leading up to the writing of his piece he told me something of its background and intent. If he had survived he would have gone on to a deeper analysis of these preliminary and as yet rather bare findings – perhaps one of his students may, in time, be moved to fill the gap. In the meantime, since he can no longer speak for himself I have taken the liberty of reproducing here what he told me. The first section of the chapter below is thus cast, as I believe he would have wished, as if his, but in my words, conveyed, as a trusted friend, on his behalf.

I have also ventured to insert some minor revisions and additions to what he himself regarded as a first draft. This is in places where, it seems to me and others, the sense is not as clear as he would have wished. I know from conversations with him more or less where he wanted to go and think he would have been pleased that, however imperfectly, I have tried to follow him.

Dear Gerhardt, may your dreams, as you so richly deserve, be sweet. [RF]

A few years ago, Ruth Finnegan approached me out of the blue. She wanted to consult me about the study of dreams – strange as, though (some) anthropologists have indeed focused on this topic, my own work up to then had been on such subjects as multi-ethnic London, immigrants and identity.[1]

But, amazingly, she was right.

From a child I have had what are sometimes called déjà-vu dreams, dreams, that is, that later turn out to have been predictive in the sense that when I came, later, to the actual real experience, I knew that this was, somehow, the second time round. Ever since childhood I have had such dreams, often several times a week.

I mentioned the subject to my group of about a dozen Ph.D. students in the University of Amsterdam, drawn from many continents in the world. As anthropologists, I could reasonably expect them to be open-minded on the subject (others might well be dismissive of this irrational topic); they might also, I thought, know of comparative accounts or case studies that I could use, as a friend, to respond to Ruth's inquiry (it was far from my thought that I could possibly be in a position to write anything on the subject myself, far less something of any substance).

To my astonishment a third of them turned out to have similar dreams. Even more amazing, the same was true for a third, again, of the following year's doctoral intake. In the context of the open give and take of our mutual learning there was no reason whatsoever to disbelieve them, either at the outset or in what they later shared with the group. It true that, as emerges in all treatments of such subjects, and certainly in this volume, there is always the epistemological issue of what is truth?, reality?, how *prove* anything? But as scientists we can only go on the evidence we have in people's actions and words. What other can we seek? For now, that has to be enough.

It was too good an opportunity to miss. My doctoral students and I set up a joint research project, where those with the experience of predictive or pre-dreaming (as I will call it) – dreaming of something that had not yet happened but in the event did so – were interviewed by the rest. Then the results were reported and, up to a point, analysed (there was no time for more).

The results were designed to feed into the question of how widespread pre-dreaming might be. Is it essentially of the far away and long ago, as commonly assumed (if people think about such a topic at all, that is)? Might it be of the present too and of contemporary import? And while we might not be surprised to find reports of such experiences among superstitious, backward and peasant people and the like (the folk as they are sometimes dubbed), could educated and modern-looking people possibly engage in what are, to many, irrational and unfounded practices? Finally, the crucial question for us as anthropologists: does the experience run across all cultures?

The results were startling, but there is of course no way they can be generalised. These were just two groups of about a dozen highly educated and culturally open individuals each. Nevertheless what they had to say was first-hand, open, often on a subject about which (like many people perhaps) they had not been prepared to speak before. Their reports furthermore acquired some validation and authority as being produced in the setting of a university and department known for their rigorous research methodologies. The findings suggest, at the very least, that it is worth conducting further research into the distribution of pre-dreaming. Given that it is a subject that it is not, in many settings, the done thing to talk about, even, as we found, in some cultures stigmatised, it may be more widespread among the population than is generally realised.

And whatever the more general conclusion, here we have at any rate a series of primary, validated and self-described case studies to add to the others in the volume. I do not know (nor does Ruth) of any other similar study, and to that extent this account must be regarded as having the value of uniqueness

(RF on behalf of GB, based on Baumann 2012–14).

Gerd Baumann with Walo Subsin et al.

To Start: What is 'Pre-dreaming'?

The first thing that all we predictive dreamers in this study shared was a heightened and sharpened recognition of *spaces* that could not be known before. All of us pre-saw future spaces, complete with furniture, lighting by windows, sunlight or lamps or in twilight, and many in buildings or other spaces they did not know before.

But though we were pretty clear, if mostly close-mouthed, about what we experienced, the terminology to speak about this in more general, agreed terms was not readily available to us. Science, it seems, has no made-up Greek or Latin name for what we mean here by our predictive dreaming , as it does, for instance, for telepathy (artificial Greek for partaking at a distance). The Greek *promnésia* (fore-memory) might have worked, but the Greeks themselves call it déjà -vu dreaming.

The matter is not so simple in other language clusters. Yedan Li, one of our group, writes:

> In China's major psychological literature, déjà-vu is called huan yi, literally 'illusional memory', or ji shi gan, literally 'it seems that you have known or have felt this before'. Some authors also use the words from Japan. As far as I know, all those words are translations from French. I cannot find an original concept of déjà-vu in the traditional literature. (Yedan Li, email of 13 March 2012)

So even Greek, Chinese and Japanese, as well, by the way, as Arabic, use either déjà-vu directly, or translate it straight from the French (was this thing a French invention of Dr Whoever who coined the word?).

The Dreamers

So let us return to the solid ground of what our informants tell us, amplifying the first description, then widening out to a measure of cross-cultural comparison.

First, how and why is this skill (or affliction?) acquired? A common thesis among the pre-dreamers was heredity. All of us trace our gift as coming through the female line: the two homosexual men through their mothers and back to their great-great-grandmothers; the rest of the sample, females, traced it to their female ancestors in straight matrilineal reckoning (cultural context and contrast did not seem to matter). There presumably cannot be a matrilineal gene for the capacity to pre-dream, so perhaps these are self-justificatory explanations for the ability that all of us are, in fact, happy to have

Our dreamers' spatial pre-dreams were also made of constellations. They were either *with* other people, or else had them around them, all in precise spatial order and surroundings. We distinguish *with* from *around* because two perspectives are possible. Some previews were at eye-level perspective, pre-seeing known or unknown, others as if the dreamer was present, seeing through a camera eye. Others were from a bird's-eye perspective, seeing through the dreamer's eyes indeed but as if floating above the action.

One strange case was Subsin, who pre-saw a place he had never imagined himself visiting:

> On my third trip back to [my native] Thailand, I saw, from bird's-eye perspective, a sun-burnt dark-skinned lone man, with one of those tourist cotton hats on, amidst kangaroos. I heard his voice, and it was like mine by voice and accent. A friend in Thailand, the English-born doctor, suddenly persuaded me, a month or so later, to fly with him for a quick holiday in Darwin, Australia. And there it was: me alone amidst kangaroos hopping like mad.

The horizontal pre-view camera, as it were, reproduces distances between the self and others. The vertical or angled pre-view camera on the other hand is close enough to recognise furniture, lighting and constellations of others in either a known or an unforeseeable space.

A camera, however, though a useful image up to a point, is not a sufficient simile or comparison. For one thing, this camera can have blurred spots. Unknown people appear with blurry faces, as they do in TV shots of people that need to be kept anonymous. None of our dreamers foresaw the faces of people they did not know, even if they had seen photos of them (as is now easy by googling or face-paging unknown people before encountering them at anything from a party to a job interview): they did not pre-dream them. All the same, the dreamers somehow recognised in what space they would meet previously un-knowns, eventually in eye-to-eye contact, or had pre-seen them as from a surveillance camera perspective. Many pre-dreamers had also helped their deficient cameras through voice recognition.

Voices always talk. It can be just snippets. Or it can be exchanges between self and others that last over four or five sentences. You recognise them just as a fieldworker remembers interviews when s/he has not had the opportunity to take notes in writing: by key words and phrases that remain in the memory until after the interview. All fieldworkers, from social scientists to social workers, and whether pre-viewers or not, know this as a mnemonic mechanism. Pre-dreamers however have, sometimes, literally heard it before.

So if all pre-dreams are 3-D, what about 4-D, including colour and sound or voice? For colour, Subsin is a fine test case, as he is colour-blind and needs friends to buy colour-matching clothes:

I was always colour-blind. When, as a child, I painted grass blue and skies pink, everybody admired my imaginative art work. At age fifteen, my art teacher told me I was colour-blind. Then I learned the names of colours from colour-seeing people, and I learned to put names to very intense colours. Yet my déjà-vus [pre-dreams] are technicolour: red surfaces burn like fire, and blue ones are cool like ice! In real life, I still need someone to say colour-match or not.

Sound recognition goes even beyond persons' voices and one's own words and sometimes afore-heard replies. Baumann, trained in musical composition and organ playing, pre-heard his (pretty incompetent) compositions and, more convincingly, pre-heard organs in their best combinations of from five to fifty registers (of which, of course, one selects any number between one and, if vaingloriously stupid, all). There were only the vaguest spatial indications of where the registers would be pulled or stopped on unknown organs: very much like the blind spots on unknown faces that we mentioned earlier.

Besides the films (so to speak) with limited vision, there were also silent films. These had more extended vision. One of these presented a time-shifting mother–daughter telepathy, as reported by Lotte about the time she had to fly to England.

> Afraid of flying, I booked the aisle seat nearest to the Emergency Exit (by the way, the most intelligent tip for forced fliers). A night or two before flying, I dreamt about my flight to England (I departed Tuesday 20 March and came back today, 24 March). I dreamt I was sitting on the plane, just two chairs away from the side exit doors. When taking off, the plane crashed and 'landed' on a road next to the airport, but it was a positive crash because nobody was dying and I escaped out of the side exit via the wing of the plain. A colleague of mine, not on the plane, was suddenly there too, and I clearly saw myself and him running on the road because people said the plane was going to explode. So we ran, nothing tragic really happened and an ambulance was arriving. Well, on the departure day, I was nervous as hell (I did not tell anyone about my dream, because when I was young I tended to 'feel' things: when a close friend of my family died, I was a baby [*sic*] and I got very wild during my sleep at the time she died. When my grandfather died, when I was eight years old, I was sitting up during my sleep and said: 'Dag, opa' ['Bye, grandad'].

On the flight this week, nothing happened, luckily, and I felt completely relieved after the departure. When I came back, I was again very nervous, because my dream felt like I was not in the Netherlands. Nothing happened. But today [the day of her return], I could finally tell my mother about this very scary dream and she finished my story: 'You were sitting right there, two away from the Emergency Exit, am I right?!' She had almost exactly the same dream just yesterday night (the night before my return)!

So, well, telepathy or not: there is something, definitely.

Telepathy with the precision of a pre-dream also happened simultaneously, albeit one-sidedly, in the same week. Subsin dreamt in Arizona of Baumann climbing the steep wooden staircase in a tiny Amsterdam shop which both had visited together once and separately often, each time with each other's wish-lists in mind. Here is Subsin on the recognition of face by voice, and at the same time the precise location:

> I had a dream the other night [Monday to Tuesday 26 March 2012] with you in it. I really didn't see your face, but I recognised your voice immediately. I saw your silhouette with bright light shining behind you from upstairs. You were calling out for Tommy. I woke up, calling out Tommy [myself], then went for a pee and back to sleep. Strange, I remembered it in the car on my way to work. I was reminded of the dream. How's your friend Tom?

Strangely, he did not recognise my face in a space he knew, but could not know I was in at the selfsame time, but space without face gave the soundtrack to the telepathy.

> It was not Baumann's friend called Tom, who Subsin knows exists, but happened at precisely the same time (treating the nine-hour time-zone difference between Subsin and Baumann as zero) and concerned Baumann's favourite shop assistant whom, unlike all other customers, he calls Pan Tommy, whom Baumann was looking for in vain in a fairly urgent matter.

Unlike telepathic dreams, prophetic dreams are recognised by probably all humans, at least in their sacred texts or myths, where they are described with pre-view-like precision. Formulated as myth or sacred texts, they were and are life-changing for all believers. Often, too, it is the same for the scholars who study them. Yet listen to this prophetic present secret of Carla Bringas, a Peruvian-born doctoral student in her mid-twenties at the Universities of Amsterdam and Osaka, Japan:

> Years later, after my scholarship for Europe was denied, I was granted a scholarship for Japan. I did not remember immediately about that dream until months later, once in Japan, some particular day I was having the same breakfast of the dream in a similar room,

and in a very irritated mood. And then . . . I was already speaking Japanese, at that moment with my Korean neighbour. My irritable mood stopped when it suddenly came to my mind, that dream. Twelve years later I remembered that dream and I thought 'Déjà-vu!'

Prophetic dreams of this kind of visual déjà-vu quality can thus not easily be sorted into wish dreams or fear dreams. The dreamers remembered them as emotionally neutral, in the style of a documentary film without commentary. All such pre-dreamers had both fear dreams and wish dreams, manifested as déjà-vu – predictive. All were emotionally neutral when they happened, and the pleasure or self-assurance only came at the moment of recognition.

The pre-viewer Subsin remembered a dream from the age of nine, perhaps earlier:

> I had, still in Thailand, a school atlas of the USA in my hands, but it slipped out of my hands. Then, I saw New York as I imagined it from postcards, I was there, again in bird's-eye perspective, and so I know I was destined to find my second re-incarnation in this one life in the USA. Visiting New York took plenty more years, but my mother managed the miracle that I could join her in the States when I was nine. I also pre-dreamed another wish fulfilment, when, on my second trip to [my native] Thailand, I realised I had been there before, receiving my Blessing as a Novice Monk in the [Buddhist] monastery above my home village.

One wish fulfilment pre-dream was to be tested by him and his lover: 'I was in Paris, and they had strange boats, all black, and with a rowing guy, rowing away at the back. You were already in it, I got in, but suddenly you vanished, and only the rowing guy was there.' The déjà-vu was received in the month while the lovers were planning a trip to Paris three months away. Whether re-premonition of Death in Venice, or Paris and Venice as the two romantic cities in Europe, clearly a wish fulfilment. 'But bad dreams, too: my childhood concussion, falling down the staircase in my grandparents' house, and the concussion, me run over by a truck, with that memory loss about some periods that I am only starting to remember.'

More comparatively, prophetic pre-dreaming of imminent deaths can mobilise the symbolisms we have learned from myths and sacred iconographies. The New Testament, for instance, consists of nothing but retrospective fulfilments of Jewish messianic prophecies, but that does not make it bad literature. By way of a simpler but equally symbolic prophecy, Baumann, then aged twenty-one, pre-dreamed the dying of his long-suffering mother. A skeleton flew across the garden and came in through the French doors of her bedroom that opened of their own accord. She died, three days later, of her own accord, to escape unbearable suffering. Another premonition of death came to Lotte, as we heard above, about the grandfather she loved.

Sampling Cultural Contrasts: Dream Management, Culture, Conventions

To chart some cultural differences in the reception and communications, we add data from five further people, all at present Ph.D. candidates in the Netherlands. We treat all eight of us one-by-one, but according to the same ordering of the information. We order them by a simple proximity of dream cultures or similarity of symbols. Since we write in a Germano-Latin language, we start with the language group that we all used to communicate, then spiral out via the Mediterranean and Hispanic mother tongues, and then further away, to China and Thailand.

Indo-EuropeanLanguage Worlds, 1: Mainly Germanic

Lotte from the Netherlands

Dreamer Profile
I think I am an average dreamer, with a déjà-vu pre-dream maybe twice a year.

Cultural Stigma?
In the Netherlands, there is not a stigma as such, but we follow the common proverb, 'Do like normal, that's mad enough by itself.' So I tell only my mother and my favourite aunt about them, and you guys in the focus group of course.

Recurring Dreams or Motifs
(here we need to give the whole conversation, as it happened, not quite by telepathy, but certainly by mutual intuition.

Lotte: A few years ago, I regularly had this dream in which I was clinging on to a very high lamp post during a storm. Sometimes, this lamp post was situated in the middle of a dark deep ocean. I had this dream once a week. It suddenly stopped. I don't have dreams like that any more now. I only have a recurring dream when I am just asleep and I am relaxing my muscles. I always get a little shock then which wakes me up. Just before that shock I always dream that I am falling from the stairs or a stoop or stumbling over an object.

GB [Gerd Baumann]: Were you maybe the first, or first young woman, in your family to make it to university?

Lotte: Now that you mention it, I am the first in our family getting into university and doing a Ph.D., never really realised that! Mention it.

Death Dream
My telepathic fear-of-death dream is described above. I had it a few days before my flight; she had it on the day of my flying back and intuited which seat I was sitting in.

Gerd from Germany/Britain

Dreamer Profile
As a vivid dreamer and notorious déjà-viewer, I have learned, like Lotte, to be reticent about it.

Cultural Stigma?
People in Germany, Britain or the Netherlands may think I lay a special claim to obscurantist knowledge, and like all of us, I am a rationalist – or wish to be.

Recurring Dreams or Motifs
Like Yannis below, I had recurring catastrophic dreams as a child: old-timer cars, my greatest love at ages five to twelve, all fell into an abyss and meant the end of the world.

Death Dreams
Like Tania below, I sought my long-dead father's approval of my re-found lover and beloved. The two shared the front bench in my father's dearest object: his first car, a pre-war wreck that he bought in 1949 and sold in 1951, before I was born. My long-dead mother, too, was introduced to my re-found lover, thirty-eight years after she died. Both dreams excluded me: once I was on the back bench of the pre-war wreck; once my mother told my lover all my secrets. My symbolic pre-dream of my mother's death was described above.

Indo-European Language Worlds, 2: Indo-European-Roman and Latin America

Yannis from Greece

Dreamer Profile
I am a vivid dreamer, but have no pre-dreamed déjà-vus. My dreams are so realistic, however, that I sometimes pinch myself to know if this is a dream. As you know, I am a rationalist, but I cannot say whether the pinching is in the dream or in the state of half-sleep.

Cultural Stigma?
There is no stigma attached to déjà-vus in Greece, so telling people would count as banal or trivial. However the Greek

Orthodox Church might see these as possession dreams, af-
flictions to be exorcised.

Recurring Dreams or Motifs
My dreams, however, are like déjà-vus, and there are two
recurring dreams: the bad one is a global catastrophe, with all
the images of disaster movies, and even with zombies in them;
but it may go back to the Athens earthquake.

Death Dreams
I had no premonitions, but I had a consolation dream: my
mother died when I was ten; at age fourteen, I saw her among
the ones she loved most, sitting around a round table: her
father, her husband and me, and she literally just fell asleep.

Vanessa from Portugal

Dreamer Profile
I am a vivid dreamer, but am not sure I have real déjà-vus.

Cultural Stigma?
There is no stigma on déjà-vus in Portugal. People are perfectly
at ease sharing moments of recognition or other so-called
paranormal experiences.

Recurring Dreams or Motifs
I have no recurring dreams as such, but a recurring motif that
always astonishes me: I fly through the air, head first and arms
back, and in a blue cape exactly like Superman. I have sometimes even picked up and flown to safety a person in danger.

Death Dreams
I never had any, since nobody I loved or love has died yet, not
even my great-grandparents. However, recently I dreamt that
I was in the old house where my grandparents have lived before
they moved. It was empty, and I ripped a piece of wallpaper

off the wall as a memento. Last night I was worried about my
grandparents.

Tania from Bilingual Canada

Dreamer Profile:
I am a vivid dreamer, and I also dream my déjà-vus. Sometimes
I wake up and know: this was the pre-dream of a déjà-vu
recognition.

Cultural Stigma?
You tell some and not others. There is no cultural pattern, it
is just about whom you trust.

Recurring Dreams or Motifs
I also fly, though not like Superman, as Vanessa does, but like
swimming breast-strokes in the air. Once I even had oncoming
traffic: an unknown woman, like me in pyjamas. The woman
said: 'Never mind, of course dreams can intersect!' I would
recognise her in the street if we saw each other. I have a few
other dreams that I am expecting to turn out to be déjà-vus.
Déjà-vus can last for up to a minute in real-life real time.

Death Dreams
I dreamed of introducing my boyfriend to my long-dead grandfather in my grandfather's house in Sicily.

Carla from Peru

Dreamer Profile
I have pre-seen déjà-vus only incidentally. The déjà-vu of a
girl in Peru speaking an Asian language in Asia came from a
dream aged eleven in Peru and became real when I was twenty-
three. I am indeed waiting for other déjà-vus to become real.
I remember them a few days before they become real. I have

no experiences of telepathy. The rest I know you have in the text.

Cultural Stigma?
I mention these dreams to friends. I guess they are hard to imagine for other people that do not experience them. And of course, it can be powerful if one discovers one has some sort of mental power.

Non-Indo-European Language Worlds: China and Thailand

Both Yedan from China and Walo from Thailand/USA speak perfect English. Yet the cultural embeddedness of dreams demands cross-cultural translations, as we shall see.

Yedan from China

Dreamer Profile
I am not sure that my déjà-vus come from dreams.

Cultural Stigma?
The Chinese phrase ji-shi-gan is focused on the feeling of recognition, and when I first learned the word déjà-vu from TV, I thought: goodness! French even has a name for it that includes the pre-dreaming! Even when I told a new Chinese friend in Amsterdam on the day before our Focus Group, he said: 'Hmm, and dreaming it before, that is a little weird!' I think I do not get my déjà-vus from dreams. In any case, normal Chinese try to explain it by watching movies or TV. The people who try not to explain it away are of the more educated classes: government officials, and business people sometimes even boast about them.

Recurring Dreams or Motifs
When I was at High School, age sixteen to eighteen, my teacher embarrassed me about my bad maths. The same dream came

back two or three times, each time with the same ending, which only much later became a realistic perspective: I will be a Doctor of Law, so I need no maths. My most recent déjà-vu was this one: on my first day at Amsterdam, I took the tram to Rokin Street, I stopped in my tracks: I had already seen this strange street with a river right down the middle, and beside it a lady parking a silver-coloured car and getting out in a striking red coat. I stood rooted to the ground and stared at her, until I felt embarrassed and walked on

Death Dreams
On the eve of 5 April, when we commemorate the dead with traditional rituals, I dreamed about my grandfather who died seven years ago, and I dreamed about the chalk circle that should be the centre of the ritual. The same night, my mother had the same dream, and on 5 April we had it together for the first time.

Walo from Thailand/USA

Dreamer Profile
People I share the bed with say I dream vividly, and mutter aloud in several languages, like Baumann. My dream memory is bad; my déjà -vus are seldom, and they concentrate on periods of crisis. Once, I had none for sixteen years.

Cultural Stigma?
None, as talking about dreams or déjà-vus is normal in Thailand, as it is with Mediterranean people.

Recurring Dreams or Motifs
On dreams I do not know, on motives I know: it is death and reincarnation.

Dreams of Death and Reincarnation
The two are the same to me, as you know. A prose poem came

to me last week, when I visited my mother after two years' absence. You should know that I was the sole surviving foetus of triplets that died in an accident at seven months' pregnancy. My mother had to eat a dead crow, so as to grant the dead kids reincarnation. I even wrote a poem about it:

Bird? or God?

I was the one that flew up in the sky,
and with my droppings I fertilised the earth.
    I have forgotten how long I was part of the earthquake
    or how many lives I lived.

In my past life as a crow, I was transporting souls
    to their destination. Doing that,
    I was shot down and then ingested.

My love for life comes from the souls I transported.
They rewarded me with this life in human form,
able to carry on this burden of living.

For now, when I see my dreams from a bird's-eye view
of the earth, they are merely glimpses of my past.

With such poetry, who wants science?

So we leave it at that. There is surely much analysis still to do and explanatory hypotheses to explore. But here at least we have a meaure of first-hand evidence from a group of carefully trained observers recounting their experiences in good faith for other scientists to augment and analyse.

Notes

[1] For example Baumann 1996, 2009.

Gerd Baumann with Walo Subsin et al.

References

Baumann, Gerd (1996) *Contesting Culture: Discourses of Identity in Multi-Ethnic London* (Cambridge: Cambridge University Press).
Baumann, Gerd (2012–14) Personal communications.
Baumann, Gerd and Gingrich, Andre (2009) *Identity/Alterity: A Structural Approach* (Oxford: Berghahn).

7

Trance and Sacred Language in Religious Daoism

Phyllis Ghim-Lian Chew*

Daoism is part of the 'Chinese religion', which comprises two other 'faiths', Buddhism and Confucianism. This eclectic mixture in the Chinese religion allows a Chinese religionist to be able to claim to be Daoist, Buddhist and Confucian at the same time. As a 'lover of nature', he is Daoist; as one 'who is serious about his duties', he is a Confucian; and finally as one who is 'aware of the transience of life', he is a Buddhist (Chew 1993). This is a syncretism illustrated in folk temples not just in Singapore but also in other thriving communities such as Taiwan, Macao and Hong Kong, where statues of Confucius, Laozi and the Buddha, the founder-teachers of Confucianism, Daoism and Buddhism respectively, are set up alongside those of traditional Daoist immortals as objects of veneration.

It should also be noted that while we are interested in expounding on the Daoist 'religion' (*Daojiao*), this is very different from Daoist 'philosophy' (*Daojia*). The latter is represented by the philosophies of Laozi and Zhuangzi, documented in the classical texts ascribed to them. On the other hand, the Daoist religion which is the popular religion of the masses is dependent on the service of spirit-mediums and monks whose main function is to communicate with the gods and spirits on behalf of humankind. Understandably, these two disparate strands have given rise to much perplexity by outside observers, one being a sophisticated philosophy and the other interwoven with elaborate rituals. Finally, while we have from the outset taken pains to differentiate between Daoist religion and Daoist philosophy, it must be noted that religious Daoists themselves draw no such distinction between the two, as is evident from the eclectic incorporation of the philosophical *Dao de jing* into their own traditions.

While religion may be a well-studied field, especially in its doctrinal or scriptural aspects, its practices in the spiritual and mystical lives of the vast masses are greatly under-researched. Most present-day scholars are also so steeped in secularism that they are often oblivious to the depth of spiritualism among the Chinese masses. This account will centre on the less understood and less known 'religious Daoism', which has mostly been under the shadow of philosophical Daoism.

Over the centuries, religious Daoism, which comprises a large dose of shamanism, has branched into many distinct sects, all with their own histories and traditions, and all differentiating themselves from each other basically through different doses of practice from the streams of shamanism, Confucianism, Buddhism and Daoism (Clammer 1993). In addition, the published studies on the Daoist religion often start from a western or Christian worldview of what a religion should be. For example, it is not uncommon to find book titles like 'Chinese magic and superstitions' or 'Chinese-medium cults' and minority terminologies such as 'cults', 'folk festivals', 'superstitions', 'polytheism' when referring to religious Daosim, which paradoxically, is the religion of the majority, i.e. the masses.

The Temple

We will enter the Daoist temple, traditionally a focal point for the Chinese community, to observe the phenomenon of trance and sacred language. It is much like a community hall –while the medium is in trance, adherents may go about their individual worship, be it the folding of incense paper, praying with joss-sticks at different altars in the temple or chatting in a corner. While silence may be golden in other faiths such as Orthodox Christian, Hindu and Buddhist, this is not the case in a Daoist temple, which is often noisy with drums, gongs, children running around, mahjong players etc. Here the practices of clairvoyance, fortune telling, exorcism, invocation and prayer are everyday affairs (Dean 2009).[1]

In Daoist temples, one may witness the ubiquitous practice of spirit-mediumship and mediums who subject themselves to extreme self-mortification practices such as piercing their cheeks and bodies with swords (Heinze 1993).[2] Mediums vary widely in age and every sort of personality, and may be of either sex. They are able through the use of special language to travel and retrieve ancient wisdom within the spiritual dimension. The medium invokes the *Shen* (spirits or deity) to take over his/her body and do the healing that is required. *Shens* are compassionate beings and manifest their generosity by answering dreams or by giving answers to questions. Mediums may also visit other worlds/dimensions to bring guidance to misguided souls and to ameliorate illnesses of the human soul caused by foreign elements. Unfortunately in the West, derogatory terms for spirit mediums abound through negatively connotative terms such as witch, wizard, shaman, magician and sorcerer.

Data Collection and the Site in Question

The site of research is Singapore, the only country in South-East Asia with a Chinese majority. It is a small thriving island city-state on the trade route between China and India. Religion appears to be alive and well in the lives of Singaporeans, and freedom of worship is enshrined in the Singapore constitution. The ten religions of Singapore (Baha'i Faith, Buddhism, Christianity, Jainism, Judaism, Hinduism, Islam, Sikhism, Taoism, Zoroastrianism) are represented at the Inter-Religious Organisation (IRO), a central body consulted by the government onreligious affairs.[3] Where the Daoist faith is concerned, there are likely to be more than 500 Chinese Taoist temples in Singapore that have some regular spirit-medium consultations. Beyond these official consultations in temples, there are also many spirit-mediums who practise in private homes across the city, and for whom no statistics are available.[4]

I belong to a familial tradition with an active belief in ancestor worship and the spirit world. I myself believe in the existence of a universal God and/or Creator and the many spirits that inhabit this world. I believe too that the 'other world', the spirit world, may 'be closer than my life vein' although it is 'hidden'. I have had detailed participant observation at Daoist ceremonies in Daoist temples as a child and now as a researcher. I have attended numerous Daoist events, such as anniversaries of particular deities, funeral rites, festivals etc. As a child, I attended Daoist festivities with relatives and witnessed many mediums in action. I have had meals with mediums when they were out of their trance; they have been relaxed, friendly and 'very human' at these occasions, In my childhood and adulthood, I must have sat through countless sessions with temple mediums as they went on with their client consultations, and shared meals with devotees. I enjoy participating in temple entertainments such as *wayangs*[5] and street possessions. In recent years, I have been able to record some of these activities on a small video camera and occasionally on my hand phone. I count a handful of spirit mediums as my personal friends. Interviews with these mediums were done during such informal occasions, conducted in the vernacular (Hokien), which also happens to be my mother tongue.

In writing this account, I read and collected data from different sources so that the final picture could be more broad-based. I have also attempted to incorporate the contributions of linguistics, political economy, history and sociology so as to provide a wider and more balanced analysis. I have had the privilege of a very modern 'western' education, notably post-graduate qualifications in linguistics from the United States and Australia, a background which has enabled me to work as a teacher-educator in the National Institute of Education for many years. While this particular research study is unconventional, being on trance and sacred language rather than on human language in the classroom, I hope to grasp the native point of view and to realise the vision of a world from the point of view of the religious Daoist.

As most writers unfortunately have been innocent of extensive association with mediums, and the number of mediums whose careers are known to us in any detail from the published literature so far are few, I have chosen two methods in this study: (1) participant observation at Daoist events where spirit-mediums were in attendance; (2) case studies of lives of spirit -mediums through one-to-one interviews. It is my hope that this account focusing on trance and sacred language in religious Daoism may give some insight and add impetus to more research on this subject.

Language and Religion

In many cultures and religions, the origin of language or speech is seen as a gift of a divine being to humankind. In the Bible John 1:1 begins: 'In the beginning was the Word . . .' Sura 96, Al Alaq, of the Quran extols the reader to 'Read in the name of your Lord . . .' In Genesis, Adam is given the power to name the acts of creation.

Resources of beautiful, poetic and powerful words, as evident in world scriptures, have been handed down from the seers and ancestors of past ages, and their legacy has been a tradition of mystical powers of healing (Finnegan 2012). Indeed in many religions, sacred words contain a mystic quality and are so powerful that most religions have imposed special restrictions on their use in the name of respect and reverence. For example, in orthodox Judaism, it is regarded as sacrilegious to pronounce the name of God, and in certain denominations of Daoism such as the Yiguan Dao[6] certain sacred words or phrases, called 'the three jewels' cannot ever be sounded to oneself or uttered to another soul until a certain time when certain rituals and ceremonies are performed (Lim 2011).

The origin of writing is also associated with religious accounts. Deities such as the god Thoth in Egyptian myths, Brahma in Hindu religion and Odin in Icelandic sagas, are regarded as the creators of speech and sometimes writing. In Chinese mythology, writing is traced to a heaven-sent 'river-horse' or turtle which appeared from a river before a legendary god-emperor. This turtle did not speak Chinese but he carried the gift of writing as a set of strokes on his back. The laws of writing were then written down. An alternative mythology of the origin of writing states the case of an 'emperor' who, after listening to the birds, and when they had flown away, silently copied the marks their delicate feet had left behind in the light sand.[7]

In addition, language enables us to traverse the vast borderland of dreams and liquid knowing, and is probably the cause of making the anthropoid human. It is species-specific. Our ability to symbolise non-concrete objects through language permits us to move conceptually thorough time and space. Our words enable us to traverse wild fantasies, describing in exquisite detail and with great emotion encounters, real or imagined. It carries us to a world where the living cannot pass.

It is unfortunate that the role of language and the power it ignites in the imagination and soul have not attracted the attention they deserve because, for the Daoist, language was certainly not the self-arranged abstruseness of accountants, lawyers and academics. Indeed, the word and the thing are often the same. Language is linked to the cosmological hierarchy with the divine at the apex. Words are believed to be inscribed on tablets of gold in the highest heavens and are imbued with a certain spirit. They are stored on the mountain of jade capital in Mystery Metropolis, the centre of the Heaven of the Grand Network. Celestials residing in these heavens transmit their wisdom either through liturgical manuscripts and scriptures handed down and recopied within lines of hereditary transmission or directly by possessing the body of a medium. The ancestral text often preserves a language or a variety for its use which has ceased to be used by the wider linguistic community. This adds to its special potency by giving it an ancient wisdom. In this sense the sacred texts in Daoism are not merely containers of divine truth but also powerful means of magic, seats of celestial potency and signs of the ultimate.

The Spirit or Sacred Language

An other-worldly spirit language is necessary if the medium is to communicate with the innumerable gods or celestials, immortals, deified heroes, forces of nature, all of whom are empowered to intervene in human affairs. Resembling in functions the imperial state bureaucracy, these spiritual beings make up a highly sophisticated structured pantheon. In the higher reaches of heaven, the immortals serve as celestial administrators along with nature gods and divinised human beings. They may empower the practitioner, granting him influence over the relevant entity and providing protection from all demonic and harmful influences.

This means that the intermediary or medium needs to possess a literary-mythological mental map which will enable him to recognise the who's who of the spiritual pantheon as he goes on his mission (cf. Pentikäinen and Simoncsics 2005). To elicit the deities' help and rapport, deeply subjective illocutionary acts such as gifting, flattering and threatening (sometimes these have to be done sequentially) must be performed, and registers and genres mastered. The *shen* or deities that are engaged all have a special affinity for the problems of daily life since they were all human beings at one time and therefore are deemed better suited to understand the frailties of the human condition.[8] However, it must be noted that it is only the minor and more insignificant *shen* who condescend to manifest themselves to humankind.[9] Some popular and 'communicative' *shens* are: Santaizi (三太子), the monkey god; Tianhou, the Queen of Heaven (天 后 聖 母,); Guan Gong (关 羽), and the child god Shan Cai Tong Zi (善財童子), who is also affectionately known as Zai Zai.[10]

I have managed to interview four mediums from different temples, while in their out-of-trance state, about the semiotics associated with the state of trance. In the following, Mediums A and B are part-timers – that is, they hold regular jobs besides their service as spirit-mediums for two evenings a week in a dedicated temple. While mediums may journey to the spirit world at any time, the purpose of an appointed time at a designated place (temple) is basically to provide a means for people to share in this religious experience. Mediums C and D are full-time mediums, in the sense that they are also the temple caretakers when they are not in trance. They receive a small stipend for their services. It should be noted that some deities do not permit their mediums to accept personal contributions to their upkeep, although clients may pay small amounts of cash for the maintenance of the deity's elaborate shrine and its daily demands of food and fruit offerings. All four mediums profess that they are called to the vocation out of a sense of 'service' to their community.

The following extracts recount their semiotic efforts to enter into the spirit world and to invoke the deity to enter the human condition through the vessel of his physical body:

Medium A: I light the joss-sticks in front of the altar and then I sit down and concentrate by closing my eyes. I chant a powerful invocation I learned as a girl. Then, gradually, Jiǔtiān Xuánnǚ (九天玄女, Mysterious Maid of the Highest Heavens) makes my body expand and I feel a heavy iron pocket of air not being able to move very well. Then I hear a click at the back of my head and I know nothing, because she takes over. Later, when she is ready to leave my body, I feel my blood steaming back – I can once again feel my fingers and toes and I feel that I have awoken from a long sleep. (A, lines 6870–6920)

Medium B: I first kneel and then I lie face down in front of Zai Zai (善財童子) (a statue on an altar). I will recite a short invocation, sometimes repeatedly, until I feel my body begin to rock uncontrollably. Then I see a shadow come over me – it seems to envelop, consume me. I am forced to vomit everything from my stomach [Medium B is not aware that there is a thick steam of bile emerging from his mouth as 'vomit'. The attendants around him take the vomit to means a purification of the body before the deity may enter]. I don't remember anything after that.

Medium C: My followers (temple attendants) begin to recite the chant to the beat of drums, the gong, the flute . . . The drums get louder and louder I close my eyes and I feel my body floating above my head and going into a different realm, very far away. It is so peaceful and I am oblivious to earthly concerns, but suddenly I hear the sound of thunder which rushes through my body, and I find myself fully awake and sitting on the dragon chair [the chair which the medium sits on is called 'dragon chair' and my followers taking off the robes of Guangze Zunwang (泽尊王) and dressing me up in my normal clothes; and then I realise that my body has already been used and I am now returned to myself.[11]

Medium D: I burn incense and practise purification on days before the trance. On the day where I must trance, I bathe, abstain from sex and abstain from meat. I do the ritual of bowing and prostrating in ten directions. I loosen my clothes to settle on a meditation cushion before Guan Gong's (关羽) altar. I visualise the seven gods of the dipper, the heavenly queen as well as Lord Lao surrounded by tigers and dragons – I call their names aloud when I see them; I use a mantra but may not finish saying it and then I just knock off – like irresistibly falling into a very deep sleep.

The above accounts show different ways of falling into trance. Some verbalise a chant they have memorised, often in front of an altar which contain visuals of the deity and other powerful talismanic signs. Still others more silently visualise images of the deity with their thought processes, bolstered with meaningful talismanic phrases until the deity 'arrives'. Some depend on music, usually rhythmic drumming to elicit a state of trance. Whatever it is, sacred language is helpful to the invocation of sacred thoughts and plays a major role in invoking trance.

In all four cases, when the deity arrives, the facial expression and bodily movement of the mediums change dramatically to take on that of the deity. This is because the deity has displaced the soul of the medium and suspended it in some kind of vacuum. Hence when a spirit-medium is in trance, his body and soul are separate and he or she is in a 'death-like' state. Jung (1960: 95, 99) has termed this the 'unconscious autonomous complexes' which appear as projections because they are not associated with the ego. This phenomenon is of course completely incompatible with common cultural assumptions and biases guiding western notions of 'self' and 'personhood' (Cohen and Barrett 2008).

Certain commonalities may be extracted from their narratives. First, the mediums are trancing in front of the altars which contain statues of their respective gods. All mediums are observed to focus on the statue of the particular deity they intend to invoke – bystanders should therefore not stand in between the medium and the deity, as this breaks the visual line of communication. I have seen photographers and spectators pushed aside when they attempt to photograph this event or attempt to obtain a closer view of what is going on. Trancing may take on different bodily postures – Mediums C and D are standing; Medium A is sitting still, while Medium B is lying prostrated on the floor. Medium D is standing and performing certain ritual theatrical steps with sacred hand gestures and incantations as his mind creates a cosmic scenario for his transformation. Music may be present: the beating and acoustic of the drum enable Medium C to achieve an altered consciousness whereby he may, if he wishes, contact an accessory from the spirit world to help him summon his host.

All four mediums were observed to transform within a span of fifteen to ninety minutes to an altered spiritual state whereby they were privy to all kinds of spiritual forces and to perform wondrous feats and to endure physical harm which are not normally possible in a human being. When 'possessed', the medium will take on the mannerisms and characteristics of the possessor through facial gestures and body movements. The purpose of this dramatic change is not so much to draw attention or create a spectacle for the audience, as many western accounts have come to believe (see Jordan 1999), but rather to lead the worshippers-seekers-adherents in a solemn ritual.

Each deity has their own special name and character, and a sacred spell must be addressed in their own terms and in their favourite way. There are special talismanic phrases and sacred words which are in use, some lasting a few seconds, others up to a few hours. The spell may be a word, a phrase or an entire text often filled with symbolic and mythological significance. This emotional belief and faith in its potency leads to tangible results, and the focused recitation gives the primordial gods the power to emerge from emptiness. Language therefore functions as the indispensable bridge to the divine.

Analysis of an Invocation

The following chant to Guangze Zunwang (泽尊王), the ancestral god of filial piety from Fujian, China, has been shared with me by Medium C. This deity is traced to one Guo Zhongfun, born to a poor family in 923 CE in Shishan, Na'an, Fujian. Guangze Zunwang's filial piety and ability to do miraculous deeds as a child led to his deification after his death at the tender age of sixteen. This well-known chant for devotees was first obtained from Shishan Fengshan Si (Phoenix Mountain) in Nan'an in particular and the sacred sites of Guangze Zunwang's cult in general. The chant may be used individually or in a congregation during trancing.

In Table 1, the Chinese words are on the left while the translation is on the right. (Note: the words in brackets are my own addition).

Table 1: Invocation to Guangze Zunwang

Invocation (in Chinese)	Invocation (translated into English)	Speech acts
广泽尊王咒	Guangze Zunwang (honorary King) Incantation	Invoking the sacred name of the deity
南无郭府大圣王 一心化身扶灵童 扶办鬼神神通大 当初小时也身在 南无	Namo, Guos family the great King the great King from Guos family devotely incarnated as (transformed into) a boy help people dealing gods and ghosts with great power even when he was a boy, he's got the [incarnation] Namo	Praising the deity by recounting the many praises of the deity, the deity's deeds the deity's attributes
香气沉沉应乾坤	strong scent fills the earth and the heaven	Inhaling the breeze of the sacred mountain abode of the deity.
应开凤山祖殿门	Opens the temple gate in Fengshan	Seeking admission at the gate to the deity's abode at Fengshan in the sacred Mount Phoenix through visualisaton

祖殿门下专拜请 广泽尊王降临来 南无	At the temple gate (we) humbly bend and request Guangze Zunwang(s) descendence Namo	Imploring the deity's descent (*kow tow* or prostration is required here)
九斩化身威猛烈 白衣童子 展威灵 惟首当年真总济	killing the nine incarnations fiercely, the boy in white exerts great power remembering all the saviour deeds he made then	Recalling (with awe, emotion and reverence) the young deity's prowess, achievements and past deeds
古今凡作人香 香 南无	until today whenever he appears the scent spreads Namo	Encouraging and visualisation of the deity's appearance
悦香关灵伏幕叩 显名千秋甚分明	in scent the spirit of the King withdrew and the curtains closed uphold (his) name for thousands of years	Revering the fact that Great spirits are only in the physical realm for the shortest duration. 'Curtain' signifies that the spirit world is here – only a curtain separates us.
稽首再拜诵真咒 复位威武降 临来	kowtow again, recite the holy incantation and request the returning of the almighty	Supplicating the deity to descend. This is accompanied by a prostration ritual.
南无，南无，南无	Namo, Namo, Namo	Revere, do homage, kowtow and trust.

The above incantation, which functions basically as an invocation, may appear simple if viewed through its English translation but read in its original classical Chinese is one of mysterious weight and beauty. As a stylised chant handed down through genealogical lines of discipleship, it brings with it the weight of historical credibility. Its grammar, syntax and lexis are arranged in an archaic fashion. It is a compelling text when memorised and internalised.

Read in the original Hokien, rhymes and rhythms enable the creation of a ladder to the gates of heaven whereby the deity may both ascend and descend. The speech acts of invocation, praising, inhaling, seeking, imploring, recalling, encouraging, supplicating, revering and trust are all intrinsically present. It is notable that the incantation is only successful when gestalt tendencies are employed, that is, that the brain sees, comprehends and self-organises a complex of information in a holistic and analogued way. The whole text is often greater than its parts, the human eye sees objects in their entirety before perceiving their individual parts, and the speaker should therefore learn the incantation as a whole, never reciting it in parts if the power, grandeur and mystical quality of the prose are to be preserved.

The invocation is set to music, making it effectively a chant which, when recited, is accompanied by the mesmerising effect of flute, drums and cymbals. It may be noted that a different temple worshipping the same saint is likely to have a different version or method of chanting and drumming, while the text may be the same. One intones the incantation a few times to internalise and feel the haunting pulsating vibration of every character. The use of the sacred word 'namo' six times in the text means 'bow, trust and do homage to the deity.'

Visualisation during recitation of the text is made easy since, in reading, the reader is in reality deciphering a series of logograms. Every character brings with it an array of historical-mythological narrative. Chinese characters are basically pictograms or pictorial representations of the morpheme represented, e.g. 山 for 'mountain' and 刀 for 'knife'. There are also ideograms which represent abstract concepts such as 'knife', 上 'up' and 下 'down', while 刃 is an ideogram meaning 'blade'. The logogram affects the mind in a different way from the speaker.

The text in Table 1 may also be regarded as a prime example of a performative as recounted in speech act theory, although there has not been much research on this in pragmatics (cf. Austin 1962: 5). Just as the priest may perform an act of legal marriage by declaring: 'I pronounce you man and wife', the medium in chanting this text is similarly performing a legal summoning of the deity.

However, performatives are often socially contested, just as a marriage may be deemed null and void if the priest turns out to be unlicensed. In our case, while the invocation may successfully persuade the deity to take over the medium's consciousness, it may not be viewed by sceptics as such since, in the first place, they do not believe that there are spirits with whom one may communicate. In addition, when sceptics try to test the invocation by using it in more restrictive laboratory conditions, it becomes no longer a performative, as the deity is unimpressed and will not cooperate. It is the emotional belief and faith which will create the reality.

The Role of Music

Music is a kind of language which may be effectively tapped to transport the soul more swiftly to another realm. Set to talismanic or sacred words, it is of particular significance in all faith traditions as it is able to create a heightened form of internal 'stirring' which will enable the soul to traverse to a higher state. In brief, it is a gateway to the soul. For this purpose many sacred scriptures are sung as mantras and chants rather than merely recited. Medium C has already recounted how rhythmic drumming transports him almost immediately to another realm.

When the questions posed by the devotees have all been answered, and the deity is ready to leave the body of the medium, music is once again employed together with other linguistic-semiotic devices. Here the attendants will burn talismanic paper and then sprinkle its ashes over the medium's head. On other occasions, the attendants will soak the talismanic paper in water before sprinkling the water on the medium's head. In addition, a trumpet may be blown, a gong sounded, or a decisive knock on wooden divination blocks may be used. It should be noted at this point that it is not the paper/metal/wood which is the talisman but rather the *sacred words* written on these materials which have the 'potency' to do what it is supposed to do. Through these measures, the medium will be suddenly jolted out of the trance and become 'human' again. The suddenly awakened medium will appear startled and 'dazed' and will attempt to shake his head, shoulders and limbs as if to 'readjust' physically to his normal condition. The medium is then helped by his attendants to the various altars where he may prostrate himself in gratitude to the deity(s) for their cooperation in their service to humanity.

Once this is done, the medium is restored to his human self and once again in possession of his own personality.

The Consultation Process

Worshippers visit the mediums to *wen shen* (ask or beg God) for both physical healing and to seek the moral advice and blessings of a higher authority. Here, the medium should be able to communicate directly with the worshippers, but it is difficult for him to do so since, as the deity incarnate, he is no longer able to use human language. Instead his language is at once elevated and 'strange', seemingly incomprehensible to all except his attendants. Hence temple mediums are often accompanied by a handful of attendants who may take turns acting as interpreter. These attendants have other functions when they are not acting as interpreters. They can be doing any of the following: wiping the altar table clean; handing ritual objects to the medium; distributing queue numbers to the crowd waiting for their turn at the consultation;[12] finding herbal medicine to be dispensed; explaining how charm papers are to be used, such as burning them, mixing the ashes with water for drinking or folding them to be worn as amulets; instructing visitors how many joss-sticks to put in the different censers, and in which sequence etc.

The deity does not speak in human language. In everyday conversation, participants share default assumptions and engage in a joint production (Sperber and Wilson 1995). Adherents understand that as they approach the medium in trance, they are speaking with a deity and not a human being. There are no shared assumptions between the deity and the human, and therefore ambiguities abound. The deity's language poses a challenge for comprehension. While most clients use the temple vernacular (Hokien) during the consultation, the deity will answer in the 'high' version, thus creating a classic diglossia of powerful-powerless. Further, the deity may not just speak in a high variety but also a different tongue. For example, if the deity is from the fifth century, he or she is likely to be speaking the fāngyán (regional language) and phonological variations (accent) of his era and region in China, making comprehension a challenge. Sometimes the deity may also break out in song, much like a Chinese opera singer, and this mode of communication also presents a different kind of challenge to comprehensibility.

I am not sure whether the language which the helper(s) attempt to translate is a form of glossolalia (cf. Samarin 1972). In two instances, I have had the opportunity to tape the speech of the medium-deity, but have not been able to make sense of it or to verify whether it is really the language of the historical period of the deity in question. What appears on my tape recorder is a phonologically structured human utterance but does not bear any resemblance to any natural language that I am aware of. I can only say for now that it is a human language, as there are accent, rhythm, intonation and pauses which break up the speech into distinct units. There are ostensibly nouns and verbs although I am not able to understand what they mean. It comprises strings of syllables, made up of Chinese sounds put together more or less haphazardly but emerging nevertheless as word-like and sentence-like units because of realistic, language-like rhythm and melody.

Unfortunately, it is not possible in this preliminary research to verify whether this is truly ancient Chinese speech, since the Chinese language is not phonetic and we have no idea of what ancient Chinese speech might sound like. While many western systems represent sounds, logographic systems such as Chinese and Japanese kanji use symbols to represent meaning directly and have no, or comparatively few, clues to pronunciation. Chinese writing has the special characteristics of not really being aligned, from the phonetic point of view, to a particular language. It uses *a posteriori* principles much like those used to create Esperanto and other modern artificial languages. The characters refer to ideas before referring to sounds, and a person can read them without knowing how to pronounce a single Chinese word, in the same way that a comic strip can be read without words. In other words, one and the same Chinese ideograph stands for a concept which can be read by people who, in the hundreds of spoken Chinese languages, do not understand each other. I know of no one who has done research on how accurate the version of classical Chinese is or whether it is a kind of glossolalia, but this is certainly an exciting research area for future scholars.

Talisman Writing and Trance

In traditional Chinese culture, the written word has always been held in high regard, and hence it is not surprising that it has been used to reinforce religious authenticity and power. Great prestige is tied to literacy since the writing and reading of classical Chinese has always been an imposing technical challenge. Literacy used to involve learning tens of thousands of distinct characters and to be very hard to learn. Literacy and the use of wényán (文言) (classical Chinese) was rare – it being the language of the literati, of diplomats and government officers – a group in imperial China which never constituted more than two per cent of the population. Paradoxically, while the temple-going population may be largely illiterate, the temple itself is adorned with many literary symbols on its walls, on its altars and on the robes of the mediums and attendants. Daoist temples use esoteric diagrams, charts of the universe, supernatural maps of sacred mountains and talismanic signs to activate the original powers of Dao. Temple walls and artefacts contain celestial signs and drawings that symbolise the essential power of god or heaven. Calligraphy is prevalent in cosmic charts or banners hung at doors and gateways. Symbols of cosmogony elements, the representations of the body, depiction of body gods or even symbolic representation of the underworld in most places abound (Kohn 2009).

The talisman is an object believed to contain certain magical properties which will provide good luck for the possessor and also protection from harm. In other faith traditions, a talisman is usually an amulet of some kind; for example, Catholics have been known to use the cross as a talisman in exorcism. However, Daoist-Chinese talismans are word-based, probably owing to the respect given to the Word.

In view of this cultural preference, the medium has on his table writing utensils to help him in talisman writing. While in the past, talismans were rectangular pieces of wood and metal, they are now, more recently, coloured paper (usually yellow, red or blue) inscribed in black or red ink with figurative signs, stylised characters and images. A special brush and ink are required for talismanic writing, although at times the ink may be redundant as the medium may sometimes write it with his own blood.[13] The words have magical powers as they are they are now handwritten by the deity and imbued with the energy of the writer. The gift of the talisman enables the receiver to carry it with him or her as a memento of the encounter with the gods – it also has the power to mediate all that he or she thinks, says and does. A talisman can only be handled and activated if the practitioner is in a high state of purity and mentally prepared to take on the powers it represents. On the talisman is the written word, written in black, white or red ink, which conceptually evokes the medium's intercession and contains the ability to provide vicarious experiences for both speaker and hearer.

The situation will dictate what the medium-deity will write on the talisman. In other words, what will be written is dependent on what one is actually asking the deity. Each talisman which is given is tailored to the person and comes with a different set of instructions such as to be displayed, to be burnt, to be conveyed or to be imbibed into the body. For a student who wishes to take an important examination, a talisman with words on it can be put in the pocket or wallet, which he can carry with him to the examination hall.

Different deities have different styles of drawings and writings. However, if a talisman is written for another deity rather than for an adherent, it is written differently. For example, when addressed to the gods of heaven, the characters point upwards and when addressed to the gods of earth, the characters point downwards. Here the seal of the medium become significant. Seals have traditionally been used by emperors, magistrates, government officials etc. as they represent authority, trust and power. When the deity-medium writes his petition to a co-deity, he will have his seal stamped on the talisman for the client. For example, a client in much distress sought the help of Medium B as he was denied the fair share of his inheritance by his sibling. The talisman-petition is than handed to the client, who is then instructed by the attendant to burn it at the respective altar of the deity to whom the petition is addressed. (There are many deities in a Taoist temple; each of them has specialised attributes and functions.)

Hence, as the client delivers the petition to the other deity in question at another altar, it is not just he himself who is asking the favour, but also the deity represented by his seal. Indeed, seals are in so much demand that during Daoist holy days and festivals, seal-stamping is often performed as a sign of luck and protection, much as one might wear a Christian cross around one's neck. Here seals are stamped on the back of the shirt conspicuously (especially in the topmost central position). Sometimes they are stamped on arms/hands or directly on the body. I have seen temple assistants stamping them on people's palms as well.

Conclusion

While an altered state of consciousness can be attained through hypnosis, meditation, prayer, mantra, yoga etc., in Daoism it is invoked by the semiotics surrounding literacy. There is no canon in popular Daoism – meanings are communicated orally with the aid of music or through visuals which manifest themselves in charts, symbols and calligraphy on the walls, tapestries, talismen and seals. Inherent in Daoism is a belief in the divine origin of language, the emotional attachment to the power of sacred words, as apparent through the use of sacred language in sacred texts, incantation, chants, visualisation, ritualistic movements, talismans and seals. As Rafael (1992) has noted, it is through language that the super-natural is made believable and is a major source for the survival of religious dispositions

There is a strong case that mystics of all persuasions (Hindu, Buddhist, Muslim, Jewish and Christian) experience the same transcendental reality, but what every medium does, as every anthropologist has shown, is that his or her experience is intrinsically shaped by the socio-cultural tradition that he grows up in. In the Chinese temple, the gestalt effect is the form-generating capability of our senses, particularly with respect to the visual recognition of figures and whole forms instead of just a collection of simple lines and curves. The meaning is acquired from the product of complex interactions pertaining to the language of invocation, chant, music, talisman and seal among other visual, musical and ritualistic stimuli present in the temple environment (cf. Carlson and Heth 2010).

In the tradition of religious Daoism, the spirit-medium is an important channel to bridge the gap between this world and the next. Not everyone may possess the rare gift of spirit-mediumship, but those who have it often regard it as a form of service and calling. The prophet-founder of a major religions may be said to be the 'medium' or 'channel' for messages or 'revelations' from the spirit world. For example, Mohammad and Bahaullah claimed that the Angel Gabriel was the source of their inspiration. Gautama Buddha sat under a Bo tree and received 'enlightenment' from a source beyond. Jesus, Moses and Elijah fasted for forty days and nights – controversies abound as to what actually took place, but their spirits were much strengthened and they returned from their sojourns committed to continue their mission. These communications from another realm occurred in altered states of consciousness with the recipient often in deep meditative absorption or an ecstatic trance. I am not claiming that the more mundane spirit-mediumship recounted in this study is equivalent to the grand revelations of Mohammad or Buddha, but only point out that in both cases, a kind of 'mediumship' was involved which channelled ideas from one dimension to another. The channelling powers of Daoist mediumships are, of course, a drop in the ocean, since the founders of the great religions have revealed relatively more lengthy and exquisite texts which are an important impetus for the revival of entire societies and the building of new civilisations.

We do not yet possess the tools to explain or dissect with any great accuracy the altered consciousness that spirit-mediums go through, but this consciousness may be likened – for want of a better analogy – to a 'dream' state. For most of us, while we may encounter myriad messages and visions as if by telepathy in our dreams, we do not remember most of them when we are 'awake', and neither do we have the expertise to interpret these messages. Sceptics may question the authenticity of these dreams or visions, especially as some 'visionaries' have been known to use their powers for self-aggrandisement and profit.

Whether the skills or 'gifts' of Daoist mediums are genuine or fake, there is no doubt that an effective medium will be sought after, and an ineffective one may fade out very fast. Unfortunately there is currently no reliable way of confirming whether a spirit medium is 'the real thing'. Reiki experts claim to be able to feel a medium's energies when in trance, as they are adept in the spiritual practice of palm healing as an alternative medicine.[14] The problem is that Reiki experts themselves are not fully recognised by the scientific community. Nonetheless, it is not the Reiki experts who may confirm the medium's authenticity but rather the clients of the medium themselves who have personally witnessed miracles of healing in their own lives.

With the rise of a materialistic ideology in Asia, there has been a corresponding loss of spiritualism, and many Daoist mediums have ceased to fulfil their former functions. Authentic mediums die, and so too their personal experiences. Most of them are also less than willing to talk with an ethnographer. In Singapore, as in many cultures, the traditional belief system has also become endangered, not least because of partial or total language shift due to the spread of globalisation and the use of English (Chew 2009). The community remembering the associated beliefs and practices of Hokien grows old and dies, and many folklore memories, songs and texts are also progressively forgotten.

Phyllis Ghim-Lian Chew

Notes

* This research is supported by a grant, SUG 20/15 CGL, from the National Institute of Education, Nanyang Technological University. I am grateful for the help rendered to me by my two research assistants as well as to all my temple informants during the course of my research.

[1] This is very evident in countries such as Hong Kong, Taiwan, Macao and rural China today.

[2] The Chinese word *wu* 巫, 'spirit medium; shaman; shamaness; sorcerer; doctor; proper names' was first recorded during the Shang Dynasty (*c.*1600–1046 BCE) – this ancient Chinese tradition continues in the spirit mediumship of contemporary China, Hong Kong, Singapore, and Taiwan.

[3] See e.g. *Straits Times*, 16 January1995. p. 19: 'Singapore First World Religion Day Draws 1000'.

[4] Information gleaned from Victor Yue, the founder and moderator of the online Taoism-Singapore interest group,

[5] A *wayang* is a makeshift stage in a field or street, a performance usually staged on the birthday of a deity for his or her entertainment.

[6] Also known as I-Kuan Tao. Currently, it is the third most popular faith in Taiwan (after Buddhism and Taoism). It claims approximately 2,000,000 members in overseas Chinese communities around the world.

[7] The earliest written language is the so-called Jiǎgǔwén 龜甲獸骨文字 (Oracle Bone Script), *c.*1500 BCE. It later evolved to Dàzhuàn (大篆) (Greater Seal) (1100–700 BCE); and then to Xiǎozhuàn (小篆) (Lesser Seal), to the Lìshū form charcters in the Han dynasty, and finally to the regular script or Kǎishū (楷書), a style which has remained the standard written style of writing until recently, a time span of about 2,000 years.

[8] For example, the Bodhisattva Guanyin, the goddess of mercy, is the 'favourite' deity of many sprit-mediums owing to her infinite compassion and mercy.

[9] Those higher on the hierarchy such as the Jade emperor or Yuhuangshandi (Tiangong, lord of heaven) and Sakyamuni Budda (Rulaifo) almost never associate with spirit-medium ship as they are held in great reverence and no human being would dare to approach such deities to take the shape of human form.

[10] Also, while some mediums are adept in invoking particular deities, others may invoke a few deities, but only one of the many deities invoked may possess his body at any one time.

146

[11] When the deity descends, the attendant will remove the medium's clothes and prepare the specific robes for the deity (depending on which particular deity has descended). The attendant will then address the deity using the peculiar address form and chant specific to the deity.

[12] The average number of devotees who turn up each time to consult the medium-deity when in session is around fifty. Queue numbers are therefore given by the attendants to the small crowd.

[13] Tang ki is not like the typical medium in the western world, but rather his body becomes the deity's. We recall that the attendants do not put on his 'god-robe' until the possession has taken place. His blood is the blood of the deity. Hence, the drawing of blood through self-immolation is part of the ritual to release the power of the god into the world – because the blood is now the blood of the god.

[14] Reiki is a spiritual practice developed in 1922 by Japanese Buddhists. Reiki practitioners believe that they are transferring universal energy (i.e., reiki) in the form of *qi* (Japanese: *ki*) through the palms, which they believe allows for self-healing and a state of equilibrium.

References

Austin, John L. (1962) *How to Do Things with Words* (Oxford: Clarendon Press).

Carlson, Neil R. and Heth, C. Donald (2010) *Psychology the Science of Behaviour* (Don Mills, ON: Pearson Education Canada), pp. 20–2.

Chew, Phyllis Ghim-Lian (1993) *The Chinese Religion and the Baha'i Faith* (Oxford: George Ronald).

Chew, Phyllis Ghim-Lian (2009) *Emergent Lingua Francas and World Order: The Politics and Place of English* (London and New York: Routledge).

Chia, Meng Tat (2009) *Sacred Ties across the Seas: The Cult of Guangze Zunwang and its*

Religious Network in the Chinese Diaspora, 19th Century–2009 (BA Hons thesis submitted to the Department of History, National University of Singapore).

Clammer, John (1993) 'Religious pluralism and Chinese belief in Singapore', in Hock Teng Cheu (ed.), *Chinese Beliefs and Practices in Southeast Asia* (Petaling Jaya, Selangor: Pelanduk Publications), pp. 199–220.

Cohen, Emma and Barrett, Justin L. (2008) 'Conceptualizing spirit possession: ethnographic and experimental evidence', *Ethos*, 36/2: 246–67.

Phyllis Ghim-Lian Chew

Dean, Kenneth (2009) 'Further partings of the way: the Chinese state and Daoist ritual traditions in contemporary China', in Yodhiko Ashiwa and David L. Wank (eds), *Making Religion: Making the State* (Stanford, CA: Stanford Univeristy Press), pp. 179–210.

Finnegan, Ruth (2012a) 'Language as talisman: a story of dreaming and waking', *Applied Linguistics*, 101: 17–27.

Heinze, Ruth-Inge (1993) 'The dynamics of Chinese religion: a recent case of spirit possession in Singapore', in Hock Teng Cheu (ed.), *Chinese Beliefs and Practices in Southeast Asia* (Petaling Jaya, Selangor: Pelanduk Publiscations), pp. 187–97.

Jung, Carl Gustav (1960) *Psychology and Religion* (New Haven: Yale University Press).

Jordan, David K. (1999) *Gods, Ghosts, and Ancestors: Folk Religion in a Taiwanese Village*, third edn (San Diego CA: Department of Anthropology, UCSD (published as a www. document. URL: *http://anthro. ucsd.edu/~dkjordan*).

Keane, Webb (1997) 'Religious language', *Annual Review of Anthropology*, 26: 47–71.

Kemp, James (n.d.) An illustrated compendium of Taoist, Buddhist and Shinto talisman of the Far East. Available from the author.

Kohn, Livia (2009) *Introducing Daoism* (London and New York; Routledge).

Lim, Francis (2011) 'The eternal mother and the state: circumventing religious management in Singapore', *ARI Research Working Paper Series*, no. 161.

Pentikäinen, Juha andSimoncsics, Péter (eds) (2005) *Shamanhood: An Endangered Language* (The Institute for Comparative Research in Human Culture, Series B, 117).

Rafael V. L. (1992) *Contracting Colonialism: Translation and Christian Conversion in Tagalog Society under Early Spanish Rule* (Durham, NC and London: Duke University Press).

Samarin, William J. (1972) *Tongues of Men and Angels: The Religious Language of Pentecostalism* (New York: Macmillan).

Sperber, D. and Wilson, D. (1995) *Relevance: Communication and Cognition*, second edn (Oxford: Blackwell).

8

Everyday Trancing and Musical Daydreams

Ruth Herbert
Faculty of Music, University of Oxford/
University of Kent, School of Fine Art and Music

Listening to . . . a symphony by Glazanow [*sic*] I had the inner vision of an unknown landscape, a wild northern bay . . . against this backdrop . . . I beheld the strangest apparitions . . . crowds of people dressed in red, also white horses, but also terrifying mythological beasts . . . (Frau Maria) (Lee 1933: 351–2)

You know just before you properly wake up in the morning . . . you're not asleep, but you're not really back in the land of the living? Sometimes I can get like that with the music – it's taking you away somewhere, isn't it? (David)

Induction

In the years immediately prior to the First World War the British writer Vernon Lee (remembered principally for her contributions to the fields of supernatural fiction and aesthetics) compiled a now all but forgotten questionnaire and interview study of the music listening experiences of 150 individuals in Germany, France, Italy and the UK. Lee highlighted two ways of responding to music: listening and hearing. For Listeners, music was the main focus of (effortful) attention. Their mode of listening was primarily autonomous – about the music. The experience of Hearers was very different: a multimodal interweaving of musical characteristics with extra-musical detail:

> moments of concentrated and active attention to the musical shapes
> are like islands continually washed over by a shallow tide of other
> thoughts: memories, associations, suggestions, visual images and
> emotional states . . . they coalesce, forming a homogeneous and
> special contemplative condition . . . Musical phrases, non-musical
> images and emotions are all welded into the same musical day-dream.
> (Lee 1933: 32)

Lee identifies two key characteristics of lived experiences of music:
(1) the presence of a fluctuating, distributed attentional focus; and
(2) a perceived move away from a baseline or normal state of
consciousness. The arts are inextricably linked to consciousness
transformation, both in terms of their creation and reception. The
process of imagination constitutes one of the most fundamental
transformations of consciousness. Without the capacity to imagine
the arts could not exist – a theme I'll return to later in this chapter.

Of all art forms, music appears to afford the most versatile means
of customising individual, subjective experience (and communal
inter-subjective experience) across a diverse number of everyday
life scenarios. As a non-verbal, multivalent means of communication, incomplete in terms of sensory information, music prompts
a performative stance to sense-making, where individual interpretation is necessary to fill in the gaps (Windsor 2000). Music's semantic
malleability makes it a potent mediator of experience, able to blend
together elements of external awareness that would otherwise
remain perceptually separated and to connect internal and external
concerns. In other words, music may function as a prosthetic
technology of the self (DeNora 2000: 46–74) to 'choreograph'
consciousness. I have suggested elsewhere (Herbert, 2011a) that
this type of interaction between music and consciousness may be
usefully conceptualised as a form of musical trancing.

Six Observations on Musical Trancing

Universalism

Transformations of consciousness (whether termed trance, entrancement, altered states, alternate states etc.) occur universally

in all cultures (Brown 1991; Nettl 2000) and are considered to have adaptive value in evolutionary terms (Dissanayake 1988; Lewis-Williams 2002). Music's association with consciousness transformation is ancient (e.g. as used in ritualistic contexts) and the transformative power of music, i.e. 'the use of music to provide some kind of fundamental change in an individual's consciousness' has been considered as a universal[1] (Nettl 2000: 468).

Relativism

The neuropsychological processes characteristic of musical trancing remain constant cross-culturally, but different trancing vocabularies attach to different cultures and, crucially, the contents and raw feel of subjective experience vary. The ethnomusicologist Judith Becker has employed Bourdieu's notion of habitus to capture the situatedness of musical experience, an embodied pattern of action and reaction in which we are not fully conscious of why we do what we do (Becker 2010: 130).

Process

Transformations of consciousness are best considered as processual, rather than as discrete 'states' (Becker 2004; Herbert 2011a, 2011b). The term 'entrancement' and the gerund 'trancing' both point towards the dynamic nature of subjective experience. The processes of imagination, falling asleep (hypnagogia), dreaming and waking (hypnopompia) may all be usefully conceptualised as instances of trancing.

Definition

Trance may be most profitably understood not as a unitary state, but as a Wittgensteinian category, a set of similar events that bear 'family' resemblances to one another (Becker 2004: 43). This accommodates empirical findings that although individual instances of trance may be quite diverse, they do share common features. Through my empirical study of musical trancing I have adopted the following inclusive definition:

> Trancing-as-process [is] an over-arching concept that subsumes
> absorption (total involvement) and dissociation (detachment) within
> it . . . I define trance as a process characterised by a decreased
> orientation to consensual reality, a decreased critical faculty, a
> selective internal or external focus, together with a changed sensory
> awareness and – potentially – a changed sense of self. (Herbert,
> 2011a: 50)

Attentional Focus
Musical trancing episodes may focus on acoustic attributes of
music, on sources specified by music (associations, memories)
which trigger imaginative involvement, physical entrainment to
music, emotions represented or induced by music, or a fusion of
aural, visual and kinaesthetic elements (i.e. a multimodal, heteronomous focus).

Research
The disciplines of ethnomusicology and anthropology have both
embraced the study of transformations of consciousness (usually
labelled as trance or altered states of consciousness (ASC). Psychological studies of musical experience however, have tended to
avoid this topic, partly because of concerns that it is not a credible,
academically respectable area of study, and partly because research
has been dominated by a focus on emotion to the exclusion of
other experiential phenomena (Herbert, 2012c).[2]

Hypnagogue (noun)

an agent that induces drowsiness or sleep (WordNet, 2010)[3]
Origin: late nineteenth century: from French *hypnagogique*, from Greek
hupnos 'sleep' + *agōgos* 'leading'

Since 2005 I have carried out a series of empirical inquiries focusing on the everyday listening practices of individuals in the UK,
driven by an interest in the range of consciousness music-listening
episodes may encompass. The primary aim has been to examine
the interaction between music, mind, culture and context via

phenomenological study (semi-structured interviews and free descriptions) of the psychological processes present in real-world musical experiences and the subjective feel of the totality of such experiences as they unfold. To date nearly one hundred individuals, from nine to eighty-five years of age, from diverse social backgrounds and with an array of musical tastes have contributed to a developing library of listening experiences.[5]

In the following section I offer some snapshots from reports of music listening, drawn from my past and ongoing research.

Musical Daydreams

Super Powers (Autobiographical Fantasy)
Soundtrack: 'Russian Privjet' (Basshunter).

I definitely use music to daydream. Quite a lot. I've got this very weird obsession since I was very young that I've got some strange power built up in me and in certain music that I will imagine myself doing some weird super power thing . . . In one piece – something by Basshunter– I just see myself in some random road which is a bit funny but yeah I just see myself floating in the air, moving stuff with my mind . . . Well, it wouldn't be a road it would sort of . . . I would be randomly in the middle of the playing fields just sort of controlling the weather, that sort of thing . . . And as the music progresses [it's] sort of a bit like a sci-fi movie. The actions and the drama gets more intense as the music gets to its climax and then it would sort of dwindle.

Basshunter's very techno-modern and it is easier to access it in the techno-modern music because it is very . . . sort of bass-dominated so you can get very strong feelings from it and . . . if the volume's at a certain pitch I find it a lot easier to access that path. I can't do it with classical music. Just really big sounds. I can get really into my imagination. I have got a bit of an overactive imagination!

It's a sort of alternate world sort of thing . . . because I don't really like my world a lot. In that [alternate] world everything is sort of right . . . so since young I sort of, it's just been a place to go. (John, aged seventeen)[6]

For John, music provides a regularly accessed forum for experimentation with identity – a common preoccupation in adolescence. Listening here is clearly multimodal and heteronomous. Musical attributes and lyrics prompt a dreamlike, filmic succession of personal and cultural associations and memories. The attentional focus is inward and there is a clear motivation to escape to an alternate world where everything is sort of right.

All the Daydreams Come Out (Fictional Fantasy)
Soundtrack: 'Luna' (Astor Piazzolla).

I have a big habit of having daydreams, and when I'm listening to music I just seem to – all the daydreams seem to come out and I might either imagine stories or I might imagine the future, or depending on the type of music I might think of different people . . .

When I was listening to Astor Piazzolla in the car there was this rather creepy track and I imagined there was someone being murdered – a small child actually, and there was this evil killer who we don't know of – no one's ever seen their face as it's hidden under a black hood. And they're the one killing all these children. And it leaves. And it sees a little poor baby. It's had some trouble with being a child in its previous life and it thinks that all children are horrible due to what's happened to it in its childhood. It looks at the child and it starts to feel sorry for the child. Then it forgets, throws it into the river and starts murdering a whole load of other kids. So that's one of – that's one of the stories. I can't really remember all of the stories I dream about. It's usually quite dramatic. (Lily, aged eleven)

Both John and Lily accept daydreaming to music as a regular mode of musical experience and both have a developed imaginative capacity,[7] revealed in their inwardly directed attention and production of spontaneous imagery. Lily's daydream possesses more of a narrative quality however – a sense of storying to music, involving fictional characters. Phenomenological reports I have collected so far suggest that this type of imaginative fantasy is more likely to arise in pre-pubescence and early adolescence.

Paper-thin Aliens (Dissociation from Surroundings)
Soundtrack: Music for 18 Musicians (Steve Reich).

> Reaching the roundabout on a dual carriageway, the sharp clarity of the yellow and black chevron pattern shouts at me to appreciate it . . . traffic slows as we approach Orpington outskirts and I feel curiously remote. Stare at some pedestrians at a junction and realise I feel almost too distant. They look paper-thin, almost alien, I have no connection with them: or rather, I do have a connection but am observing it and them. (Will, aged fifty-seven)

Subjective experience is reconfigured as repetitive patterns within a minimalist piece of music blend with and heighten perception of repetitive patterns in external surroundings (the chevron pattern). The initial absorption afforded quickly shifts to a dissociative, semi- dreamlike experiential vantage point (no connection) where objects assume a preternatural quality (pedestrians seen as paper-thin, almost alien).

Hallucinogenic Notes and Chords (Absorption in Sound Attributes)
Soundtrack: 'The Mythical Laboratory' (Mikhail Karikis).

> Listening to CD on the train. Fascinating textures, no melodies dreamy and very relaxed. Love the hallucinogenic quality of sustained notes and chords with endlessly repeated rhythms. Drift for a while into smile-inducing vacancy . . . timbres, rhythms for their own sake with no particular rational attempts to make associations . . . fifty per cent experiencing them as hypnotic, and fifty per cent noticing that they had hypnotic qualities. The latter impinges on the former. (Max, aged forty-six)

In contrast to the previous excerpts, subjective experience here does not encompass visual elements (real or imagined), but relies solely on a fascination with acoustic attributes. The episode features a relaxed critical faculty and a reduction in thought (vacancy). Max explicitly recognises that his conscious awareness has been altered (hallucinogenic, hypnotic), but the subjective feel of the experience is influenced by a belief that certain musical qualities will act to transform consciousness, i.e. that music is a stimulus capable of inducing specific effects.

The Comfortable Non-state. (Dissociation from Self – Partial)
Soundtrack: 'When I see scissors I can't help but think of you' (Dead Texan).

> The sounds consist of very little more than looped string sections, which are layered to allow for slow and quite subtle thematic shifts . . . I have selected well and this allows me to drift into the comfortable non-state . . . I wander around town and pop in and out of the quirky little shops, just browsing and apparently advertising my insularity . . . the whole point is to be as unaware of my physical self as is realistically possible – the music allows for gradual and deeper dislocation. Like a waking dream I think, where I am the conductor and the real-world activity . . . is really just a game in which I am choosing to whimsically dabble in. I'm lost in the music – it is feeding my spacelessness. This works well until I visit the market and am asked a question as I browse the CD stall . . . I am roused from my reverie and all of a sudden thrust into the 'onmode' again . . . I wander away and realise that something new has to be chosen. I will remain disconnected and insular. (Gary, aged thirty-three)

As in the first of these six musical daydreams, there is the suggestion of a rehearsed, established listening behaviour. For John (Super Powers) the intention was to access a powerful fantasy identity and alternate world; for Gary it is to enter the comfortable non-state, i.e. to detach from self – particularly negative mentation. As in Will's experience, where music afforded a preternatural, fantastical sense of external surroundings, Gary's perception of reality is altered by his engagement with music which provides an insulatory auditory bubble that allows for dislocation. The objective world is experienced as emotionless and dreamlike, as if through the eyes of another.

Somewhere Else to Go (Dissociation from Self – Total)
Soundtrack: 'False Freedom' (While She Sleeps).

> On the bus listening [to metal] I start looking out and I do know I
> am looking out and then eventually there is just a fade where I am
> just unaware that I am unaware . . . kind of inside the music,
> disappearing . . . it's not positive or negative, just about an alternative
> space, somewhere else to go . . . I am not aware of myself, I am just
> aware of the track, like the track is my thoughts. (Jake, aged fifteen)

A particularly common form of musical daydreaming for
teenagers appears to involve the use of music to dull consciousness by flooding it with sensation (here, extremely loud techo
metal). Jake's field of awareness becomes narrowed and the
alternative space he disappears into acts to provide absence from
all aspects of self. The experience is neither positive nor negative
in valence, instead providing a dissociation from affect – and
from the effort of functioning as a separate being (the track
becomes my thoughts).

Hypnopomp (noun; neologism)

relating to the state immediately preceding waking up (Oxford
dictionaries. com).[4]
Origin: early twentieth century: from Greek *hupnos* 'sleep' + *pompē*
'sending away'

'An Experience Economy'

'The fourth phase of the experience economy is here. We call it
virtuality and involvement' (SOTT trend research and innovation
agency web statement, 2012).[8] The concept of an experience economy, originally a business philosophy (Pine and Gilmore 1999),
has exerted a growing influence during the last decade on marketing
strategies across a range of industries and organisations – from
tourism, hospitality, leisure and the arts to education and healthcare.

Key is the notion that consumers (particularly in affluent societies) value experiences rather than material objects (of which they have plenty).

Two current manifestations of this in the music business are: (1) the growth in the number of music festivals and live music events; (2) the promotion of tours via record albums, rather than the previous promotion of albums via tours.[9] The established trend research and innovation agency Science Of The Times's recent research on the experience economy highlights public demand for both memorable experiences and experiences that reference fictional or virtual realities. Clearly, music fits into the realm of the experience economy rather than simply being a service or product for consumption (Pearce 2013: 5) because it is a complex stimulus which affords a multifaceted interaction to the perceiver. The mental, physical and social worlds of the music consumer all help define an experiential encounter as opposed to a service or material object purchase (Pearce, 2013: 5).

It may be tempting to dismiss the experience economy label as a glib, cynically manufactured and over-hyped business construct. Yet, evident alongside the unashamed manipulation is a recognition of the active, creative nature of mental engagement. And in highlighting the human propensity for experiences which take us somewhere else, trend researchers and strategic marketing experts are keying into behaviours that, in the fields of ethology, cognitive archaeology, evolutionary psychology and ultradian studies, are considered to be psychobiologically inevitable and crucial to the process of enchantment. The final section of this chapter offers a brief overview of this multidisciplinary territory.

Dreaming, Imagining, Artifying, Musicking

An important and persuasive multidisciplinary cross-section of research suggests that the processes of dreaming, imagining and making and receiving art are inextricably intertwined. In warm-blooded vertebrates at least, sleep constitutes the most evolutionarily ancient form of consciousness transformation (Opp 2009). Significantly, although all mammals and birds are thought to experience REM or dream sleep (Jouvet 1999), only humans are thought to be capable of recalling their dreams.

The cognitive archaeologist David Lewis-Williams (2002) has theorised that it was the development of long-term memory that made recollection of imagery in dreams (or ritualised trancing) possible, in turn promoting the development of the imaginative faculty, and that such imagery was then artified by being engraved or painted on cave walls. On this view, once the capacity to imagine was established, the emergence of the arts was inevitable. The ethologist Ellen Dissanayake (1988, 1992) considers such artifying to constitute a process of making special which carried adaptive value in evolutionary terms – partly because it enhanced routine tasks, facilitated sharing of concepts in ritualistic contexts etc., but also because the transformations of consciousness accompanying artifying promoted innovative thinking, relief from trauma and psychophysiological recuperation.

Lewis-Williams's (2002) theory stresses the shared perceptual territory between alterations of consciousness, imagination, the arts and the REM stage of sleep. The REM state, identified by the pioneer of sleep research Nathaniel Kleitman in 1953, is a period of rapid eye movements that occurs approximately every ninety minutes during sleep,[10] and that corresponds with times when dreams take place. Kleitman maintained that this cycle of REM/non-REM sleep persisted in the form of a basic rest/activity cycle (BRAC) in waking hours (Kleitman, 1982). Although evidence supporting this theory is inconclusive, the notion of a waking BRAC has been the subject of an intriguing empirical study, employing diary and questionnaire methods (Duchniewska and Kokoszka 2003). The authors noted that rest episodes were passive in nature, featuring an inwardly directed attentional focus, and increase in imaginative activity. They observed that culturally accepted behaviours, e.g. leisure activities (including listening to music, reading and other aesthetic activities), could accompany such episodes (2003: 155). The tantalising possibility the notion of a waking BRAC offers of the interaction between artistic engagement and trance awaits further research.

Across the industrialised West trance has tended to be mis-represented, misunderstood, mistrusted and undervalued as a phenomenon. As Judith Becker emotively puts it: 'We have no reputable trance states, no awards for revelations from mediums, no summer camps for learning to trance, and no serious attention from the scientific community . . . we have written off trance' (Becker, 2004: 13).

Yet, a growing body of evidence from evolutionary psychology and chronobiology indicates that the capacity for consciousness transformation – for entrancement – is a human given, an essential contributor to effective daily functioning and psychophysiological well-being. One key function of the arts from their first origins appears to have been to access alternate states of mind. Music seems to be a particularly versatile mediator of everyday entrance-ment, a conclusion supported by the prevalence of secular musical trancing in everyday life.

Notes

[1] The use of music to afford consciousness transformation may be con-sidered to constitute an 'absolute' universal, i.e. a phenomenon that has been identified from the ethnographic record as occurring across *all* cultures.

[2] Within the field of music and affect studies, it is now accepted that emotions do not account for the entirety of subjective experiences of music. See for example the revised *Handbook of Music and Emotion* (Juslin and Sloboda, 2010: 940).

[3] The ASCs experienced by almost all ordinary people are dreaming states and the hypnogogic and hypnopompic states, the transitional states between sleeping and waking. (Tart 1972:1203; Princeton University 'Hypnagogue', WordNet (Princeton University. 2010: <*http://wordnet.princeton.edu/*>)).

[4] <*http://oxforddictionaries.com/definition/english/hypnopompic?q= hypnopompic*> (accessed 14 September 2013).

[5] Detailed discussion of experiences gathered between 2005 to 2007 can be found in my book *Everyday Music Listening* (Herbert 2011a) and elsewhere (e.g. Herbert 2011b, 2012a, 2012b, 2013).

[6] All names have been changed.

[7] John and Lily's accounts are taken from my current study of young people's musical engagement. As part of that study participants completed a range of psychometric measures. Both participants scored highly on the Creative Experiences Questionnaire (Merckelbach et al. 2001) and Modified Tellegen Absorption Scale (Jamieson 2005), which tap the capacity for imaginative involvement.

[8] *http://scienceofthetime.com/study/mentality-trends/virtuality-involvement/* (accessed 20 September 2013).

[9] As evidenced by PricewaterhouseCooper's global entertainment and media outlook: 2013–17, *http://www.pwc.com/gx/en/global-entertainment-media-outlook/segment-insights/music.jhtml* (accessed 14 September 2013).

[10] It can thus be considered as an example of 'ultradian cyclicity' – a biological cycle that occurs more than once during a twenty-four-hour (circadian) period.

References

Becker, J. (2004) *Deep Listeners: Music, Emotion, and Trancing* (Bloomington: Indiana University Press).

Brown, D. E. (1991) *Human Universals* (New York: McGraw-Hill).

DeNora, T. (2000) *Music in Everyday Life* (Cambridge: Cambridge University Press).

Dissanayake, E. (1988) *What is Art For?* (Seattle and London: University of Washington Press).

Dissanayake, E. (1992) *Homo Aestheticus: Where Art Comes From and Why?* (Seattle: University of Washington Press).

Duchniewska, K. and Kokoszka, A. (2003) 'The protective mechanisms of the basic rest–activity cycle as an indirect manifestation of this rhythm in waking: Preliminary report', *International Journal of Neuroscience*, 113: 153–63.

Herbert, R. (2011a) *Everyday Music Listening: Absorption, Dissociation and Trancing* (Aldershot: Ashgate).

Herbert, R. (2011b) 'Reconsidering trance: cross-cultural differences and cross-disciplinary perspectives', *Ethnomusicology Forum*, 20/2: 100–27.

Herbert, R. (2012a) 'Modes of music listening, modes of subjectivity', *Journal of Sonic Studies*, *http://journal.sonicstudies.org/vo102/nr/a05*

Herbert, R. (2012b) 'Musical and non-musical involvement in daily life: The case of absorption', *Musicae Scientiae*, 16/1: 41–66.

Herbert, R. (2012c) 'Conceptualizing the subjective experience of listening to music in everyday life', in E. Cambouropoulos, C. Tsougras, P. Mavromatis and K. Pastiadis (eds), *Proceedings of the 12th International Conference on Music Perception and Cognition and the 8th Triennial Conference of the European Society for the Cognitive Sciences of Music* (Thessaloniki), pp. 421–2.

Herbert, R. (2013) 'An empirical study of normative dissociation in musical and non-musical everyday life experiences', *Psychology of Music*, 41/3: 372–94.

Jamieson, G. A. (2005) 'The Modified Tellegen Absorption Scale: a clearer window on the structure and meaning of absorption', *Australian Journal of Clinical and Experimental Hypnosis*, 33/2: 119–39.

Jouvet, M. (1999) *The Paradox of Sleep: The Story of Dreaming* (Cambridge, MA: MIT Press).

Juslin, P. N. and Sloboda, J. A. (2010b) 'The past, present, future of music and emotion research', in P. N. Juslin and J. A. Sloboda (eds), *Handbook of Music and Emotion: Theory, Research, Applications* (Oxford: Oxford University Press), pp. 933–55.

Kleitman, N. (1982) 'Basic rest–activity cycle – 22 years later', *Sleep* 5/4: 311–17.

Lee, Vernon (1933) *Music and its Lovers: An Empirical Study of Emotional and Imaginative Responses to Music* (New York: E. P. Dutton and Co Inc.)

Lewis-Williams, D. (2002) *The Mind in the Cave: Consciousness and the Origins of Art* (London: Thames and Hudson).

Merckelbach, H., Horselenberg, R. and Muris, P. (2001) 'The Creative Experiences Questionnaire (CEQ): a brief self-report measure of fantasy proneness', *Personality and Individual Differences*, 31: 987–95.

Nettl, B. 2000 'An ethnomusicologist contemplates universals in musical sound and musical culture', in N. L. Wallin, B. Merker and S. Brown (eds), *The Origins of Music* (Cambridge, MA: Massachusetts Institute of Technology), pp. 463–72 .

Opp, M. R. (2009) 'Sleeping to fuel the immune system: mammalian sleep and resistance to parasites', *BMC Evolutionary Biology*, 9: 8, http://bmcevolbiol.biomedcentral.com/articles/10.1186/1471-2148-9-8

Pearce, P. (2013) 'From Dischord to Harmony: Connecting Australian Music and Business Through the Experience Economy', in P. Tschmuck, P. L. Pearce and S. Campbell (eds), *Music Business and the Experience Economy: The Australasian Case* (Berlin and Heidelberg: Springer-Verlag), pp. 1–10.

Pine, B. J and Gilmore, J. H. (1999) *The Experience Economy: Work Is Theater and Every Business a Stage* (Boston: Harvard Business Press).

Tart, C. T. (1972) 'States of consciousness and state-specific sciences', *Science*, 176: 1203–10.

Windsor, W. L. (2000) 'Through and around the acousmatic: the interpretation of electroacoustic sounds', in S. Emmerson (ed.), *Music, Electronic Media and Culture* (Aldershot: Ashgate), pp. 7–35.

9

An Angel of Modernity: Karlheinz Stockhausen's Musical Vision

Morag Josephine Grant
Independent researcher, Scotland and Germany

In the score to *TRANS* (1971) for orchestra by the German composer Karlheinz Stockhausen (1928–2007) we read the following:[1]

> The composer experienced TRANS in a dream during the night of 9th–10th of December 1970. The next morning he wrote down in captions and a few sketches what he had heard and seen in the dream . . . The work was written in Kürten from July to September 1971. (Stockhausen 1971: IX)[2]

Stockhausen, who came to prominence in the early 1950s, is both one of the twentieth century's most famous and also most controversial composers in the western art music tradition. An early pioneer of both electronic music and the total serial method of composition, he and his contemporaries were often accused of over-intellectualising musical creation, and of creating works so radical that meaningful communication with a larger audience was impossible.

What, then, are we to make of the composer's statement that *TRANS* came to him in a dream? It is not a unique occurrence, either: from roughly the 1960s onwards, Stockhausen increasingly talked of the role of dreams and visions in his music, and of being a mere transmitter for ideas from a different domain; he also occasionally talked about being a visitor to earth from the star Sirius, also known as the Dog Star. The impact on the reception of his music has been significant. Where his earlier work is often viewed as overly rational and abstract, Stockhausen's later works have been subjected to the opposite accusation: of celebrating an irrational and personal spiritual mythology. This criticism has been levelled especially at the major opera (life-)cycle *LICHT* (*LIGHT*), on which Stockhausen worked exclusively for over twenty-five years.

This chapter will look more closely at the issue of dreams, visions and related forms of communication in Stockhausen's thinking about music, including a discussion on the role of angels – those archetypical communicators between domains who also feature frequently in Stockhausen's biography and music. These themes, so central to Stockhausen's music, also help situate his life's work within much broader traditions and practices which are central preoccupations for this book as a whole.

Dreams

Stockhausen spoke often about the role of dreams in his work, and several of his compositions had their origins in dreams.[3] Though the number of these is not overwhelming relative to the extensive catalogue of completed works, the 'dreamworks' (Toop: 2008) include many of the composer's most famous compositions, and several which were turning points in his compositional development. *TRANS*, for example, is one of the first full-scale realisations of what the composer called 'ritual scenic music'. The score gives the following instructions for the presentation of the piece:

> At the beginning of the performance the curtain is closed. The hall lighting goes out. The curtain opens slowly over a period of ca. one minute (or longer). The whole stage is steeped in a violet-red, misty light. This colour is hard to describe; the nearest thing to it is the violet-red light that occurs in the early stages of a sunrise over the North Pole – seen from an airplane – and the violet-red light over the horizon near the end of a sunset in a clear sky at sea; yet this light should be diffuse and misty. To achieve this colouring effect in the theatre, one needs a thin gauze curtain (the thread-texture of which should be invisible, as far as possible), onto which light is beamed from violet lamps on the stage apron. (Stockhausen: 1971: ix)

When the stage finally becomes visible, the audience sees the string section of the orchestra seated in two straight, parallel rows, the row behind on a raised platform of 45 cm height. Behind the strings, and not visible due to a thick curtain, stand the conductor and four further groups made up of wind and percussion instruments. Additionally, loudspeakers placed at specific points throughout the hall transmit the sound of a weaving-loom shuttle. The greatly amplified loom shuttle – the effect of which is rather like the sound of the slide-changing mechanism on an old-style slide projector – also aids the temporal coordination of the piece, with the transition to each new cluster chord played by the conductor-less string section marked by the loom shuttle.

The Stockhausen expert Richard Toop has drawn attention to the importance of visual aspects in the composer's dreamworks (Toop 2008: 195). But though the staging instructions certainly reach a new level in *TRANS*, Stockhausen's music very often contains scenic elements, and theatre and ritual are fundamentally important to his output. From the very earliest stage of his career, he sought to replace the sterile ritual of the contemporary concert hall with a new musical practice which reconnected with the spiritual role music plays in so many cultural traditions (cf. especially Stockhausen 1957). He would later suggest that the future of music lay in 'polyspatial musical rituals' featuring

> performers of ritual scenic music, who do not, like traditional musicians, simply 'play through' the piece the same way any other musician would, but who would play as personifications of arche-typical and never before existent figure in new, musical and spatial rituals. (Stockhausen: 1986: 432)[4]

Though such tendencies are thus the exception rather than the rule in Stockhausen's oeuvre, *TRANS* remains a useful piece to open our discussion for various reasons. We could begin with the very title of the piece, with its obvious connotations of *trans*-cendence and *trans*it between domains, and simultaneously the state of *trance*, which is etymologically related. According to Toop, *TRANS* was originally to be entitled *Musik für die nächsten*

Toten: Requiem für Orchester (*Music for the Next to Die: Requiem for Orchestra*); Toop points out that the relationship between dreaming and death is obvious in another of Stockhausen's dream-works, *HIMMELS-TÜR* (*HEAVEN'S-DOOR*, 2005), in which a percussionist plays (or knocks) on a huge door made of different types of wood, created especially for the piece (Toop 2008: 195).

The scenic presentation of *TRANS* is also relevant for us, particularly the presence of both visible and invisible elements, whereby the most active instruments are those concealed behind the curtain. There are also examples of transition between the two: at several points in the score, a soloist from behind the curtain makes a brief appearance in front of it. Stockhausen stressed the importance of the invisible elements being heard but not seen, since 'Then it becomes much clearer what is meant by the title *TRANS*' (Stockhausen 1975: 182). Thanks to the gauze curtain, however, even the visible elements are seen as if through a haze, and a haze of a very particular colour. Stockhausen had dreamt of a pulsating hexagon of the same violet-red colour some two years previously (Stockhausen 1981: 216), and he described a similar colour in connection with the piece *GOLDSTAUB* (*GOLDDUST*) from *AUS DEN SIEBEN TAGEN* (*FROM THE SEVEN DAYS*, 1968).[5] In a later interview, Stockhausen mentioned this colour again in connection with recurring visions or, perhaps better, state of consciousness, in which he was physically aware of the presence of God – or more specifically, of being part of God, since in Stockhausen's spirituality, we are all atoms of God (Stockhausen 1981: 190–1).

Probably the most famous of Stockhausen's dreamworks is also the most spectacular – the *HELICOPTER STRING QUARTET* from the opera *WEDNESDAY* from *LIGHT*. This spectacular composition requires that the members of a string quartet quite literally take flight, each in one of four helicopters; their perform-ance is relayed back to the audience by a live video link. Like many people, Stockhausen often had dreams of flying, and beings who can fly are found in some pivotal works from the 1970s which also stemmed from dreams and visions. *MUSIK IM BAUCH* (*MUSIC IN THE BELLY*, 1975), which was 'dreamt from A to Z' (Stock-hausen 1975: 577), features a large model of a bird-man called Miron, albeit one who does not actually fly during the piece. This is only one of many references to mythical bird figures in Stockhausen's writings, inspired in part by Sufi and ancient American ideas.[6]

Anthropologists and historians of religion have pointed to the connection between birds and angels in some traditions. In the case of Stockhausen, the angels make a first obvious appearance in *DER JAHRESLAUF* (*THE COURSE OF THE YEAR*, 1977) for Japanese gagaku ensemble, which again derived from a highly complex vision. The piece presents a figurative race of time in which time's progress is defended by an angel-headed character against the most devious attempts to halt it by a devil-figure. *DER JAHRESLAUF* was the starting point for the seven-opera cycle *LIGHT*, and was reworked into the first act of *TUESDAY* from *LIGHT* (1991). In the cycle, *TUESDAY* is the day of battle between Michael and Lucifer, celestial beings that appear in various forms in different mythologies and who are two of the three main pro-tagonists in *LIGHT* (the third, Eva, likewise needs no introduction). *LIGHT* and the unfinished cycle which followed it, *KLANG: THE 24 HOURS OF THE DAY* have another and more indirect relation-ship to dreams and communication in the state of sleep: both draw extensively on *The Urantia Book*, said to have been communicated to the American couple William S. and Lena Sander via a celestial being who spoke through the voice of a middle-aged man who was in a deep sleep. *The Urantia Book* contains ideas and references common in Christian and related spiritual traditions, but adds to these new elements concerning life on other planets within and beyond our own galaxy.[7]

Angels

Theologians and other researchers into what is known as angelology have often suggested that the development of angels as distinct beings is related to an increasingly hierarchic and transcendent idea of the divine: as the deities become further and further removed from humanity, mediators – the angels – are required. According to Wolfgang Speyer,

The concept of the divine messenger – both male and female – in Homeric epics, which are for us the beginning of Greek literary tradition, in the first place tell us about man [*sic*]. He appears as a being standing between the sensual phenomena in time and space and the world of the divine, of the superhumanly powerful which is perceived by the spirit-soul. At the same time this expresses the tension and the basic contrasts that concern the world and man: One contrast concerns the cosmos, the other man. As light and darkness, heaven and earth, are placed in opposition to one another, so spirit and body as well as internal and external perception are inside man. As the senses inform about the external world, so does the spirit, which surpasses the merely logical faculties of reason, about the operating of the divine. (Speyer 2007: 35)[8]

Divine messengers, then, become important at precisely the same time as different cosmological domains become not only increasingly distant from one another, but increasingly polarised – a mode of thinking which would prove profoundly important in the history of western thought. By contrast, polytheistic belief systems, such as that of ancient Egypt, recognise several greater and lesser deities whose characters are rarely split neatly between the 'good' and 'evil' polarisations which become important for Judaism, Christianity and Islam, possibly under the influence of Zoroastrianism (see e.g. Hutter 2007). Such polarisations are thus not very useful for understanding these other belief systems (Schipper 2007: 1).[9] Nor indeed are they strictly useful for understanding Stockhausen's own angelology in *LIGHT*, although the topic of polarisations, and overcoming them, is central to Stockhausen's thinking, as I shall discuss in conclusion.

The role of angels in Stockhausen's life and work is not limited to LICHT/LIGHT. He spoke several times about having a guardian angel, and of knowing of the existence of angels for as long as he could remember (e.g. Stockhausen 2000); the archangel Michael was also of great importance to him from an early age. As well as his incarnation in *LIGHT*, Michael is present by implication in another of Stockhausen's most famous compositions, *GESANG DER JÜNGLINGE* (*SONG OF THE YOUTHS*, 1955–6).

This tape piece – one of the greatest works of early electronic music – combines material generated electronically with a manipulated recording of a boy singing the 'Song of the Youths' from an apocryphal source of the biblical Book of Daniel. The youths concerned are the three young friends of Daniel thrown into a furnace by Nebuchadnezzar: they emerge unharmed, with witnesses saying they had seen a fourth man in the furnace with them, who had the appearance of an angel; in many interpretations, this protecting angel is taken to be Michael. In an interview from 1998, Stockhausen gave very personal reasons for being inspired by this story in the 1950s:

> The special fascination of the 'Song of the Three Youths in the Fiery Furnace' from the Third Book of Daniel resulted from the fact that I myself felt like a young man in the furnace at that time. Everything I did was aggressively turned down and damned by the music journalists and musicologists of the time. There was a professor Blume, chairman of the German Musicological Society, who in a large text wrote that Stockhausen was laying the ax to the roots of music and was destroying all of occidental music. Therefore, I felt so like the young men in the furnace, and I could only pray that St. Michael would come and pull me out of the blazing fires. (Stockhausen quoted in Peters 1999: 100)

Other works by Stockhausen from *LIGHT* onwards have more obvious references to angelic beings. These include the *ANGEL PROCESSIONS* (2007) from *SUNDAY* from *LIGHT* (see here especially Henkel: 2016), and *UNSICHTBARE CHÖRE* (*INVISIBLE CHOIRS*, 1979), an electronic composition on biblical texts which forms part of *THURSDAY* from *LIGHT*. In *FREUDE* (*JOY*, 2005) from the series *KLANG* – written for two harpists dressed in white, who while playing also sing the text of the pentecostal hymn *Veni creator spiritus* – the angelic symbolism could hardly be more obvious.

An angel also features in one of Stockhausen's earliest compositions, which – perhaps not insignificantly – was revised and published in the same period as *TRANS* and other key works discussed here. The *DREI LIEDER* (*THREE SONGS*, 1950) for alto and orchestra were composed while Stockhausen was still a student, unsure whether his future lay in music or in literature. He submitted the pieces to the jury of the recently initiated International Summer Courses for New Music in Darmstadt, West Germany, but they were rejected. On hearing from the music critic and jury member Herbert Eimert that, amongst other things, the lyrics (written by Stockhausen himself) were too disturbing, Stockhausen replaced the text of his first song with the German translation of the poem 'The rebel' by Charles Baudelaire. This poem tells of an angel who 'dives to the earth like an eagle', and in his anger uses means as much violent as spiritual to insist upon obedience to the law of love of all humanity. In Stockhausen's setting, following the rhetorical structure of Baudelaire's text, special emphasis is given to the final line, with the damned's response to the angel: 'Doch immer sagt der Gottverfluchte: Nein!' ('But the damned one always says: No!').

It is tempting to read Stockhausen's setting of this poem as a sort of prelude to *LIGHT*, and this although the style of the *DREI LIEDER* is radically different from Stockhausen's mature style, which dates from *KREUZSPIEL* (1951). The introduction to his setting of Baudelaire's poem gives a prominent role to the trumpet, the instrument also used to represent Michael in *LIGHT* (the three central protagonists of *LIGHT* are each represented by an instrumentalist and dancer as well as a singer). This may be a coincidence: the instrumental role of Michael was clearly created for Stockhausen's son, the trumpeter Markus Stockhausen, and the use of the militaristic trumpet in the first of the *DREI LIEDER* may have more to do with the text which Stockhausen replaced – a reflection on recent historical events – as with the angelic imagery of Baudelaire's text. Indeed, though the archangel Michael is often portrayed as leading God's army, Stockhausen claimed later that he was unaware of representations of Michael playing the trumpet until after he had commenced writing *LIGHT* (Stockhausen 1981: 208).

Other aspects of the representation of Michael and other angels do however show the influence of a number of world traditions, particularly Jewish and Christian. The conflation in Stockhausen's presentation between Michael and Christ may derive from *The Urantia Book*, but also reflects the elevation of Michael to the role of the supreme angel and an almost God-like status in Second Temple Judaism (see e.g. Berner 2007). A possibly more direct influence on Stockhausen's conception comes from the Dead Sea Scrolls. Angels play an important role here, notably in the War Scroll, which 'anticipates an end time war when a celestial host will annihilate all the evil forces, both human and demonic' and the Community Rule in which 'the Sons of Light are governed by an archangel, the Prince of Light', sometimes interpreted as Michael (although it is Lucifer whose name has the literal reference to light; Wassen 2007: 499). Wassen describes the war detailed in the War Scroll as utopian in character, following a 'strict predetermined timeline in which the war is divided into seven parts over a period of 40 years, during which time even the enemies observe sabbatical years'; God is absent from the war as it happens, but clearly oversees the proceedings and has already determined the outcome (Wassen 2007: 511).

The parallels between this and Stockhausen's rendering of the bloodless battle between Michael and Lucifer over the course of a year in *TUESDAY* from *LIGHT* are at the very least highly interesting. A note on the sketches of *THURSDAY* – the first of the operas to be composed, though as we have seen the relevant scene from *TUESDAY* just predates it – specifically references the Qumran sect (assumed to be the authors of the Dead Sea Scrolls), indicating that this was one of many sources Stockhausen consulted when developing his own version of the recurring battle between the forces which Michael and Lucifer represent (Stockhausen 1978: 418).

Perhaps the most striking coincidence between the cosmological worldview of the Scrolls and Stockhausen's beliefs is the fact that, to quote Wassen again, 'Rather than mediators the angels appear as heavenly beings that humans can join to transcend the human sphere and come close to God' – an experience she says seems to have been most profound in the moment of worship, particularly musical worship (Wassen 2007: 515–19). This tallies exactly with Stockhausen's view: for him, angels are not messengers from above, but a state to which human beings should aspire, with music one of the main ways this can be achieved. Thus, despite his belief that a further and devastating global conflict was inevitable in the near future (apocalyptic ideas and angels have always gone together), Stockhausen was fundamentally optimistic: 'We need have no doubts about the future, because it is of a new nature [*Geist*], and this nature is young, and because, after *homo faber* and *homo ludens*, it announces *homo angelicus*, the musical, winged, cosmic human being' (Stockhausen 1986: 450).[10]

Communication

> A modern artist is a radio receiver conscious of itself in being conscious beyond itself. (Stockhausen 1969a: 301)[11]

Sleep, and dreaming, is only one form of consciousness that can open the door to visions. *TELEMUSIK* (1966) derived from a vision Stockhausen had in Japan after several jet-lagged nights without sleep, his mind overloaded with the new sights, sounds and customs of Japanese culture. Two years later, following the traumatic breakdown of his second marriage to artist Mary Bauermeister, Stockhausen emerged from a week in which he had hardly eaten or slept to write the texts which became *AUS DEN SIEBEN TAGEN* (1968). This and other pieces from the same year are of profound significance for the development of Stockhausen's ideas on musical communication. With regard to *STIMMUNG*, a piece for six singers that employs techniques of overtone singing and the intonation of sacred and magic names from various cultures, Stockhausen stated that a prime aim was to hone singers' and audiences' receptivity by encouraging them to hear into the sound. In *KURZWELLEN* for ensemble and *SPIRAL* for a soloist, the musicians' sensitivity and receptivity is heightened by instructing them to react to transmissions picked up by short-wave radios during the performance – something that is impossible to predict beforehand.[12] According to Stockhausen, the effect in the case of *KURZWELLEN* was that even in the very first performances we had the direct experience of a lasting, suprapersonal submission to inspiration, extended stillness, a complexity, freedom, spaciousness and a medial relinquishing of the self, which went beyond all our previous experiences and which heralded something completely new in the interpretation of music in toto.

At the moment I can report no more regarding *KURZWELLEN* than that times and spaces within which we are used to make music have been transcended and the possibility is becoming apparent of connecting with levels of consciousness which were previously closed to us or which could be accessed only in the briefest moments of intuitive submission. (Stockhausen 1968–9: 113–14)[13]

In a second programme text written a year later – and two months before Neil Armstrong set foot on the moon – Stockhausen is more specific about the further implications: 'Does not much of what we pick up with the short-wave receivers not sound like it came from very different regions, beyond language, reportage, "music", morse signals?' (Stockhausen 1968–9: 115).[14] Such comparisons are not uncommon in the history of modernist composition: the most obvious example is the line from the poet Stefan George – 'I feel the air of other planets' – which Arnold Schoenberg inserted into the score of the last movement of his second second quartet, regarded as the first of his pieces to abandon tonality. Also, since the very first experiments with electronic composition, composers and public alike had often used metaphors about outer space in describing this music. Stockhausen, however, is suggesting a more literal possibility of picking up signals from extraterrestrial sources. A few years later, after reading the Christian mystic Jakob Lorber's writings on the star Sirius, Stockhausen began to have dreams that he said revealed to him that he himself was a messenger from Sirius, a topic which formed the basis for a work with same title composed in 1975.

The idea of transforming material, including pre-existing music, according to certain rules dates back to *PLUS MINUS* of 1963, and became a staple of performances Stockhausen gave with his ensemble in the later 1960s. The use of radio added a new dimension, however, which corresponded well to Stockhausen's developing ideas on his own role as 'receiver' and 'interpreter' of messages from another domain. With regard to *PLUS MINUS*, he had stated that

> I am beginning to listen as if on an adventure, I am discovering a music that I produced; I sense that I am an instrument in the service of a much deeper power that I cannot grasp, a power that can only be experienced musically, in sound poetics. (Stockhausen 1965: 43)[15]

The text 'Litany', which forms an instruction to *AUS DEN SIEBEN TAGEN*, announces a new stage in this process: the aim is 'to connect you, the player, to the currents that flow through me, to which I am connected' (Stockhausen: 1968). His role as a composer is thus to assist the musician in reaching the same level of receptivity to these influences which he had possessed since birth.

Stockhausen noted in 1969 that while individual performances of *AUS DEN SIEBEN TAGEN* clearly differed a great deal from one another, different performances inspired by the same text shared certain similarities, which he called 'musico-genetic characteristics'; this led him to suggest that 'The point would seem to be the discovery, through the different texts, of different archetypes of musical processes, which lead to highly individual musical events' (Stockhausen: 1969b, 124). Although these claims need to be balanced against the fact that the performances concerned all involved largely the same group of people over a relatively short time period – and always under the direction of Stockhausen himself – the references to musical archetypes is as significant as his later discussion, in the same text, of a supra*rational* concept of music. Stockhausen vehemently rejected the attribute 'irrational' often applied to his music from this period onwards, and recognised that the roots of such an attribution lay in the fact that ours is a culture which lays very much weight indeed on rational thinking. 'Musical meditation', he countered, 'has nothing to do with emotionalism (*Gefühlsdüselei*), but with a heightened state of awareness and – in its most brilliant moments – creative ecstasy' (Stockhausen 1969b: 125).

In many works of this period, Stockhausen's approach to meditation is closer to Eastern tradition, particularly yogic ideas, than to the religious cultures of Europe and the Near East. This is most obvious in the texts of *AUS DEN SIEBEN TAGEN*, which are often reminiscent of instructions for yogic meditation; the structure and sound-world of *STIMMUNG* also has a great deal in common with practices of mantra-singing.[16] Stockhausen read the teachings of the influential yogi Sri Aurobindo towards the end of the infamous seven days that resulted in *AUS DEN SIEBEN TAGEN*, days in which he has described himself as being psychologically in a state near death (Stockhausen 1973b: 528–9). Satprem's book on Sri Aurobindo had been sitting on his bookshelf for a while, but – according to the composer – he was only moved to pick it up and read it at that point. Describing this event, he stated that, while he had always felt led 'like a child', he had 'never before consciously experienced that I just *had to do* what was communicated to me' (Stockhausen 1973a: 529).[17] But if, as he by that point increasingly believed, Stockhausen really was a transmitter, what was the message?

Karlheinz Stockhausen's Musical Vision

Two beings succeed in moving from a mode of existence beyond that which can be physically represented and perceived into a temporally and spatially limited area. They are connected by virtue of being each the polar opposite of the other. (Stockhausen 1952: 13)[18]

This quotation comes from Stockhausen's description of the basic idea behind one of his earliest compositions, the *Schlagquartett*, which was withdrawn and reworked into the *SCHLAGTRIO*. Its resemblance to a recurring theme in angelology – the idea of beings that move between the corporeal and incorporeal realms, between limited time and eternity – is striking. More importantly, the concept of two elements which are polar opposites but approach one another to the point where one could, theoretically, become the other, is an early expression of Stockhausen's reading of the serial principle in music.

Scholarly and popular understanding of the avant-garde compositional movement known as total serialism has tended to focus on the desire to create a completely unified musical form freed from the strictures of conventional harmonic and thematic thinking. Serial method sought to achieve this by generating whole compositions from numeric series applied to almost all the main musical parameters (pitch (or sound), rhythm/time organisation, amplitude and timbre). Misunderstandings regarding this venture, coupled with the fact that the music associated with serial composers has the reputation of being extremely difficult, has however meant that further aesthetic and philosophical foundations of serial thinking are often overlooked.[19] The serial technique developed as a way to balance different musical entities – individual sounds or groups of sounds – in a way that counters the structures of argument, counter-argument and resolution that were the basis for older ideas of musical form in western art music. In 1963, talking about the piece *MOMENTE* (1962), Stockhausen described his journey of the previous decade as one in which, disturbed by the prevailing dualism of western thinking, he tended first towards monism, but then through this to an increasingly polyvalent view of the world (Stockhausen 1963: 31–3). A programme note to the theatre piece *ORIGINALE* (*ORIGINALS*, 1961) also includes a passage that foreshadows many of his later descriptions of the serial principle, simultaneously drawing them together with his interest in ritual and theatre:

> The one tips over into the other – opposites are mediated. Black is a degree of white; scale of grey values.
>
> Things separated in time and space – people, activities, events of life (nothing acts as if, nothing is meant; all is composed, everything means) – are packed into one space, into one time: Theatre. (Stockhausen 1961a: 109)[20]

This process of mediation, and transformation – simultaneously respecting the inherent qualities of each element in the process – is not always immediately apparent from the complex-sounding structure of the works. There are exceptions, however, such as the meeting of the boy's voice and the electronic music in *GESANG DER JÜNGLINGE*, and the famous moment in the electronic part of *KONTAKTE* (*CONTACTS*, 1958–60) where a swirling pitch line is slowed down to reveal that it is not a line at all, but a series of pulses.[21]

A very different example is presented by the late work *NATÜR-LICHE DAUERN* (*NATURAL DURATIONS*, 2005–6), a set of twenty-four pieces for piano from the series *KLANG*. The first pieces in this set are marked by a succession of clear and stark distinctions – polarisations, we could say – between the music played by the left and right hands. In the first piece, for example, the right hand plays single notes, beginning near the top of the piano's range, while the left alternates with dyads and chords in the middle and lower ranges. Gradually, the right hand moves down, until it meets the register of the left hand; at this point, the single notes switch to the left and proceed down to the bottom of the piano's range while the chords and dyads rise upwards again. This may well be the clearest representation in all Stockhausen's music of the idea of crossing and transformation of thus neutralised polarities. Over the course of the next few pieces of *NATÜRLICHE DAUERN*, however, the void between the extremes is filled out. Notes enter in quicker succession, and increase in number, until the surface character of the piece is transformed into the type of high-energy statistical forms so familiar from classically 'serial' works written half a century before. Thus, the initial polarities are revealed to be but single instances of a complex and dynamic network of interconnections and relationships.

Though Stockhausen did not employ the serial technique in the strictest sense throughout his career, the underlying philosophy remains fairly constant. From 1970 onwards – after the brief hiatus of pieces like *AUS DEN SIEBEN TAGEN*, which consists solely of a set of prose instructions – Stockhausen used a method he called formula composition. Formula compositions are based on a relatively short, exactly notated 'formula' from which the entire piece is derived. Unlike in serial music, however, there is a significant degree of freedom in how this is applied, as long as the basic idea

– e.g. each section of the piece might correspond to an individually defined note in the formula – is adhered to. This is how a single 'superformula' made up of three individual formulas for each main protagonist can generate the colossal entity that is the seven operas of *LIGHT*. One telescopes out, as it were, from each moment of the formula, a falling-together of temporal realities that is a recurring preoccupation in Stockhausen's musical thinking, not to mention reflecting how we feel we dream of events taking place over hours or days, only for scientists to quietly inform us, when we wake, that the actual time-span of the dream was mere minutes.

For many of Stockhausen's contemporaries, serialism was an aesthetic and political rather than a spiritual philosophy. And while other composers of the post-war avant-garde are frequently accused of being too rational, Stockhausen is probably the only one simultaneously felt to be too rational *and* too irrational. Perhaps the problem is actually the type of binary thinking which it was Stockhausen's express aim to transcend. That this modernist's music is simultaneously deeply rooted in an interest in, and appreciation of, a whole gamut of world traditions, is likewise not the contradiction it may appear. Günther Peters has suggested that the idea of striving beyond current limitations and towards the divine is the essence of Stockhausen's message (Peters 1999: 121). He also warns that we should refrain from trying to find a coherent 'system' or 'interpretation' in the way Stockhausen integrates ideas from different traditions and belief systems: 'Stockhausen does not set up a sterile play of legends. Instead, he mixes cultural codes, he breaks up traditional images and, thus, makes room for the development of new things' (Peters 1999: 117).

There is much still to be explored and written regarding Stockhausen's interpretations of the archetypical figures that in *LIGHT* bear the names Michael and Lucifer. And if the connection between music and the divine, and in particular music as a means of mediating and communicating between our own and other realms, seems far-fetched to contemporary western readers – whether with regard to Stockhausen, or countless other examples – perhaps we should bear in mind that it is a commonplace even of more 'rational' discourse on music to speak of it as something magical, a source of power beyond us and over us which we cannot quite grasp. At the same time, the special powers of music are not something we need seek beyond ourselves. We forget too easily that, as Arthur O'Shaughnessy famously put it, '*We* are the music makers / And we are the dreamers of dreams' (my emphasis). The wonder of music is the wonder of humanity itself.

Stockhausen seems to have shared something of this sentiment when he gave Michael the following text in the piece appropriately called *VISION*, which introduces the audience of *THURSDAY* to the central cosmological themes of the cycle. *VISION* relates the tale of Lucifer's fall from grace when he had disagreed with the cosmological hierarchy's decision to create humankind. Michael, on the other hand, took a quite different approach, and a quite different route from the one Stockhausen projected for the rest of us: he did not develop from a human into an angel, but for a time became one of us. For, as he sings,

> I wanted to know what it is, to be human
> I wanted to sense everything that only a human can sense
> I have experienced the human's pain, the pettiness in them,
> > the ludicrous in them.
> I have felt their childlike nature and their joy, their happiness [. . .]
> And I know that many of you will laugh at me
> when I sing you this:
> > I have fallen hopelessly in love with humanity
> > with this earth and its children
> > despite LUCIFER
> > despite Satan –
> > despite everything . . .[22]

Notes

[1] In this chapter I have adopted Stockhausen's convention of capitalising the names of his published compositions. Where English versions of the names of pieces are appropriate or common, I have included these at the first mention of the piece in question. An exception is the days

of the week from the series *LICHT*, which like the title of the cycle as a whole I have given in English throughout.

[2] Kürten is the small town in Nordrhein-Westfalen, western Germany where Stockhausen lived from the 1960s until his death.

[3] Stockhausen said with regard to these works that while the basic form and idea were generally very clear to him from the dream, the micro-structure often required careful calculation; nevertheless, in these works the process of writing was almost automatic (Stockhausen 1975: 576–7).

[4] 'Darsteller ritueller *szenischer Musik*, die nicht nur wie traditionelle Interpreten ein Stück "abspielen", was andere auch abspielen können, sondern die als Personifizierungen von archetypischen und nie dagewesenen Figuren in neuen, musikalischen Raumritualen spielen wurden.' My translation.

[5] 'GOLDSTAUB refers to the experience of being, with eyes closed, in a state of total relaxation (no images or thoughts) and concentrating on a "colour" that, from an initial black-grey, develops through a warm, reddish violet to *golddust* – even in the deepest night' ('so meint GOLDSTAUB die Erfahrung, sich bei geschlossenen Augen völlig entspannt (ohne Bilder oder Gedanken) auf die "Farbe" zu konzentrieren, die nach anfänglichem Schwarz-grau über ein warm-rötliches Violett zu *Goldstaub* wird – auch in finsterer Nacht' (Stockhausen 1973a: 149). My translation.

[6] Stockhausen's interest in Sufi mysticism derived from his reading of Hazrat Imyan Khan, whose writings provided texts and titles for several pieces in the later 1960s and early 1970s. His knowledge of ancient American belief systems is due in large part to his friendship with the anthropologist Nancy Wyle.

[7] For more on the importance of *The Urantia Book* for Stockhausen, see Bandur 2004; Ruch 2016.

[8] Speyer also suggests that the idea of genius which became so important in ancient Rome is linked to the developing belief from Hellenistic culture forwards in a number of divine signs, but also personal divine messengers who could take the form of birds or voices.

[9] Schipper notes that the Egyptian god Thoth is sometimes viewed as the archetype for the archangel Michael. Thoth is one of the many deities and figures mentioned by Stockhausen as corresponding to Michael: see Stockhausen 1980: 153.

[10] 'Wir brauchen keine Zweifel für die Zukunft zu haben, weil es neuer Geist ist, weil dieser Geist jung ist und weil es nach dem *homo faber* und dem *homo ludens* den homo angelicus ankündigt, den musizierenden, beflügelten, kosmischen Menschen.' My translation.

11 'Ein moderner Künstler ist ein Radioempfänger mit Selbstbewußtsein im Überbewußtsein.' My translation.

12 John Cage also made extensive use of radio. Stockhausen's approach differs in the quite typical way that he calls on musicians actively to respond to and shape musical form in conjunction with what the radios transmit. In Cage's thinking, on the other hand, the form of the piece and not just the content of the radio broadcasts are typically generated by chance and do not, as in the case of Stockhausen, depend upon the musicians' active reaction to and interaction with this content.

13 'So haben wir schon in den ersten Aufführungen die direkte Erfahrung einer andauernden überpersönlichen Eingebung, ausgedehnter Stille, einer Vielschichtigkeit, Freiheit, Weiträumigkeit und einer medialen Selbstentäußerung gemacht, die alle unsere bisherigen Erfahrungen übersteigen und etwas entscheidend Neues in der musikalischen Interpretation überhaupt ankündigen. Ich kann im Augenblick über die *KURZWELLEN* nicht mehr berichten, also daß Zeiten und Räume, in denen wir bisher gewohnt waren, Musik zu machen, aufgehoben sind und die Möglichkeit sich abzeichnet, mit Bewußtseinsschichten Verbindung aufzunehmen, die uns bisher verschlossen oder nur in äußerst kurzen Momenten intuitiver Eingebung zugängig waren.' My translation. I have rendered the German *Eingebung* as *submission* and *submission to inspiration* here as this seems more appropriate to the collective and suprapersonal state Stockhausen is describing than the more usual translation of *inspiration* or *intuition*.

14 'Klingt nicht schon vieles, was wir mit den Kurzwellenempfängern auffangen, als käme es aus ganz anderen Räumen, jenseits von Sprache, Reportage, "Musik", Morsezeichen?' My translation.

15 'Ich beginne, abenteuerlich zu hören, ich entdecke eine von mir hervorgerufene Musik: ich spüre, daß ich – als Instrument – einer viel tiefer liegenden, mir unfaßbaren Kraft diene, die nur musikalisch, klangpoetisch erlebbar ist.' My translation.

16 The composition *MANTRA* for two pianists (!) and live electronics from 1970 demonstrates this debt in the very title. Significantly, this piece marked a return to through-composed music for Stockhausen after several years working with the practice of intuitive music. It is also the first piece to use the technique of formula composition, discussed further below.

17 'Ich bin immer geführt worden wie ein Kind [. . .] Aber ich hatte vorher nicht bewußt erlebt, daß ich nun direkt tun mußte, was mir durch Nachrichten mitgeteilt wurde.' My translation.

[18] 'Zwei Wesen gelangen aus einem Zustand, der jenseits des physikalischen Darstellbaren und Wahrnehmbaren ist, in einen zeitlich und räumlich begrenzten Bereich. Sie sind als Pole aufeinander bezogen.' My translation.

[19] Discussed in detail in Grant 2001.

[20] 'Eins schlägt ins andere um – Gegensätze sind vermittelt. Schwarz ist ein Grad von weiß: Skala der Grauwerte. Zeitlich und räumlich getrenntes – Personen, Tätigkeiten, Ereignisse des Lebens (nichts tut so, als ob, nichts ist gemeint; alles ist komponiert, jedes meint) – gerafft in einen Raum, in eine Zeit: Theater.' My translation.

[21] The psychoacoustic phenomenon whereby a series of pulses, if their succession is fast enough, is perceived by human ears to be a distinct and continuous pitch rather than rhythm, was the basis for Stockhausen's conception of the 'unity of musical time'; see here especially Stockhausen: 1961b. This is a perfect demonstration of the idea that not only can any one thing be transformed stage by stage into another, but also the underlying unity of all things that makes this possible.

[22] 'Ich wollte wissen, was es ist, ein Mensch zu sein. / Ich wollte alles spüren, was ein Mensch nur spürt. / Ich habe des Menschen Leid, das Kleine an ihm, das Lächerliche erlebt. / Ich habe seine Kindlichkeit und seine Freude, sein Glück gefühlt [. . .] Und ich weiß, daß viele von Euch mich verlachen / wenn ich Euch singe: / Ich habe mich unsterblich in die Menschen, / in diese Erde und ihre Kinder verliebt – / trotz LUZIFER – / trotz Satan – / trotz allem.'

References

Author's note: For better chronological orientation, writings by Stockhausen which appear in his collected writings are listed here by their date of original publications or the date of the original interview: the date of publication of the volume is included at the end of the relevant entry.

Bandur, Markus (2004) "'. . . alles aus einem Kern entfaltet, thematisch und strukturell". Karlheinz Stockhausen und die Rezeption des Urantia Book in LICHT', in Imke Misch and Christoph von Blumröder, *Internationales Stockhausen-Symposion 2000: LICHT: Musikwissenschaftliches Institut der Universität zu Köln, 19. bis 22. Oktober 2000. Tagungsbericht* (Münster, Berlin and London: LIT-Verlag), pp. 136–46.

Berner, Christoph (2007) 'The four (or seven) archangels in the First Book of Enoch and early Jewish writings of the Second Temple Period', in Reiterer, Nicklas and Schöplin (eds), pp. 395–411.

Fischer, Alexander A. (2007) 'Moses and the Exodus Angel', in Reiterer, Nicklas and Schöplin (eds), pp. 79–93.

Grant, M. J. (2001) *Serial Music, Serial Aesthetics: Compositional Theory in Post-war Europe* (Cambridge: Cambridge University Press).

Hannah, Darrell D. (2007) 'Guardian angels and angelic patrons in Second-Temple Judaism and early Christianity', in Reiterer, Nicklas and Schöplin (eds), pp. 413–35.

Henkel, Georg (2016) 'Angel of Joy: Stockhausen's "mirrors in sound" and the audibility of the inaudible', in M. J. Grant and Imke Misch (eds), *The Musical Legacy of Karlheinz Stockhausen* (Hofheim: Wolke), pp. 138–47.

Hutter, Manfred (2007) 'Demons and benevolent spirits in the Ancient Near East: A phenomenological overview', in Reiterer, Nicklas and Schöplin (eds), pp. 21–34.

Peters, Günther (1999) '". . . How creation is composed": Spirituality in the music of Karlheinz Stockhausen', tr. Mark Scheiber and Günther Peters, *Perpectives of New Music*, 37/1: 96–131.

Reiterer, Friedrich V., Nicklas, Tobias and Schöplin, Karin (eds) (2007) *Angels: The Concept of Celestial Beings – Origins, Development and Reception*, Deuterocanonical and Cognate Literature Yearbook 2007 (Berlin and New York: Walter de Gruyter).

Ruch, Christian (2016) '". . . but what I've heard, I think, it's true": Karlheinz Stockhausen and the Urantia Book', in M. J. Grant and Imke Misch (eds), *The Musical Legacy of Karlheinz Stockhausen* (Hofheim: Wolke), pp. 148–57.

Schipper, Bern U. (2007) 'Angels or demons? Divine messengers in Ancient Egypt', in Reiterer, Nicklas and Schöplin (eds), pp. 1–19.

Speyer, Wolfgang (2007) 'The divine messenger in Ancient Greece, Etruria and Rome', in Reiterer, Nicklas and Schöplin (eds), pp. 35–47.

Stockhausen, Karlheinz (1952) 'Schlagquartett' (1952), in Karlheinz Stockhausen (ed. Diether Schnebel), *Texte zur Musik, Bd. 2: Aufsätze zur musikalischen Praxis 1952–1962* (Cologne: DuMont, 1964), pp. 13–18.

Stockhausen, Karlheinz (1957) 'Musik in Funktion', in Karlheinz Stockhausen (ed. Diether Schnebel), *Texte zur Musik, Bd. 2: Aufsätze zur musikalischen Praxis 1952–1962* (Cologne: DuMont, 1964), pp. 212–14.

Stockhausen, Karlheinz (1961a) 'ORIGINALE (1961)' (programme note), in Karlheinz Stockhausen (ed. Diether Schnebel), *Texte zur Musik,*

Morag Josephine Grant

Bd. 2: Aufsätze zur musikalischen Praxis 1952–1962 (Cologne: DuMont, 1964), pp. 107–9.

Stockhausen, Karlheinz (1961b) 'Die Einheit der musikalischen Zeit', in Karlheinz Stockhausen (ed. Diether Schnebel), *Texte zur Musik, Bd. 2: Aufsätze zur musikalischen Praxis 1952–1962* (Cologne: DuMont, 1964), pp. 211–21. English translation: 'The concept of unity of electronic music [*sic*]', tr. Elaine Barkin, *Perspectives of New Music*, 1/1 (1962), 38–9.

Stockhausen, Karlheinz (1963) 'MOMENTE (1962)' (programme note), in Karlheinz Stockhausen (ed. Christoph von Blumröder), *Texte zur Musik, Bd. 3: 1963–1970: Einführungen und Projekte, Kurse, Sendungen, Standpunkte, Nebennoten* (Cologne: DuMont Schauberg, 1971), pp. 31–9.

Stockhausen, Karlheinz (1965) 'PLUS-MINUS' (programme note), in Karlheinz Stockhausen (ed. Christoph von Blumröder), *Texte zur Musik, Bd. 3: 1963–1970: Einführungen und Projekte, Kurse, Sendungen, Standpunkte, Nebennoten* (Cologne: DuMont Schauberg, 1971), pp. 40–3.

Stockhausen, Karlheinz (1968–9) 'KURZWELLEN für sechs Spieler' (two programme notes), in Karlheinz Stockhausen (ed. Christoph von Blumröder), *Texte zur Musik, Bd. 3: 1963–1970: Einführungen und Projekte, Kurse, Sendungen, Standpunkte, Nebennoten* (Cologne: DuMont Schauberg, 1971), pp 112–15.

Stockhausen, Karlheinz (1969a) 'Ein Mundstück', in Karlheinz Stockhausen (ed. Christoph von Blumröder), *Texte zur Musik, Bd. 3: 1963–1970: Einführungen und Projekte, Kurse, Sendungen, Standpunkte, Nebennoten* (Cologne: DuMont Schauberg, 1971), pp. 300–2.

Stockhausen, Karlheinz (1969b) 'AUS DEN SIEBEN TAGEN' (two programme notes), in Karlheinz Stockhausen (ed. Christoph von Blumröder), *Texte zur Musik, Bd. 3: 1963–1970: Einführungen und Projekte, Kurse, Sendungen, Standpunkte, Nebennoten* (Cologne: DuMont Schauberg, 1971), pp. 123–5.

Stockhausen, Karlheinz (1971) *TRANS* (musical score), Vienna: Universal Edition.

Stockhausen, Karlheinz (1973a) 'GOLDSTAUB' (liner notes for Deutsche Grammophon recording), in Karlheinz Stockhausen (ed. Christoph von Blumröder), *Texte zur Musik, Bd. 4: 1970–1977, Werk-Einführungen, Elektronische Musik, Weltmusik, Vorschläge und Standpunkte zum Werk Anderer* (Cologne: DuMont Schauberg, 1977), pp. 149–51.

Stockhausen, Karlheinz (1973b) 'Zweites Gespräch', in Karlheinz Stockhausen (ed. Christoph von Blumröder), *Texte zur Musik, Bd. 4: 1970–1977: Werk-Einführungen, Elektronische Musik, Weltmusik,*

186

Vorschläge und Standpunkte zum Werk Anderer (Cologne: DuMont Schauberg, 1977), pp. 526–49.

Stockhausen, Karlheinz (1974) 'TRANS für Orchestra' (programme note), in Karlheinz Stockhausen (ed. Christoph von Blumröder), *Texte zur Musik, Bd. 4: 1970–1977: Werk-Einführungen, Elektronische Musik, Weltmusik, Vorschläge und Standpunkte zum Werk Anderer* (Cologne: DuMont Schauberg, 1977), pp 181–2.

Stockhausen, Karlheinz (1975) 'Interview III: "Denn alles ist Musik …"', in Karlheinz Stockhausen (ed. Christoph von Blumröder), *Texte zur Musik, Bd. 4: 1970–1977: Werk-Einführungen, Elektronische Musik, Weltmusik, Vorschläge und Standpunkte zum Werk Anderer* (Cologne: DuMont Schauberg, 1977), pp. 569–86.

Stockhausen, Karlheinz (1976) 'Die sieben Tage der Woche', in Karlheinz Stockhausen (ed. Christoph von Blumröder), *Texte zur Musik, Bd. 6: 1977–1984: Interpretationen* (Cologne: DuMont, 1989), pp. 152–71.

Stockhausen, Karlheinz (1977) 'LICHT-Blicke' (interview with Michael Kurtz) , in Karlheinz Stockhausen (ed. Christoph von Blumröder), *Texte zur Musik, Bd. 6: 1977–1984: Interpretationen* (Cologne: DuMont, 1989), pp 188–233.

Stockhausen, Karlheinz (1978) 'Excerpt from sketches to DONNERSTAG', in Karlheinz Stockhausen (ed. Christoph von Blumröder), *Texte zur Musik, Bd. 5: 1977–1984: Komposition* (Cologne: DuMont, 1989), pp. 418.

Stockhausen, Karlheinz (1979) 'Elektronische Musik seit 1952' (interview with Marietta Morawska-Büngeler) , in Karlheinz Stockhausen (ed. Christoph von Blumröder), *Texte zur Musik, Bd. 8: 1984–1991: DIENSTAG aus LICHT u.a.* (Cologne: DuMont, 1998).

Stockhausen, Karlheinz (2000) 'Wunderbare Zeichen' (interview with Robert Baumann), in Karlheinz Stockhausen (ed. Imke Misch), *Texte zur Musik, Bd. 16: LICHT-Reflexe – Seitenzweige – Klangproduktion/ Klangprojektion* (Kürten: Stockhausen-Stiftung für Musik, 2014), pp 411–13.

Toop, Richard (2008) 'Dreamworks', in *Gedenkschrift für Stockhausen* (Kürten: Stockhausen-Stiftung für Musik), pp. 194–201.

Wassen, Cecilia (2007) 'Angels in the Dead Sea Scrolls', in Reiterer, Nicklas and Schöplin, pp. 499–523.

Acknowledgements

Thanks to Imke Misch and Gustavo Oliveira Alfaix Assis for tips and ideas.

10

How do Singers and Other Groups Synchronise to Form Communities?

Guy Hayward
Centre for Music and Science,
University of Cambridge

Chanting is often used to form communities. This chapter explores whether and how it is possible, in general terms, to characterise the 'community' that is formed by group singing, created through 'entrainment': the process through which two or more rhythmic beats somehow come to synchronise with each other (Clayton 2012; Clayton et al. 2004). In particular it will ask whether this community exists as something beyond a collection of individual relationships.

This means examining how the process of group synchronisation works from a scientific perspective. Both anthropological and scientific approaches towards group dynamics provide insights at different levels of explanation that can inform each other. The principal question I address here is how top-down and bottom-up approaches might illuminate the dynamic processes of group synchronisation. Most of the theoretical basis for understanding this dynamic process comes from systems theory (also known as 'complex systems theory', 'complexity theory', 'complexity science', or 'systems biology') in the form of Artificial Life and Autopoiesis. Research on real-life collective animal behaviour like flocks of birds and schools of fish and jazz improvisation can also throw light on the dynamic process of collective synchronisation behaviour in the context of complexity theory.

We can think about collective synchronisation in music at the level both of the group and of the individual. Here the tension between community and individual in the process of group synchronisation in music is analogous to the way that the 'top-down' collective agreement of a stable pulse interplays with 'bottom-up' individual perturbations of timing through error or improvisation. Complex systems theory describes the dynamics of how this 'collective agreement' might emerge out of the interaction between individuals and the 'system' of the pulse.

Just as there is always tension between structure and chaos, so there is always tension between any dualistic conceptions of a phenomenon – in this case, top-down versus bottom-up organisation of synchrony in group entrainment. I will not argue for the dominance of one form of organisation over the other. And although an integrated synthesis of both upward and downward causation may be ultimately desirable, my aim is more modest than that: to clarify the ways in which both forms of organisation operate.

Social Interaction at the Group Level

In thinking about phenomena such as society, culture and the individual, writers on human nature have until quite recently focused on such concerns as the nature of human brains, the structure of cognition, the origins of language and its innate structures, and the high levels of social cooperation shown by our species (Levinson 2006: 39). Levinson argues that the near-exclusive focus on these aspects of human reality has meant that the very nature of everyday human interaction has been largely overlooked – perhaps the aspect that is most easily studied and likely to have the most wide-ranging implications. Because of the importance of singing and chanting in many societies around the world, and musical activity *in general*, it is essential, I believe, for cross-cultural linguistic research to consider the interactional structure of both speech *and* music if an understanding of the 'human interaction engine' is going to be possible.

Studying human interaction at the group level is very difficult however: it is hard enough to study the interaction between just two people, let alone unpick the complexity of group interaction. Going even further, Mitchell (2012: 178) holds that 'it is likely that all the factors contributing to the complete cause of some physical event, say a window breaking when hit by a rock, cannot be represented by any single theory in the syntax of logic or even the language of physics.' If we cannot even gain a full understanding of a rock breaking a window then gaining an understanding of human social behaviour is even more of a challenge.

The search for understanding is made even more difficult given that, from an academic perspective,

> [human interaction lies in an] interdisciplinary no-mans land: it belongs equally to anthropology, sociology, biology, psychology, and ethology but is owned by none of them. Observations, generalizations and theory have therefore been pulled in different directions, and nothing close to a synthesis has emerged. (Levinson 2006: 39).

The attractiveness of a synthesis would be that we might be able to understand a little more about universal aspects of social interaction.

Levinson (2006) holds that cultural variation may not contradict his 'universalist' project, because the evidence suggests that the fundamentals of human face-to-face interaction can be observed in most societies. Though aspects of human interaction – such as spacing, posture, gesture and linguistic form – do show significant cultural variation, the actual fundamental structure of normal everyday human conversation is fairly stable across the world; e.g. the rhythm of who speaks when, or who gives and takes when (Levinson, 2006: 46).

The case of unison singing or chanting is fundamentally different from conversational rhythm because everyone makes a sound at the same time, i.e. there is no turn-taking. Interaction is characterised by expectation of close timing, produced for example by a hand wave that sets an immediate response. Interaction between individuals in unison singing is therefore even more immediate. Furthermore, group singing involves many more individuals than those involved in typical one-on-one conversations. Investigating group singing is not easy however. Any form of social interaction that involves many individuals is best viewed as having 'emergent properties arising from the interactions of component parts . . . [However] if we know the parts can we put them together and get a complete working whole?' (Moore, Szekely and Komdeur, 2010: 540).

The Top-down vs Bottom-up Dynamic in Group Interaction

Here a top-down influence refers to a level of organisation that is distinct from 'the sum of the parts' – the sum of parts being the aggregation of the actions of the individuals within the group – and this top-down influence yet influences those individual actions. A better translation of Aristotle's famous phrase 'more than the sum of the parts' is 'the whole is over and above its parts, and not just the sum of them all' (Mitchell, 2012:).

Understanding top-down influences as 'over and above' the sum of their parts is a reasonable starting point to investigating collective action, given that 'everywhere we look in nature, at whatever level or scale, we find wholes that are made up of parts that are themselves wholes at a lower level' (Sheldrake 2012: 50). For example,

the structure and meaning of this sentence could not be worked out by a chemical analysis of the paper and the ink, or deduced from the quantities of individual letters (e.g. 'a') that make it up . . . the structure of the whole depends on the way they are combined together in words, and on the relationships between the words.

The same goes for music, and notes are part of bars, in phrases, in sections, in movements, in pieces. A community of singers is embedded in its local, regional and global environment. Thus, wherever one looks one finds organised systems that exist in *nested hierarchies*.

'The sum of them all' can refer to what is termed 'aggregation' in complexity science. 'Aggregation' is defined as 'a particularly simple kind of compositional relationship between component parts and the whole. The weight of a pile of rocks being the aggregate of the weight of each component rock is an example' (Mitchell 2012: 174). Therefore, in contrast with top-down explanations, bottom-up explanations of group interaction come from individuals whose actions, when aggregated, make up the collective action of the group.

Top-down influences tend to be more stable because a group's unity depends on the whole group adhering to principles that are 'above' any one individual. The point is that although the lower-order actions of the individual are often necessary for the maintenance of higher-order stability in the group, they may also act as destabilising influences.

Bottom-up aggregation is a linear part-whole relationship; however, in more complex systems as witnessed in social behaviour, the part-whole relationships can be represented by non-linear dynamics which are based on 'dynamical instability in which a physical system could end up in wildly different end states depending on very small differences in its initial state' (Mitchell 2012: 179). Non-linear dynamics depend on feedback loops between individual components, with interactions going both ways: up towards stable structure and down towards instability. It is through these feedback loops that small variations in a system's initial state are amplified to the extent that a system can end up in wildly different states. Therefore, 'even if a behaviour, described at a higher level of organisation, is determined by the interactions of entities at a lower level of organisation, if the dynamics are nonlinear, the behaviour will not be predictable' (Mitchell 2012: 180). Hence the behaviour of non-linear systems is unpredictable due to the fact that both bottom-up and top-down influences interplay with each other.

An example of a non-linear system of living organisms in which the individuals move more freely is the way bees assess their colony's nutritional status. However, for simplicity, this is a relatively stable non-linear system. Seeley (1989) describes how in a bee colony forager bees fly out of the hive to forage for food. When they return they 'unload' their haul to a younger 'unloading' bee who transfers the food to an empty cell. What communicates to the forager bee whether to leave the hive again either to carry on foraging or to stop foraging is the relative difficulty of finding an unloading bee, which is dependent on how easy it is for an unloading bee to find an empty cell. The relative difficulty of offloading to an unloading bee tunes the number of foragers to the rate of nectar intake in the hive.

Mitchell (2012: 183) relates this tuning process to the dynamics of emergence, an important concept in complexity theory, with the 'emergent structure' being the amount of stored nectar: 'the amount of nectar stored in a hive is not a property of any of the individual bees, although it is the sum of the results of their individual behavior.' The emergent structure at the higher level emerges from the actions of the individual bees and the amount of stored nectar in turn affects the subsequent actions of the individual bees, creating a feedback loop.

Mead (1932) first proposed the concept of emergent structure as relating to 'the spontaneous evolution of structure and meaning'. Emergence is also a useful concept in thinking about other social activities; for example, emergent meaning in conversation, and emergent structure of interaction in sport when a team starts playing like a single organism. Emergent structure also relates to musical synchronisation which I will return to after discussing complex systems theory and its various manifestations.

Luhmann's Systems Theory

Luhmann's 'systems theory' (1982) is primarily 'top-down'. He argued that a theory of social systems does not need to concern itself with the individuals who are part of that system (Gershon 2005: 100). What matters from Luhmann's perspective is that a system can determine what is system and what is environment, and individuals are merely 'environment' from a system's perspective – their individual agency is irrelevant. Though it is of no use in analysing person-to-person social interaction, his ideas do help us understand something about how individuals are influenced by overarching systems that to a large extent delimit their behaviour. Similarly Durkheim:

> Precisely because society has its own specific nature that is different
> from our nature as individuals, it pursues ends that are also specific-
> ally its own; but because it can achieve those ends only by working
> through us, it categorically demands our cooperation. Society
> requires us to make ourselves its servants, forgetful of our own
> interests. (Durkheim, 1995: 209)

Durkheim's work on *recreative effervescence* was an attempt to
show on the level of culture how society encourages an individual
to conform to a societal system.

Luhmann's conception of a system is one of reduced complexity
in comparison with its far more complex environment. Gershon
(2005: 102) describes how '[a] system is constantly reformulating
the noise and chaotic complexities that leave the environment and
enter the system into order. But creating order is also always creating
a simplification; it is reducing complexity to what is manageable.'
A system can only bring order to complexity to a limited degree;
if the environment becomes too complex the system will not be
able to bring it into order. A system therefore can only select a
limited amount of information from its environment. This 'limit'
changes as the system adapts by changing its ability to structure
its environment. As Luhmann has said, 'Contrary to what is
commonly thought of it, the focus of modern systems theory is
not identity but difference, not control but autonomy, not static
but dynamic stability, not planning but evolution' (Luhmann 1982:
137).

The principles of difference, autonomy, dynamism and evolution
cannot exist when only top-down processes are functioning because
it would mean that nothing could create difference, create the need
for autonomy, stand in the way of systemic influence, or prompt
evolution and adaptation. That is obviously not how things are.

There are examples of collective human behaviour which suit
Luhmann's theory where it seems that the bottom-up influence of
the 'individual' is greatly diminished, and a top-down 'common
goal' is dominant. For example, as Canetti (1973: 32) says about
crowds: 'A goal outside the individual members and common to
all of them drives underground all the private differing goals which

are fatal to the crowd as such. Direction is essential for the continuing existence of the crowd . . . A crowd exists so long as it has an unattained goal.'

In the context of the *haka* (New Zealand pre-rugby team ritual), 'the tribe feel themselves a crowd. They make use of it whenever they feel a need to be a crowd, or to appear as one in front of others. In the rhythmic perfection it has attained the haka serves this purpose reliably. Thanks to it their unity is never seriously threatened from within' (Canetti 1973: 34). The top-down 'common goal' in the *haka* is rhythmic unity: group activities reduce individual perturbation and increase singularity of purpose and action.

Similarly, a school of fish moves in such ways as to demonstrate a single purpose. Here, large groups of individual fishes swim 'in tight formations, more or less parallel to each other, changing direction and reversing in near unison' (Sheldrake 2003: 117). This is similar to what is observed in collective singing and in chanting. Furthermore, most species of fish, including herring and mackerel, form schools without leaders or hierarchies, suggesting – as do the collective achievements of ants and termites – the dominance of top-down organisation.

Complex Systems

These are systems whose behaviour

> cannot be extrapolated from the behaviours of its individual components . . . found in fields as diverse as particle physics, ecology, economics, neurology, sociology and computer science. Their behaviour cannot be controlled or designed in a hierarchical way. (Worrall, 2004: 121)

'Emergent structure' is a core concept in complex systems theory: 'novelty, unpredictability and the causal efficacy of emergent properties or structures, sometimes referred to as downward causation' (Mitchell, 2012: 173). As with a choir, it emerges ultimately from the complex interactions between individual components, and therefore arises from a 'bottom-up' synthesis of the network of local interactions.

Emergence is also a key concept in another systems theory of complex behaviour, *autopoiesis*, which refers to a closed system that can create itself (*auto* meaning 'self' and *poiesis* 'creation' or 'production'). Autopoietic organisation is defined as 'a unity by a network of productions of components which (i) participate recursively in the same network of productions of components which produced these components, and (ii) realise the network of productions as a unity in the space in which the components exist'. The central tenet of the philosophy of autopoiesis is that of a bottom-up synthesis:

> the properties of a unity [i.e. a cell, organism, etc.] cannot be accounted for only through accounting for the properties of its components . . . the living organisation can only be characterised unambiguously by specifying the network of interactions of components which constitute a living system as a whole, that is, as a 'unity' (Varela et al. 1974: 187)

It is the network of interactions itself that is considered as a unity (a 'system'), the concept which binds the multiplicity of local interactions.

'Artificial Life' is an applied version of systems theory that relates to the concept of autopoiesis. The 'artificial' in Artificial Life (hereinafter ALife) 'signifies that the systems in question are human-made; that is, the basic components [i.e. computer representations] were not created by nature through evolution' (ibid.). ALife is

> devoted to understanding life by attempting to abstract the funda-mental dynamical principles underlying biological phenomena, and recreating these dynamics in other physical media, such as computers, making them accessible to new kinds of experimental manipulation and testing. (Sipper, 1995: 1)

The most important properties of ALife systems are those which emerge at higher levels, and ALife systems can be seen as large collections of simple, basic units.[1] Like autopoiesis, ALife aims not to define the properties of the individual components of a system, but to define the properties of the network of mutual relations between individual components. ALife is thus *synthetic*, attempting to construct phenomena from their elemental units, as opposed to *analytic*, trying to break down complex phenomena into their basic components (which is characteristic of traditional biological research) (Sipper, 1995: 1). Therefore ALife is, like autopoiesis, a *bottom-up* project.

It remains to be seen whether autopoietic and ALife models can model the complexity of living systems situated within their ever-changing environment and it seems unlikely that either autopoiesis or ALife will ever be able to look at living systems in all their complexity, nested as they are within systems within systems. In any case the power of mathematical models declines rapidly as systems become more complex when one moves from physics to biology let alone social psychology – though specialists rather seldom reveal this to the public at large:

> Many animals exhibit remarkable collective behaviour. Social insects gather in large numbers – swarms – to forage and build nests. The ability of flocking birds to coordinate their motion in order to avoid obstacles and to rapidly change direction of flight is well known to us all. (Blackwell and Young 2004: 123)

Thus, it is argued, in swarm complex systems

> [the] collective behaviour does not necessarily derive from central organisational control or leadership, but arises from the local behaviour and interaction of (relatively) simple organisms . . . each swarm member is only aware of other members in its immediate neighbourhood. A dramatic example is to be found with the huge shoals of migrating herring, sometimes up to seventeen miles long and with millions of members; it is hard to conceive of any centralised method of communication that can account for this collective behaviour. (Worrall, 2004: 121)

This seems to differ in small and large groups. In a small flock of ten pigeons the flock's movements were hierarchically organised (Nagy et al. 2010). But in large flocking or schooling groups a response governed by leaders or hierarchical structure in both flocking and schooling behaviours in large groups would not be effective. Unless the leader(s) happened to detect a predator directly, the group as a whole would not react and their safety would be threatened (Cavagna et al. 2010: 1).

The Complexities of Flocking Behaviour and its Study

So how can schooling, flocking and such group behaviour be coordinated?

Rupert Sheldrake notes how, in contrast to the numerous attempts to simulate swarming and flocking behaviour on computers, there have been 'surprisingly few studies of the detailed behaviour of [real-life] flocks of birds' (2003: 113). And this despite the comment by Cavagna et al. that 'Of all distinctive traits of collective animal behaviour the most conspicuous is the emergence of global order, namely the fact that all individuals within the group synchronise to some extent their behavioural state' (2010: 1).

Sheldrake (2003: 113) goes on to explain how the two-dimensional boids model, based on complex systems theory, starts from individual boids that are programmed to behave according to three simple rules:

1. Steer to avoid being too close to neighbours.
2. Steer towards the average direction that neighbours are heading in.
3. Steer to move towards the average position of neighbours.

However, he argues that while these rules, based on local interactions only, allow a computer screen to convincingly imitate flock behaviour (e.g. in Lion King and Batman Returns), 'it bears little relation to the behaviour of real, three-dimensional flocks of birds' (2003: 114), probably because Reynolds developed the boids program starting from the perspective of ALife rather than data about real birds.

Using the concept of 'a chorus line' (bringing us back again to music), real-life biological research by Wayne Potts attempted to explain the banking movements of large flocks of dunlins. By analysing films of their movements he found that

> a single bird may initiate a manoeuvre which spreads through the flock in a wave. The propagation of this 'manoeuvre wave' begins relatively slowly but reaches mean speeds three times higher than would be possible if birds were simply reacting to their immediate neighbours. These propagation speeds appear to be achieved in much the same way as they are in a human chorus line: individuals observe the approaching manoeuvre wave and time their own execution to coincide with its arrival. (Potts 1984: 345)

Potts argues that dunlin flock coordination is achieved through visual communication, leading to his chorus line hypothesis (similar to the 'Mexican wave' phenomenon) that the neighbours that follow the initiating bird 'will be delayed by at least their own reaction time but, further away, response times should fall as birds are able to estimate the arrival of the approaching manoeuvre wave'. This fits with his research on human chorus lines, which indicates that 'rehearsed manoeuvres, initiated without warning, propagate from person to person approximately twice as fast (107.7 +/- 6.8ms, n=3) as the 194ms human visual reaction time' (Potts 1984: 345).

In line with his theory, Potts found that where initiators of banking movements and their neighbours were discernible in the films the movements were initiated by one or a few individuals and that the waves that 'radiated' outwards from the initiating bird travelled along every major axis, even from back to front, suggesting that any region of the flock could initiate a manoeuvre, travelling at speeds nearly three times faster than if the flocks were following the actions of their neighbours. He did not observe any unison manoeuvres, which also supports the chorus line hypothesis, and would suggest that flocking behaviour of dunlins arises from bottom-up organisation. However Rupert Sheldrake (2003) argues that Potts's assumption that the birds exclusively employ the visual channel to coordinate the movement of the flock would entail

> practically continuous, unblinking, 360-degree visual attention. Even assuming total, continuous attention, how could this work when birds were reacting to waves approaching from behind [which are common in dunlin flocks, which are not V-formation flocks]? No birds have 360-degree vision, whether they have their eyes at the front, like owls, or at the side of their head like geese, dunlins and starlings. (Sheldrake, 2003: 114–15)

Sheldrake also points out that banking manoeuvres are far more than well-rehearsed standard human chorus line manoeuvres: the dunlins would have to sense exactly how to turn as well as sensing the advancing wave in order to change the overall pattern of flight within a densely packed flock without bumping into each other, and this would involve coordinating both the speed, angle and duration of any turning movement (Sheldrake, 2011: 362). Speed, angle and duration relate to the three simple rules of the boids model (average inter-individual distance, average direction and average overall position). Moreover, what is particularly intriguing about banking movements is that this precise and complex organisation happens faster than a startle reaction such as a response to a sudden flash of light.

Indeed, the implications of flocking behaviour get even more remarkable in light of further observations by Cavagna et al. (2010) of flocks of starlings near Rome. The researchers measured the velocity fluctuations of different birds and determined to what extent they were correlated with other birds. They found that every bird in the flock was influenced by every other bird, however large the flock, and that the behaviour of any one individual was influenced by all the other individuals in the group, making the group respond as one. Since that individual was influenced by the behavioural change of all other individuals in the group, the group itself could not be divided into independent subparts. The implications of such findings are hard to accommodate within complex systems computer models, given that such correlations are non-local and computer models of complex systems are often based on the assumption that any emergence arises from local interactions.

Another finding by Ballerini et al. (2008b: 210) was of the characteristic shape of flocks: thin in the direction of gravity and more extended perpendicular to it, organised in a way that maintained its proportions. This poses such questions as 'If the individual birds are responsible, how do they achieve this, starting from a purely local perception of the aggregation?' the findings above led Cavagna and his colleagues (2010) to invoke the concept of '*the collective mind*'.

Similarly, but in a different study, taking into account other factors in addition to velocity Cavagna et al. (2010) found that each bird coordinated with a fixed number of interacting neighbours during motion, approximately seven, irrespective of their distances, though with an 'exclusion zone' around them that is comparable to the average wing span of an individual which means they do not collide. This also means that for parameters apart from velocity, correlation is not scale-free. Even so, Cavagna et al.'s hypothesis of collective mind is still an option given that we still do not know which channel of communication the starlings are using, taking into account Sheldrake's point that an explanation by the visual channel only would require unblinking 360-degree vision given the complexity, spontaneity and speed of their movements.

One of the interesting developments in computer modelling of flock behaviour is that several models have now been proposed that attempt to improve upon the boid-type models by treating the flocks as a *field*, often basing this on an analogy with magnetic fields or with the flow of fluids where physicists 'do not start with individual atoms or molecules, but rather with the fluid as a whole' (Sheldrake 2003: 116). Of course, there is a fundamental difference between animal collective behaviour and magnetism: individual animals, unlike individual magnetic domains, 'each move with respect to another, so that the interaction network (i.e. who interacts with whom) changes in time' (Cavagna et al. 2010: 2). However, what is particularly interesting about this field analogy is that it is similar to Potts' chorus-line hypothesis of how a 'manoeuvre wave' moves through a line of singing humans, with the individual magnetic domains starting to line up in a particular direction, with others following suit with an implication of some top-down influence from the field as a whole.

Fish Schooling Behaviour

A school of fish, at least visually, could be said to resemble a large composite organism, often with millions of individuals 'wheeling and reversing in near unison' (Potts 2011: 357), one striking feature being the parallel arrangement of the members, with the distance between individuals uniform, and the motion of individual fishes is synchronised, thus maintaining the structure (Niwa 1994: 123; see also van Olst and Hunter 1970). The tendency of the fish to remain at the preferred distance maintains the 'structure' in a similar way to how magnets polarise the arrangement of their individual filings. The fish have no leaders in that

> speed and heading are not closely related to those of any other single fish. The strong correlations are observed between the velocity of the individual and average velocity of the entire school . . . Thus, in a sense, the entire school is the leader and an individual is a follower. This raises the question of self-organisation. (Haken, 1983)

Schooling would thus seem to be non-hierarchical. Fish may have preferred positions in relation to their neighbours, but with continual movement and reorganisation within the schools (Partridge 1981: 494). The 'school as leader, individual as follower' observation would suggest a dominant top-down influence in comparison with the normal mutuality between upwards and downwards causation of complex systems.

The most interesting schooling phenomenon is the speed of the so-called 'flash expansion', in which each fish simultaneously darts away from the centre of the school if the group is attacked. The complete expansion may take only 20 milliseconds, with the fish accelerating to a speed of 10 to 20 body-lengths per second within this short time (Partridge 1981: 492). The most extraordinary fact in all of this is that they do not collide: 'not only does each fish know in advance where it will swim, if attacked, but it must also know where each of its neighbours will swim [like the dunlins above]' (Partridge 1981: 492). Such behaviour is difficult to explain in terms of sensory information from neighbouring fish: it happens far too fast for nerve impulses to move from the eye to the brain and from the brain to the muscles (Sheldrake 2003: 117).

Even more extraordinary, schools of fish can swim at night in pitch-black water, and in laboratory experiments fish have still schooled normally even when fitted with opaque contact lenses to blind them temporarily: vision is thus clearly not essential. Neither is the detection of pressure changes in the water essential, as demonstrated in an experiment where the fishes' pressure-sensitive organs – the lateral lines which run along their length – were lacerated, and yet they could still swim as a school in the normal way (Sheldrake 2003: 117; also Partridge 1981).

What is clear from all of this is that the 'bottom-up' approach starting from individuals and their neighbours needs to be complemented by a model of the group as a whole. With hundreds, thousands, even tens of thousands of fish or birds performing complex movements, it would make sense to have a simplified, collective form of organisation because of the vast number of interactions in the whole flock or school.

Implications for Musical Group Interaction

The concepts of complex systems theory can also be applied to the process of group musical synchronisation, also referred to as 'entrainment'. Entrainment is organised by a pulse (tactus, or beat) that functions as an 'emergent property' of the performance. Of course, metre, as a hierarchy of pulses, can be constructed individually around this pulse, and on occasion the level of coordination is such that the term metre is appropriate. However, I will refer to a shared 'pulse' here because it applies over a wider variety of cases.

The pulse can be said to have a downward causation if we assume that the organisation of mutual interactions between individuals in music-making depends on a shared focus to synchronise with the pulse. For example, if performers attempt to join a performance that is already in motion, they need to synchronise in the same way as the whole group: the pulse is 'over and above' the individual performers. Other aspects of the form of the musical performance can change (e.g. the melody, who is participating), but in most cases a performance can only be described as 'together' if the group of performers align themselves with a shared pulse. In a Luhmannian sense the pulse can be thought of as a centralising mechanism which reduces the complexity of multiple factors in musical process.

However, due to the non-linear feedback interaction between top-down and bottom-up organisation, it is not obvious whether a pulse arises from negotiation between the individual performers (not centralised), or exists 'over and above' individual interactions. For large groups of singers it is possible for a pulse to be maintained even when one or two individuals are not entrained with it, which would suggest that pulse can operate at the system level of organisation, being able to tolerate environment 'noise'. On the other hand, for groups with few performers, the direction of causation is more likely to be bottom-up because the whole system is less complex and does not require a rigid top-down influence to the same degree. Bottom-up causation is desirable in small ensemble contexts because it means the performers can be more flexible. It is unclear whether one can determine the critical number of individuals before a musical performance system becomes primarily top-down or bottom-up, because there may be other factors involved such as the complexity of the music, the competence of the individuals or the varying degrees of hierarchy between performers, where even in small groups one performer may lead more than others.

The tension between top-down and bottom-up primacy in complex systems is analogous to the tension between the uncertainty and spontaneity that underpins any live musical performance on the one hand and, on the other, the stability and structure that often emerges within it. Uncertainty may be a universal feature of music-making: 'a physical and inevitable fact which is essential to the character of being live' (Visell 2004: 151). An individualised bottom-up influence is uncertain because individuals are unpredictable, and often act in such a way that they contradict and disrupt the action of whole. A centralised top-down influence on the other hand creates stability by maintaining the coherence of the whole.

'Stable' music-making creates the conditions for top-down primacy because this form of music-making is highly predictable, thus easy for a group to follow as a whole and more difficult for individuals to disrupt. 'Uncertain' music-making creates the conditions for bottom-up primacy because this form of music-making is highly improvisational and therefore unpredictable, because each member of the group can improvise individually and contribute to the group. The fact that stable music-making is *primarily* top-down and uncertain music-making is *primarily* bottom-up implies that both forms of music-making are subject to both top-down and bottom-up influence, and it is just a question of which level of organisation is dominant.

The apotheosis of *stable* musical performance is perhaps the ceremonial mantric chanting of the East, when short melodies accompany short phrases of text repeated often hundreds of times, and thousands of people can participate for long periods at a time. At the other extreme, the free improvisation of modern jazz or the communal cacophonies of some indigenous tribes represent *uncertain* musical performance. In these 'uncertain' cases, the degree of uncertainty is dependent on 'the presence (or absence) of *a priori* agreements, whether explicit or tacit' (Blackwell and Young 2004: 124). One *a priori* agreement might be 'an emphasis upon collective (rather than individual) improvisation' – i.e. each member of the group is able to improvise, rather than a solo individual improvising with the rest of the ensemble accompanying. Another agreement might be 'the avoidance of recourse to notation or other pre-existing materials [or memorised songs]' (Blackwell and Young 2004: 124).

Music-making can be both 'stable' and 'uncertain'. Live musical performance changes with each separate performance and therefore the specific structure that emerges in that performance is 'uncertain'. There are also the more 'static' structures in which the live performance is embedded; e.g. institutional, personal, political, social, self-consciously subcultural. Thus free jazz collectives in the 1970s often spent 'almost as much time discussing the political context of what they were doing as doing it' (Cross 2013). More typically the free improvisation strands of modern jazz and western classical music attempt to distance themselves from outside influences, seeking ever-newer creative contributions by participants in performance, and are thus 'deliberately and self-consciously uncertain' (Blackwell and Young 2004: 124), resisting classification in terms of any one genre or influence. Although, it may seem impossible to hold this ideal, given that the prior learning, practices and habits (whether individual or culturally determined) of individual performers will constrain their own individual performances. Indeed, the groups themselves, not just individuals, may also build up their own experiences and practices and habits.

In more general musical improvisation there are more explicitly top-down influences at play, such as stylistic training, rehearsed performance approach, the pulse, etc. At the pulse level, the 'rhythm' players in early jazz were expected to 'establish and maintain a clear and easily heard rhythmic pulse you could orient yourself to as you played, always knowing "where [beat] One was"', such as the "oompah" rhythm: a strong bass note on the first and third beats of a bar, a firm chord in the right hand on two and four' (Faulkner and Becker 2009: 125). This is a good example of how pulse can act as a stable top-down structure to which individuals can refer, even in the context of improvisation.

But it is also often the case that when someone starts to move in a musically new way the group can often flow with that individual to create a new framework for performance. One example in jazz performance might be the group process of 'substitution'. Every time a melody is repeated, an individual might spontaneously decide to change a given note/chord/harmony/rhythm in a melody, which is then picked up by the rest of the group. The next time the melody is repeated, the previous modification may or may not become the norm, depending on whether the change is accepted by the group. The process is then repeated many times, sometimes to the point where the melody is almost unrecognisable from the original, yet agreed upon by the band. In this way spontaneity/ uncertainty can give rise to an emergent structure, and, if a group disagrees about accepting or rejecting each individual substitution, this structure is held in tension with uncertainty.

This form of jazz improvisation, i.e. from spontaneity to structure, is created by each player responding to each other player in a series of 'local interactions' which eventually produce dynamic 'structure' after multiple iterations from the 'bottom-up'. However, the emergent structure is often fragile and can change quickly. The process of emergence and its dissolution relates to timing relationships in jazz too. For example, Doffman (2008) found that, in order to achieve the desired jazz 'groove', timing relationships cannot be reduced to a single form of entrainment (see Clayton, 2012: 54). Instead, 'the ideal relationship is inherently dynamic and playing jazz involves meaningful variations within the permissible range of looseness and out-of-phaseness' (Doffman 2008). For example, one player is quoted by Faulkner and Becker (2009: 8) as saying 'If sometimes I might play a phrase differently from another man, it's not that critical. As long as we're together most of the time.' The relationship between pulse and timing in jazz is thus dynamic and constantly shifting.

There is also a more fixed hierarchical structure in how musicians interact with each other in live performance. Even though the goal of free jazz is musical 'freedom', in reality each musician within the group will have a place within the hierarchy, depending on competence and experience, and at different times will have specified functions; a drummer has a primarily rhythmic function whereas a saxophonist would likely have a more melodic function. Vallacher and Jackson (2011: 1228) have suggested that within the timing of embodied interaction, factors such as power asymmetry and role relationship may result in one person's behaviour lagging behind the other's. Although they were referring to interaction between two people, asymmetrical entrainment behaviour due to power relationships is likely between members of a group too.

You learn that it's the bassist, not the drummer, who has the greatest responsibility for maintaining the beat, and at some basic level of near incompetence, it's actually much more important to keep playing boom boom boom at a steady tempo on some indecipherable low note than to get the changes right while dragging the rhythm. You are the rock upon which the band rests. (Faulkner and Becker, 2009: 123).

Indeed, it is arguable that for most people the existence of at least some perceivable structure within musical parameters like melody and rhythm is essential if a piece is to be enjoyable, even within improvisational music.

Emergent Structure in Musical Interaction

The power hierarchy in a jazz ensemble will have a relatively static top-down influence on the performance, but even this static influence can become dynamic, given that the function and hierarchical position of each performer may change during the performance. By contrast the 'emergent structure' within the actual music is dynamic, which implies that the structure does not exist before the moment it emerges. As Blackwell and Young put it, 'In improvised music, the macro-level [i.e. the overall form of a performance] can only be described with the benefit of hindsight and reflection, once the complex interactions that cause structure to emerge are complete' (2004: 125).

A structure is only emergent when it can affect local interactions by downward causation. I argue that the emergence, and therefore self-organisation, functions at a level 'over and above' local inter-actions, precisely because of the notion of a system 'self' doing the organizing. I suggest therefore that the most likely explanation of how group musical performance works needs a holistic view of non-linear dynamics between higher-order and lower-order com-ponents of a system, but where the higher-order components of a system are distinct from the lower-order components.

This creates a problem for computational analysis because the higher-order components cannot be defined in terms of character-istics of local components, or even the network of relationships between them. Indeed from a scientific perspective it is easier to measure and model physical motor behaviour than mental 'shared realities', which is the reason for the current trend to study measurable aspects of entrainment behaviour such as body movements and sounds: the 'embedded-embodied approach' (Marsh 2011). Interestingly such studies invoke Toner and Tu's (1998) 'mean field theory' for flocking and schooling movements of groups of birds and fish, as a foundational principle of their embodied social psychological approach (see Marsh et al. 2006: 14).

Focusing on body movement in musical performance is to focus on the bottom-up side of organisation. Yet the distinguishing feature of autopoiesis (relevant in the context of musical group entrainment) is the top-down idea that the product of a system's operation is necessarily the system itself, and if this systemic reproduction is disrupted the system disintegrates (Varela et al. 1974: 192). In the context of musical entrainment one kind of network of production – a shared pulse – applies to both new and existing performers. The shared pulse is an emergent structure that produces itself acting downwards on the individual actions of performers. In the case of metrical organisation of a pulse, for a metrical unit (e.g. a 4/4 bar) to be performed successfully performers must base their actions on the timings of the previous metrical unit, i.e. the next metrical unit 'reproduces' the previous unit.

We will never fully understand any system unless we also acknowledge that it will always be embedded in other systems which are also embedded in further systems and so on. However, in the context of studying bodily entrainment,

> there are diminishing returns in expanding the level of analysis to include systems at the macro end (e.g., culture) or the micro end (e.g., neural dynamics) when attempting to capture mental and behavioral processes of interest to social psychologists. Where one draws the line, however, is an unsettled matter and warrants further consideration, particularly on the part of those who are wedded to the embedded–embodied approach (Vallacher and Jackson 2011: 1227).

The pulse is arguably a good level of analysis for understanding musical performance because it is system of organisation that comes somewhere between 'culture' and 'neural dynamics', and is directly observable in the performance itself through the body movements and sounds produced by performers.

Synchronisation in Group Singing

The reason I have examined social systems in disciplinary domains such as sociology, complex systems theory, embodied psychology and animal behaviour was to integrate the complementary approaches by which different disciplines investigate group behaviour, each with its own valuable perspective. In terms of empirical studies of musical activity, music psychology is progressing in understanding how synchronisation ('entrainment') works in laboratory settings, but almost exclusively in the context of dyadic interaction (just two people). I am interested here in how synchronisation occurs in systems that are much more complex when many individuals perform together, each with their own perspective, in real-life contexts.

It is fair to say that probably no choral singers know *how* they synchronise their own singing with their fellow choristers, or at least to the level of empirical detail referred to in this chapter. However, in line with Potts's chorus-line hypothesis, it is likely that each choral onset of sound starts with some initial movement from one or a few individuals setting in motion a very fast chain reaction which results in the process of synchronisation, as opposed to a perfectly unison movement where every chorister sings exactly at the same time as everyone else. Therefore, bottom-up neighbour-to-neighbour interaction cannot explain *unison* sounds or movements.

Of course, in those cases when a choir has a conductor, one might say it is the conductor who provides a single focus that reduces their dependency on being aware of other choristers, and therefore the 'chorus-line hypothesis' may not be appropriate there. However, conductors sometimes ask their choir to 'triangulate';

i.e. to look at other choristers as well as the conductor in order to improve the cohesion of the choir (e.g. in Anglican and Catholic churches, when two 'sides' of the choir face each other). This would suggest that visual contact with as many singers in the group as possible improves group synchronisation, which is compatible with the chorus-line hypothesis. Given the obvious synchronising benefit of having a conductor, one must also ask whether, in the absence of a conductor, one or a few confident singers function as 'leaders' so as to reduce effort and increase accuracy, or whether the choir as a whole organises its own actions. This chapter has attempted to explore some of these suggestions.

In unison choral singing everyone makes a sound at the same time, whereas in conversation participating individuals actively avoid speaking at the same time, and instead take turns to speak. In order to explore how a choir is able to sing at the same time one might think in terms of how the timing of actions of individual singers are related to each other through webs of relationships, including feedback loops, which is a fundamental tenet of systems theory. However, an approach based exclusively on individual dynamic interactions between local component parts is incomplete because, for a musical performance to hold together, all performers need to have a top-down 'static' collective understanding of how their individual role fits in to the performance as a whole. Of course, this collective understanding must also be tolerant of individual variation that happens 'in the moment', such that when an individual does something unexpected the group can flow with that individual and maintain a shared framework of performance.

The bottom-up computational approaches, e.g. ALife and autopoietic organisation, although useful for understanding musical performance when performers speed up or slow down pulse, are based on fundamental assumptions of their algorithms – the most important assumption being that emergent structures or 'systems' can be modelled exclusively on their bottom-up local interactions. Reynolds's boids model, a computer programme based on this assumption, was designed to emulate the real-life behaviour of flocking movements. Potts challenged the exclusive focus of the boids model on neighbour interactions with his chorus-line hypothesis, arguing that members of a flock anticipate an incoming 'manoeuvre wave'. However, the near-instantaneous collective movement implied by scale-free correlations of collective velocities in flocking movements rules out even a 'maneouvre' wave interpretation.

It is clear from analysing real-life behaviour of flocking movements that the boids programme is designed to emulate, that the speed, complexity, diversity and 'scale-free' correlations of the flocking movements combined suggest that the metaphor of a 'collective mind' might be more appropriate for thinking about flocking behaviour, as opposed to the top-down concept of an 'emergent structure' which is based on neighbour-to-neighbour interactions. This would suggest that bottom-up explanations of flocking behaviour based on merely the sensory channel of vision are limited (communication by hearing too is unlikely given the cacophony of thousands of birds).

The movements and sounds of mass choirs of humans singing in unison are similar to flocking behaviour in that a group of individuals (sometimes in the hundreds or thousands) often move and sing together with astonishing levels of precision and synchrony. So to understand complex group entrainment both in animals and humans we need an explanation that integrates bottom-up and top-down process; i.e. local-to-local interactions as well as a 'collective mind'. Computationally, understanding musical performance in this way is a huge challenge because it would require that the computer model's assumptions are representative of musical process from both embodied and mental perspectives. This would require a total understanding of all factors involved in musical performance that, in turn, could be expressed in computational language. As we saw, this is impossible given that even a simple event like a rock breaking a window cannot be represented by any single theory in the syntax of logic, let alone complex musical interaction.

This may seem a disheartening conclusion. But it should not stop us from inquiry into the important area of musical interaction in general, or entrainment processes in particular, drawing on the fascinating insights from the study of collective animal behaviour.

Notes

[1] ALife is different from traditional artificial intelligence (AI), which is *top-down* in that complex behaviours (for example, chess playing) are identified and an attempt is made to build a system that presents all the details of this behaviour.

References

Ballerini, M., Cavagna, A., Orlandi, A, Procaccini, A., Zdravkovic, V. (2008) 'An empirical study of large, naturally occurring starling flocks', online, *arxiv/org/pdf/0802.1667.pdf*.

Blackwell, T. and Young, M. (2004) 'Self-organised music', *Organised Music*, 9/2: 123–36.

Bonabeau, E. and Dorigo, M. (1999) *Swarm Intelligence* (Oxford: Oxford University Press).

Canetti, E. (1973) *Crowds and Power* (Harmondsworth: Penguin).

Cavagna. A. et al. (2010) 'Scale-free correlations in starling floocks', *Proceedings of the National Academy of Sciences of the Unitied States of America*, 107/26: 11865–70.

Clayton, M. (2012) 'What is entrainment?', *Empirical Musicology Review*, 7/1–2: 49–56.

Clayton, M., Sager, R. and Udo, W. (2004) 'In time with the music: The concept of entrainment and its significance for ethnomusicology', *ESEM CounterPoint*, 1: 1–45.

Cross, I. (2013) Personal communication.

Durkheim, É. (1995 [1912]) *Elementaary Forms of Religious Life* (Glencoe, IL: Free Press).

Doffman, M. R. (2008) 'Feeling the groove' (Ph.D. thesis, The Open University).

Faulkner, Robeert R. and Becker, Howard (2009) *'Do You Know?' The Jazz Repertoire in Action* (Chicago: University of Chicago Press).

Gershon, I. (2005) 'Seeing like a system: Luhmann for anthropologists', *Anthropological Theory*, 5: 99–116.

Levinson, S. C. (2006) 'On the human "interaction engine"', in N. J. Enfield and S. C. Levinson (eds.), *Roots of Human Sociality: Culture, Cognition and Interaction* (Oxford: Berg), pp. 39–69.

Luhmann, N. (1982) 'The world society as a social system', *International Journal of General Systems*, 8/3: 131–8.

Luhmann, N. (2002) *Theories of Distinction: Redescribing the Descriptions of Modernity* (Stanford, CA: Stanford University Press).

Marsh, K. L. (2011) 'Sociality, from an ecological, dynamical perspective', in G. R. Semin and G. Echterhoff (eds), *Grounding Sociality: Neurons, Minds, and Culture* (London: Psychology Press), pp. 53–82.

Mead, G. H. (1932) *The Philosophy of the Present* (Chicago: University of Chicago Press).

Mitchell, S. D. (2012) 'Emergence: logical, functional and dynamical', *Synthese*, 185: 171–86.

Nagy, M., Akos, Z., Biro, D. and Vicek, T. (2010) 'Hierarchical group dynamics in pigeon flocks', *Nature*, 8/464: 890–3.

Niwa, H. S. (1994) 'Self-organising dynamic model of fish schooling', *Journal of Theoretical Biology*, 171: 123–36.

Partridge, B. (1981) 'Schooling', in D. McFarland (ed.), *The Oxford Companion to Animal Behaviour* (Oxford: Oxford University Press).

Potts, W. (1984) 'The chorus-line hypothesis of manoeuvre-coordination in avian flocks: how do flocking birds move in unison?', *Nature*, 309: 344–5.

Reynolds, C. (1987) 'Flocks, herds, and schools: A distributed behavioural model', *SIGGRAPH '87*, 21/4: 25–34.

Seeley, T. (1989) 'Social foraging in honey bees: How nectar foragers assess their colony's nutritional status', *Behavioral Ecology and Sociobiology*, 24: 181–99.

Sheldrake, R. (2003). *The Sense of Being Stared At and Other Aspects of the Extended Mind* (London: Arrow).

Sheldrake, R. (2011) *The Presence of the Past: Morphic Resonance and the Habits of Nature* (London: Icon Books).

Sheldrake, R. (2012) *The Science Delusion: Freeing the Spirit of Enquiry* (London: Coronet).

Sipper, M. (1995) An Introduction to Artificial Life: Explorations in Artificial Life (special issue of AI Expert) (San Francisco: Miller Freeman), pp. 4–8; online *www.cs.unibo.it/~babaoglu/courses/cas00-01/papers/Alife/Intro.pdf/*

Szekely, T. and Komdeur (2010) *Social Behaviour* (Cambridge: Cambridge University Press).

Thom, R. (1975) *Structural Stability and Morphogenesis* (Reading, MA: Benjamin).

Toner, J. and Tu, Y. (1998) 'Flocks, herds, and schools: A quantitative theory of flocking', *Physical Review E*, 58/4, 4828–58.

Vallacher, R. R. and Jackson, D. (2009). 'Thinking inside the box – dynamical constraints on mind and action: Comment on Marsh et al. "Toward a radically embodied, embedded social psychology," this issue', *European Journal of Social Psychology*, 39: 1226–9.

Van Olst, J. C. and Hunter, J. B. (1979) 'Some aspects of the organisation of fish schools', in M. S. Love and G. M. Cailliet (eds), *Readings in Ichthyology* (Santa Monica: Goodreads).

Varela, F. G., Maturana, H. R., and Uribe, R. (1974) 'Autopoiesis: The organisation of living systems, its characterisation and a model', *BioSystems*, 5: 187–96 (Amsterdam: North-Holland).

Varele, V. (2004) 'Complex systems in composition and improvisation', *Organised Sound*, 9/2: 121–2.

Vissell, V. (2004) 'Spontaneous organisation, pattern models and music', *Organised Sound* 9/2: 151–65.

11

The Un-speak-able Language of United Sensing: Taste the Wine!

Gianmarco Navarini
Department of Sociology and Social Research,
Bicocca University, Milan

I will explore the question of how far we can capture and understand our human senses through verbal language – in other words the relationship between synaesthesia (mutually uniting the senses), language and sense-making activities. I will attempt to do so through the example of tasting a glass of wine, whether this practice is by a 'layman', sipping merely with curiosity and attention (Caro 1990), by a so-called *amateur* or wine lover, or by a trained wine taster.

Looking at the people involved in the most ordinary and popular events of the contemporary wine world, in particular in wine-tasting courses and public wine-tasting sessions, and observing them as either novices or regular members of a community of practice (Lave and Wenger 1991), I will consider 'taste' not as a passive or determined state, but for what it really is in these situations – an *activity* (Hennion and Teil 2004). It involves united sensory experiences of a micro-world (in-the-glass and then into-the-mouth) and a discourse – *description* – about the reality of this world as related to that of the senses at work.

The first question, then, is how one goes about making wine intelligible through language. The second is what is involved in the language of sensations – 'the wine language' – when we deal with what most fascinates a novice wine taster: the attempt to describe smells, flavours, and taste. Looking at tasting as a social interaction, the way one deals with these two practical problems is through a constructed *language game*, so that novices are, like Wittgenstein playing with famous propositions of his *Tractatus*, using them as ways of framing and sharing the relationship between language and sensory experiences. Putting myself in the shoes of the novice, I will try to show how and why tasting is a tacit activity of synaesthetic knowing, both unspeakable-about and yet realised by descriptions which imply the physical-biochemical concept of wine as consisting of a whole of interconnected life-worlds, which tasters, so as both to analyse and to better enjoy the wine, wish ever to discover and to criss-cross.[1]

'Whereof one cannot speak, thereof one must be silent'

Novices and experts have at least four things in common. The first two are that every glass of wine is sensed as if being a world they wish to make intelligible while tasting it. To achieve this, they have to engage in the hidden work of attempting to forge meanings between words and sensations. The third is that, as was highlighted by an authority on the study of the taste of wine, in this *subjective* area the relationship between sensation and expression, between the word and the quality it describes, is not as straightforward as it could be elsewhere (Peynaud 1983). Tasting a wine implies a *bodily and practical* relationship between the so-called 'language of wine' (Aitchison 1999, 2003) – with its ambiguity and opacity, its power to make the wine intelligible, its freedom of expression and in some cases its snobbery, comical or even idiotic social status (Lehrer 1983; Barr 1992; Gluck 2009) – and the complexity of perception, and therefore description, which is inherent in the very nature of wine.

> Think, for a moment, of an almost paper-white glass of liquid, just shot with greeny-gold, just tart on your tongue, full of wild-flowers scents and spring-water freshness. And think of a burnt-amber liquid, as smooth as syrup in the glass, as fat as butter to smell and sea-deep with strange flavours. Both are wine. (Johnson 1966/1974, 9)

Wine lovers know about *Wine* (the simple title of the first master-piece by Hugh Johnson, the great pioneer in the spreading of wine culture, not only in the British world), and also about Robert Parker, the influential American critic and wine guru, who opened up wine in the popular culture of the United States. As reported by a scholar who does not like this kind of guru,

> Parker tasting notes are evocative, and his enthusiasm is often infectious. This is because he described, among others, a 'sexy, supple, fleshy, hedonistic' Cabernet, a Zinfandel as 'balls to the wall', he likened a Margaux to 'a towering skyscraper in the mouth', and one Châteneuf-du-Pape as 'pure sex in a bottle' . . . 'This will make even the most puritanical American rethink his antidrinking policy'. (Colman 2008, 119)

Over and above the popular enthusiasm (or scepticism) for Parker's *metaphors*, wine lovers can read more 'sober' or plain but specialist descriptions, for example, like

> Classy and harmonious. Peach, vanilla, lemon custard and mineral notes mingle effortlessy with the creamy texture, all supported by vibrant structure. The intensity builds to a long, long finish. (*Wine Spectator* (January–February 2007), 260, about a German Riesling Spätlese)

> Le vin est concentré, aussi bien dans la couleur que dans la texture. Un vin tout en nuances, allant de notes toastées, torréfiées, cacaotées, vers des notes de mûre et de myrtille. C'est du pur velours en bouche, avec una trame ensuite plus tannique, carrée [. . .] Bâti pour vieillir. Un monument! (GaultMilau (June–July 2006), 95, about a famous Château)

Finally, the wine world is crowded with ludicrously poetic descriptions, sometimes ironically collected, as in the case of an Italian wine journal advising readers to beware of language excesses. This sort of 'poem' is a good example:

Its softness of extreme berry maturity, its glycerinous density, the action of sap and warmth that has thickened the juice with pulp. Concentration on the touch, made thick and dense by the intense smell and the mellow, persistent taste. Then the colouring is a majestic plum. And for the clarity of the oenological transformation, one appreciates the primary base of the flavour, grape, and its original virgin cleanness. Radiance that illuminates the scent of fruity hints of berries [. . .] Veins and spices mixed in [. . .] enhance the brilliance, so that the sparkling facets of the warm spirit, limitless, dazzling and mellow, reveal themselves to our sensibility. One of the best Pinot Noirs ever, the tops. (collected by *Il Mio Vino* (October 2012), 21)

In short, wine language can be seen – rightly – both as a special language and also as a form of poetics, highly pertinent to the radical question of how we can articulate sensory complexity and make sense of it. Its very peculiarity – if we look at its *use* while tasting wine – is to be a sort of paradigm of human attempts to work on, and then to communicate, a whole world of private sensations within and through the limits of our language (Moore and Carling 1998).

Therefore – the fourth and most interesting thing – what wine tasters share in their *subjective* practice and experience is like sensory work, both enabled by and entrapped in some of the famous propositions in Wittgenstein's *Tractatus* – a private work that is concretely shared in wine courses and collective wine-tastings, when description and discovery are taken as a common task. Wittgenstein's propositions in this task become the very object of the inner *language game*, which ultimately constitutes tasting as a social interaction devoted to making wine and its sensations intelligible. So the novice, like Wittgenstein, jumps between two main propositions as ways to frame the flow of experience and work on them as practical problems: 'the limits of my language mean the limits of my world', and 'whereof one cannot speak, thereof one must be silent' (Wittgenstein 1961[1923], §§ 5.6, 7).

But as we have seen, the wine world is anything but silent. Apart from the question of wine snobbery, much of the popular scepticism about the 'language of wine' is due to the hidden question: is wine language a useful idiom or idiot-speak? This is the problem that afflicts the experience of a serious wine writer, and also of any wine taster. Trying to answer it, Gluck (2003, 107) argues that special languages are cover-ups: 'What are we wine writers trying to hide? Answer: our struggle to communicate.' In my view, this struggle presupposes a search for the link between synaesthesia and words to make sense of this in our private and public language.

'Synasthesia', a term which literally means experiencing the 'union of senses', and, in the language of neurophysiology and psychology, stands for the rare (or abnormal) production of a sense impression relating to one or more senses or parts of the body by stimulation of another sense or part of the body, always brings with it the problem of how one can make intelligible to others the *real* sense of this subjective world of simultaneous, concomitant, joined sensations. The basic tool we all have for doing this work in society is natural language. But it is precisely in talking about synaesthesia that language seems at the same time to demonstrate its expressive limits, at least for the speaking subject, and to arouse in other people the suspicion that the sensation – if it is not abnormal – could be real but only as a metaphor or literary trope. Moreover, observed in medical-scientific terms, the phenomenon has a liminal, marginal status, usually associated with experiences of hallucination produced by taking drugs.[2]

Even more interesting is the interpretation of synaesthesia in people who do not take drugs, and are therefore not conceived as in some 'altered state'. If we are to believe a neuroscientist expert on this topic, 'its phenomenology clearly distinguishes it from metaphor, literary tropes, sound symbolism, and deliberate artistic contrivances that sometimes employ the term "synesthesia" to describe their multisensory joinings' (Cytowic 1995). So the problem – the paradox – is that, for some scientists, this phenomenon is not really a matter of language, even though language – through metaphors, literary tropes and so on – is the only means by which these scientists and the so-called 'synaesthete' can talk to them about this un-speakable experience.

In some ordinary activities, as in the practice-world of wine tasters, this paradox does not arise in the same way since the

221

speakers refer to a concomitant experience which they are having together. Obviously, there is a difference in saying that when touching a stone slate with your eyes closed one hears a 'green silence' or feels a 'young Riesling from the Saar'. But what is one to say about a wine that tastes 'green' or is 'round'?

'The limits of my language mean the limits of my world' – and Vice Versa

Recently, mainly in the field of consumption and marketing strategies, synaesthesia has beeen connected to language as the subject of empirical experiments, usually about how thoughts primed by music (e.g. in supermarkets) influence what people perceive via another sense (North 2011). Unlike these cases, a wine taster must deal with synaesthesia not as artificially induced, but as an *endogenous* phenomenon, intrinsic to the nature of sensing wine independent of any musical background or other external influence. In this way, the most common practice to make wine intelligible is to analyse it, thus attempting to *dis*-join what is really a flow of joined sensations.

So, in the international language of wine tasters, a distinction is made by 'categories' that reflect the three basic steps of sensory analysis (technically called organoleptic analysis): *look, smell, taste.* These categories are then split – e.g. *look* usually means watching 'clearness', 'tone', 'resonance', and smell is for the nose's work through subcategories as 'frankness' (absence of defects), 'intensity', 'harmony' or 'balance', 'refinement' or 'elegance' and others (it depends on the methods used) – and it is by this practical articulation that tasters describe – and judge – a wine. Leaving aside the complexities of colour (Goodwin 2003), let us focus just on the categories of *aroma* and *scent* which are in practice what most fascinate a novice wine taster.

The classic starting problem is that when tasting a wine one feels *something* of the whole, but (*à la* Wittgenstein) does not have the words to express what the senses are grasping, or rather, to identify this specific 'something' as 'real'. Novices smell or sip a wine and receive a sensation they call – as a first result – 'perfume' or 'aroma'.[3] The success of this silent analytical operation is tied to a preliminary classification capability, the use of a lexicon that allows one to distinguish scents and flavours from other things received through the senses.

But what aroma is it? This second operation, usually also crucial in accounting for why the wine is liked or not, requires the use of a vocabulary related to the class of things called 'flavours' or 'aroma'. Now, if this language – that is used for describing the experiences of odours in the everyday world – lacks words such as, for example, 'balsamic', 'incense', 'spicy', 'mineral', 'tar', it will be highly unlikely to recognise these things as flavours, and this will result in their *not* being perceived. Thus the limits of my language seem to match the limits of the world of sensations that wine gives me tasting it.

However, if someone perceives something like a 'note of mineral', this means that the taster is able to isolate a specific sensation among the many others (see descriptions of *Wine Spectators* and *GaultMilau* mentioned above). The word 'note' suggests that one is working in this way, but also that this note is intertwined with other sensations. Anyway, assigning a name to the note makes it subjectively significant, more sense-ible; and then speaking the word, makes intelligible to others tasting the same wine. They can negotiate together to recognise what their senses can grasp or have captured. Asking if it is really 'of mineral' or 'of incense' is a typical way to start a language game.

In this process, passing from private sensation to public expression, language acts as a creative tool. In practical and social sense-making, naming means recognising and vice versa. To isolate a feeling is equivalent to demarcating something in the flow of wine that enters our body, so that (now) the limits created by language mean *boundaries* drawn inside the world that we want to know. Without these useful boundaries, usually created by a metaphor, the wine sensation-world would have no identities and differences: one could only say 'um . . . this is a wine.'

But the use of 'note', borrowed from the lexicon of music, does not only indicate a natural fallback into the field of metaphor. The term suggests, or rather makes vivid, the way in which the senses are operating: it is *as if* the wine, entering our body, is acting as a symphony of which the amateur can grasp at least the notes. Other terms, such as the French *nuance*, perform the same service: the flow of wine *is like* a 'musical picture' – think of a painting by Kandinsky (1911) or a symphony intertwined with images and light; think of the works of the Russian composer Alexander Scriabin from the early twentieth century, which arouse the deepest feeling of *movements* and *sensory fusion*. That is what we usually call synaesthesia. For a wine taster, to isolate the elements of the 'composition' means making intelligible the wine sense through an analytical process. It is as if the wine and its sensing were disassembled and then reassembled in order to capture its overall properties – the constituent parts of the sensory fusion. One can then talk of 'style', 'character', 'elegance', 'bouquet' (in the more complex wines), using metaphors that hide synaesthetic experience.

So the two-way sense of Wittgenstein's proposition fits well the way one moves into the relationship between a word and the sensation it names: the limits of my world of bio-chemical experience, of my synaesthesia mean the boundaries of my language *used* to make intelligible the wine. In any case the term 'nuance', or better *'toute nuance'* – as in *GaultMilau*'s description – can be seen as a way of implicitly saying how synaesthesia is ever present as sensations in movement: a way of making these limits 'speakable'.

Criss-crossing Worlds

As we all know, odours – and flavours – do not have a name. What we call them corresponds, by convention, to the name of the source from which the smell normally comes: odours we detect in everyday life are always odours *of something*. In addition, the odours that are intelligible for us at any given time are the ones that recall or remind us of the smell of something we have already experienced (Engen 1982, 1987, 1991). Thus smell itself works in terms of association between what one is living in the present and has previously lived elsewhere, and the use of the verbs 'remember', 'recall' suggests how we usually operate in our body-mind (Aitchison 2003). Moreover, as claimed by Le Breton in his monumental work on the anthropology of the senses,

> odour represents the elementary form of the unutterable. Describing an odour to someone who does not smell it or does not know it is an impossible enterprise [. . .] The reference to an odour resorts to periphrasis and metaphor. We always talk about the aura of smell, its surroundings; the smell never in its singularity. (Le Breton 2007, 258)

In wine as in the world, the specific smell is thus un-speakable, and the recourse to metaphors seems to stand for the limits of our language when we think or speak of flavours in wine. But when tasting a wine, these limits somehow become 'speakable', with the primary double function – both sharing and sense-making through the creation of bridges – that metaphors perform (Goode 2008; Burnham and Skilleas 2008). Wine-tasting is a language game that involves criss-crossing worlds via these bridges; embarking on the mission impossible of describing our recollection of smells through the natural tool of language becomes a natural way to play it as a learning game which implies a new wish to criss-cross.

A typical wine taster's expression is 'I sense something that recalls, reminds me of . . . rose, violet, incense, balsamic, mineral, cardamom, ginger, cedarwood, pastry, the crust of freshly baked bread, etc.' Potentially, almost all the smells of the great world of life can be found in the little world of sensations that, in just a few moments, wines give us.[4] Moreover, tasting itself is an activity in which tasters socially negotiate the sense of both the metaphors used and the recollection of smells, so that a sort of auto-adjustment is constantly put into play. But, if I have never had experience of incense, cardamom, ginger and so on, it will be hard for me to recognise such flavours in wine. Also, the intensity of the life experience is essential to forming a sensory memory ready for use, a repertoire of feelings to put into play in order to make sense of what we taste. The distraction in experiencing the 'smells of the world' (Roubin 1989), as well as a life in aseptic environments or the lack of such experiences, provides the basis for an acknowledgement of our limits in making sense of our taste. Thus, the limits of my life-world mean the limits of my wine language, and the only way to overcome – or extend – these limits is to dive more deeply into the world, the world that wine tells me exists beyond mine.

To say, 'This wine has something like cinnamon', is to use a spice metaphor which is self-explanatory, in that the aroma of cinnamon cannot be described without using the single word that defines it. The same applies to the flavours that match the common names of fruits, flowers, herbs and spices. But suppose that we know the name and the odour of 'apple', 'rose', 'rosemary', 'cardamom', 'tobacco', 'coffee', 'tamarind' and even 'citrus myrtifolia' (which many find in a good Pinot Noir), at a more sophisticated level we can describe these aromas by differentiating *within* these categories, for example by distinguishing between different varieties of apple (green, golden, from Trentino Alto Adige, Kashmir etc.), cigars (Cuban, Tuscan, island of Sumatra etc.), or coffee (from Guatemala, Nicaragua, India, Brazilian, grown in Kenya etc.). The description itself – an irony of wine snobbery – brings to mind more or less unknown worlds (botanical, geographical, cultural) that the taste of a wine invites us to explore. The same may hold true for some snobbish descriptions in tasting notes, such as a nuance of 'fresh centifolia rose, thickening the petals until they become slightly dry'.[5]

So, laugh at the snob-writers and open up to the world of smells that exist in the world of life. This is the commandment that one breathes when tasting with attention. This is the main synaesthetic virtue of metaphor.

Playing with Synaesthesia: The Sense of Descriptions

Something similar applies to 'taste', which is the name properly given to a *tactile* sensation (Miller 1997): another analytical category in the language of tasters. This is how one makes some properties of a wine intelligible through a description of what is going on when it enters the mouth. The sense of *touch* is technically the sense of taste, which is a set of perceptions obtained by what touches (is touched by) the wine – i.e. the tongue and palate. To explain how to work this sense, teachers (in taster courses) usually ask students to carry out a simple exercise such as 'Try to taste the wine holding your nose well-sealed with your fingers . . . and now try again with it free.'

This method of sensing 'taste dis-joined' is also useful for treating synaesthesia as a *flow* of joined sensations to be grasped through analysis. For example, looking at 'tone' and 'resonance' through the glass one might *see* the wine as elegant or balanced, and then measure oneself by confronting these expectations with all smells, flavours and qualities of taste in the mouth, in order to say, at the end, whether the wine is truly elegant and balanced. Anyway, the taste is given not only by flavours – for which the internal organ of smell is responsible, connecting the tongue to the brain – but also by the material substance of the wine. Separated from aromas, taste is given by the *weight* (the 'body' of the wine is the sense of its weight on the tongue), *shape* (e.g. a 'flat' or 'flabby' wine lies down and slips down the tongue), *structure* (also in the sense of musculature, encumbrance in the mouth), *texture* (e.g. the feeling of touching silk, velvet, gelatin, a coarse cloth etc.), its *heat* (alcohol), and so to speak, by its *behaviour*. So synasthesia is again the only way to describe a sensation in the mouth.

For example, one can say a wine is tannic because the taster 'feels astringency'. But what is astringency? The term is commonly used as a *descriptor*, but if I am a novice, in order to grasp its practical significance – and then with my senses – I need a description. This means describing a descriptor, and a reference to 'behaviour in the mouth' can do it. So the astringency 'is the passage of the wine that provokes the retraction of the mucous membranes, which can be experienced even after swallowing, passing the tongue on the teeth'. The most common description of a strong astringency refers to the sense 'provoked by an unripe persimmon that makes its way in the mouth and clings to the teeth and gums'. Again the taste is unutterable unless one plays with synaesthesia.

The same applies to the use of anthropomorphic terms. Sensing the wine as behaviour means for many speaking about 'character' in the sense of the wine as a living person interacting in the mouth with the taster. So we get adjectives like 'masculine' or 'feminine' (in Burgundy, they mean a continuum from brawny to delicate Pinot Noir), 'sincere' or 'honest', and even the so-called 'vins putain' (whore wines), but also the most common 'young', 'old', 'decrepit', 'evolved' (well grown or not). In short, the wine's behaviour in the mouth is also like a 'parable of human life' (for experts this parable is used for comparisons, e.g. tasting the same wine of different vintages).

For a scientist like Cytowic (1995) synaesthesia, being statistically rare, is 'abnormal'. But it is very normal for a wine taster both as joined senses and as description. These are not hallucinations or inebriations but a *practical method*. Synaesthesia perfectly embodies the reflexive and practical character of the descriptive language of the senses *at work* (Goodwin 2003). Moreover, it is often said that it is rare for smell and taste to be either the trigger or the synaesthetic response, so that it is abnormal to find someone in whom sight evokes smell. This limit, however, is not a problem for tasters: they do not see smells, indeed, to sense them better they are recommended to taste the wine with their eyes closed (it helps concentration). Finally, a famous work on this topic (Cytowic 1993) held that a 'man who tasted shapes' is a bizarre medical mystery because it seems to act both as trigger and response by language. But every wine taster is a someone who (also) tastes shapes, and we can easily find many in whom smells or aromas evoke something like sight: images and memories of other wines already tasted (Melcher and Schooler 1996), various scenes of work in the vineyard and other oenological activities (Rosso 2004) more or less tied to direct experience. Expert tasters explain or analyse certain aromas by imagining processes embedded in work-places (Dilworth 2008). For example, the 'notes of yellow apple bruised' in a white wine blind-tasted may suggest a Chardonnay made from relatively mature grapes or a slightly oxidised (but very nice) Champagne. Also, when in Italy or France one says, 'This wine is *green*', which means that it is 'harsh' or 'vegetable' (such as a Cabernet Sauvignon that tastes like green pepper), and 'harsh-ness' means – in general – that grapes were harvested not fully ripe (the stalks and seeds *are* green), so that at the same time I feel the green in my mouth and I see the green 'behind' the wine.

But let us see what it means, in practice, to describe playing with synaesthesia.

Can one Say 'Mineral' or 'This wine is round'?

The term 'mineral' is used by many tasters, most often as a typical descriptor of fine white wines such as a Riesling. Let us get into the shoes of the novices. To recognise the sense of terms like 'mineral' it is necessary that we agree, first among ourselves, on *what* we are talking about. That means grasping, describing, the descriptor. This issue has taken on an international dimension especially since, as in the United States, it has sparked a lively debate about the concept of 'minerality'.

On 6 May 2007, an article titled 'Talk Dirt to Me', in the 'Style' section of the *New York Times*, with a foreground picture of a rock in a bottle of wine, invited readers to treat this mysterious concept with scepticism. Text and picture continued the argu-ments set out six months before in the magazine *Wine and Vines* (Wine Communications Group, California), with an article by Tim Patterson entitled 'Inquiring winemaker: the myths of minerality'. Here, in summary, is the author's thesis:

> Fruit and oak have their place in great wine, but the top prize among wine attributes probably goes to minerality – the expression of rocks and soil in the aromas and flavours that end up in the glass. But for all its desirability and status, minerality is only vaguely defined and not well understood. In fact, the one thing we do know is that it has very little to do with minerals.

The author's purpose was to deconstruct the mineral as a concept at the basis of a sort of theory, perhaps of interest, but which has not much to do with the sense of that taste.[6] However, Patterson is right when he says that 'minerality is only vaguely defined', and this also applies to some in Europe who do not believe in the myth. This is interesting because it seems to confirm, unlike other popular descriptors appreciated as qualities, that 'minerality' rests in a sort of limbo, near the limits of the relationship between language and the world.

But what is minerality? Many tasters include it within the domain of descriptors, in terms of both the smell and the aroma in the mouth. This means that they are able to recognise what they call minerality with their senses – which presupposes, from a practical point of view, that they know how to describe the descriptor (Brochet and Dubordieu 2001). So I asked some of these tasters to describe this sensation that everyone considers, as they themselves have confirmed, 'one of the most difficult to describe'.

Sometimes, talking about cheap but good white wines, I was told that it refers to

> A shade that slips from stone to mineral salts [. . .] a subtle, fresh, airy and slightly wrinkled note of sapidity, not brackish [. . .] a feeling that roughly recalls the sensation that remains on the lips, as when we were kids and directly drank from a bottle of water with frizzina or idrolitina added.[7]

Another kind of description refers to a particular environmental sense: 'it's like in the mountains, after a heavy rain, when the sun comes out and everything evaporates, then you feel the wet rock, the metal, the carbolic acid.' A sense of 'crystalline and ferrous' is also one of the items often used to describe minerality: 'it recalls the feeling you get in the mountains, when you drink from a stream and your lips touch the stones on which the water is flowing'; or 'it is close to the sense you feel drinking from the tap of a public source, such as a mountain village, a clean but ferrous feeling joined to that of a water that seems made of stone' – for many, tasting the wines from the Saar in the Mosel region, this stone is slate.

Finally, among the most common descriptions, related to complex wines such as Riesling or Chablis:

I would say mainly the slight sensation of flint and steel, surely not dusty nor too dry, on the move between moist and dry. The feeling you get sniffing a flint-lock, or rather a steel that fails to light.

The flintstone . . . I mean pyrites, or even better the chert used for weapons. Imagine smelling the flintstone, first heated by the sun and afterwards dipped in cold water; then put the two sensations together.

Now, these descriptions may be significant not only for their poetic or evocative quality (though useful), but also for the fact they are periphrases which invoke the idea of synaesthesia – and therefore they work well as practical and body-reflexive discourse. Hearing them during a tasting, novices can really recognise the notes of mineral and then record their sense of this perception. For tasters, to describe a descriptor constitutes a *practical method* (Garfinkel 1967).

Another example may show the language game by synaesthesia in relation to a descriptor of textural qualities that are very difficult to describe, for instance the 'round' character of a wine. For a serious taster there are only two possibilities: avoiding this word or using it with a describable sense. Knowing how to describe the term has become a sort of social necessity, perhaps because (even more than others) this adjective triggers both popular curiosity and suspicion about tasters' language.

Some scholars have observed that, in the United States, 'integrated' is often used as synonymous with 'round' and 'complete' (Costello 2006). Here we are dealing with a wine that lacks nothing, whose components (odours, flavours, taste) are well embedded in a sort of community in which they live peacefully, having resolved any potential conflicting relationships. However, it is still unclear what this community has to do with 'round'. At first popular only in France, the term has caught on in the New World after being authorised by authorities like Émile Peynaud and Ann Noble. Nevertheless, an aura of suspicion still hangs over the word because it tries to depict a feeling that many tasters do not quite know how to define. Normally, someone employing it means that the wine – usually red – is very balanced, at least as regards the relationship between two components, acidity and tannin, which 'are very delicate in the mouth, blunt or softened, barely perceptible'. So, 'round' corresponds to a set of adjectives such as 'soft, smooth, embracing, uniform' but, above all, to the sense derived from feeling a certain behaviour of the wine in the mouth.

Without going into all the descriptions gathered, what seems to me the most effective is this: 'the sensation of wine's movement, smooth and plastic, seamless and without interruption, effort, clash, angularity, jumps and gaps – as if the wine is a sphere which finds in the tongue and palate its natural environment to perch and roll'. As well as being effective as a practical discourse, this allusion to 'sphere' is important since it captures, inter alia, one of the ways in which wine is metaphorically conceived, which is through the sensory imagination of forms. According to the most authoritative contributions in the field, the ideal and cherished form of a wine is precisely 'the sphere', seeing that it represents the *locus* in perfect balance (Peynaud 1983). Hence, at the other end of this line of sensory imagination, there are wines that (for some experts) are like 'a star in the mouth'.

> Wine that is not integrated is far easier to describe than wine that is. One can taste and talk about the 'points' of acidity or tannin or oak – like a *star* in the mouth. By comparison, an integrated wine presents itself like a *sphere* in the mouth. So round, so harmonious that one cannot easily fasten onto any single component, sensorily or intellectually. (MacNeil 2001, 4)

In short, wine tasters – and wine writers – are people who really taste shapes.

By Way of Conclusion

The limits on speaking about synaesthesia mean the limits of language concretely used to know wine. These limits are those that language games, metaphors and periphrasis aim to overcome. The activity of tasting itself is an inner game that redraws these limits, turning them into boundaries to work on. The sense of synaesthesia and its description – dis-joined, then re-joined – is one of the two key elements of this ongoing work. The other lies in the search for a new vocabulary, and in the attempt to expand the one we have. But the acquisition of this vocabulary – if it is fruitful – implies playing with synaesthesia. So this phenomenon in wine can be seen as a reflexive and ongoing product of the relationship between biochemical sensations, language practices and the practice of language in order to learn how to use it to talk about this relationship (e.g. by descriptions of descriptors).

The synaesthete-wine taster resorts to descriptions that imply a form of imagination, also based on memories of life experiences, and then on experiences of a life that maybe still has to be lived. They re-live in the mouth something similar to what they have already sensed in other situations of contact with the world, using hands and body for knowing that world. We re-live and taste behaviour, shapes, sights, places and colours. We see again in our mouth something similar to what has touched the skin of our body, such as atmospheric conditions, a bathe in a stream, a storm in the mountains, and so on.

But observed from a practical point of view, the real character of synaesthesia lies not in the poetic imagination of the descriptions. The most important thing is that these descriptions really work in order to sense the wine.

In the end, incorporating synaesthesia reflexively and contributing to the extension of appropriate vocabulary corresponds to a collective 'demand for happiness' and being 'in the creative *flow*' (Csikszentmihalyi 2002) of tasting. Having direct experience of it means to be invested with a 'sense of transition' (Howes 1991). The result of this work, therefore, is to live ourselves, an activity that opens up to the world, in the wine tasted as well as in the world of everyday life. Synaesthesia means to sense multiple worlds together.

In tasting a wine we experience a criss-crossing between a world imagined, a déjà-world, and a world yet to be explored. So playing with the un-speakable – the *sublime* – has this last implication: a wish to travel, to live more closely the worlds in which we live and where we might live – thanks to the wine!

Notes

1 My observations are based on a multi-sited ethnographic research (tasting courses, wine festivals, wine-tastings, international wine competitions, wine auctions, and participant observations of practices in vineyards and cellars) carried out in the last seven years, not in Italy alone, and on the collection of more than a hundred interviews, about fifty recorded tastings, and innumerable conversations between professionals, wine makers, wine growers, wine judges and wine lovers (Navarini 2015). Ethnography means participation, so that the research saw me passing from layman to novice wine taster, and from wine taster to novice wine judge. In this sort of career, I came to know wine lovers of the Old and New World, but also tasters from other countries. Particularly the conversations with these 'others' helped me in dealing with this 'wish to discover' as a cosmopolitan – maybe universal – issue related to synaesthesia.

2 For example, in approximately 1,300 pages of the monumental *Encyclopedia of Neuroscience* (Academic Press, 2009), the word appears only once, on p. 595, in an article on 'Substance Abuse and Dependence', merely pointing to the fact that 'Hallucinogens can produce an altered state of perception, including synesthesia (mixing of sensory modalities; e.g. "I feel orange")'.

3 Aromas or flavours are the olfactory sensations collected in the mouth (via the retro-nasal organ), while perfumes or scents are those perceived by the nose, the glass held still after being swirled. Perfumes and scents are odours, with an implicit positive connotation.

4 Discussing the problem of a vocabulary of wine, arguably too expanded in the last thirty years (Garrier 2005), would take us beyond the limits of this essay. Anyway, it should be noted that animal smells (e.g. 'sweating horse') have also found a place in this lexicon (typically to define defects or imperfections, such as an attack of *Brettanomyces*).

5 *Spirito di Vino*, 49 (2012), 65.

6 Specifically, his job is to dismantle the myth of *terroir* as it has long been celebrated in trade-marketing between France and United States, namely the 'theory' that soils *have* the same flavours which can be found in wines made with grapes grown in these soils.

7 Powder solutions (sodium bicarbonate, malic acid, tartaric acid) used for home-making sparkling water, popular in Italy in the sixties and seventies.

References

Aitchison, J. (1999) 'Tasting Terms and Linguistics', in J. Robinson (ed.), *The Oxford Companion to Wine* (Oxford: Oxford University Press), p. 395.

Aitchison, J. (2003) *Words in the Mind: An Introduction to the Mental Lexicon* (Oxford: Blackwell).

Barr, A. (1992) *Wine Snobbery: An Exposé* (New York: Simon and Schuster).

Brochet, F. and Dubordieu, D. (2001) 'Wine descriptive language supports cognitive specificity of chemical senses', *Brain and Language*, 77: 187–96.

Burnham, D. and Skilleas, O. M. (2008) 'You'll never drink alone: Wine tasting and aesthetic practice', in F. Allhoff (ed.), *Wine and Philosophy: A Symposium on Thinking and Drinking* (Oxford: Blackwell), pp. 157–71.

Caro, G. (ed.) (1990) *De l'alcolisme au bien boire*, vol. 1 (Paris: L'Harmattan).

Colman T. (2008) *Wine Politics* (Berkeley: University of California Press).

Costello, C. (2006) 'Toward an Integrated Discourse of Wine' (Senior Honors Thesis, Department of Comparative Studies, Ohio State University).

Csikszentmihalyi, M. (2002) *Flow: The Classic Work on How to Achieve Happiness* (London: Rider).

Cytowic, R. E. (1993) *The Man Who Tasted Shapes: A Bizarre Medical Mystery Offers Revolutionary Insights into Reasoning, Emotion, and Consciousness* (New York: Putnam).

Cytowic, R. E. (1995) 'Synesthesia: Phenomenology and Neuropsychology. A Review of Current Knowledge', *Psyche*, 2/10 (July), *http://psyche. cs.monash.edu.au/v2/psyche-2-10-cytowic.html/*

Dilworth, J. (2008) 'Mmmm . . . not Aha! Imaginative vs. analytical experiences of wines', in F. Allhoff (ed.), *Wine and Philosophy: A Symposium on Thinking and Drinking* (Oxford: Blackwell), pp. 81–94.

Engen, T. (1982) *The Perception of Odors* (New York: Academic Press).

Engen, T. (1987) 'Remembering odors and their names', *American Scientist*, 75: 497–503.

Engen, T. (1991) *Odor Sensation and Memory* (New York: Praeger).

Garfinkel, H. (1967), *Studies in Ethnomethodology* (Englewood Cliffs, NJ: Prentice Hall).

Garrier, G. (2005) *Histoire sociale et culturelle du vin* (Paris: Larousse).

Gluck, M. (2003) 'Wine language. Useful idiom or idiot-speak?', in J. Aitchison and D. M. Lewis (eds), *New Media Language* (London and New York: Routledge), pp. 107–15.

Gluck, M. (2009) *The Great Wine Swindle: How Snobs are Ruining Your Wine* (New York: Gibson Square).

Goode, J. (2008) 'Experiencing wine: Why critics mess up (some of the time)', in F. Allhoff (ed.), *Wine and Philosophy: A Symposium on Thinking and Drinking* (Oxford: Blackwell), pp.137–53.

Goodwin, C. 2003, *Il senso del vedere: pratiche sociali della significazione* [*The Sense of Sight: The Social Practices of Meaning*] (Rome: Meltemi).

Hennion, A. and Teil, G. (2004) 'Discovering Qualities or Performing Taste? A Sociology of the Amateur', in M. Harvey, A. McMeekin and A. Warde A. (eds), *Qualities of Food* (Manchester: Manchest University Press), pp. 19–37.

Howes, D. (ed.) (1991) *The Varieties of Sensory Experience: A Sourcebook in the Anthropology of the Senses* (Toronto: University of Toronto Press).

Johnson, H. (1966/1974) *Wine*, second edn (London: Hodder and Stoughton).

Kandinsky, V. (1911) *Über das Geistige in der Kunst: Inbesondere in der Malerei* (Munich: Piper & Co.).

Lave, J. and Wenger, E. (1991) *Situated Learning: Legitimate Peripheral Participation*. (Cambridge: Cambridge University Press).

Le Breton, D. (2006) *Le saveur du monde. Une anthropologie des sens* (Paris: Éditions Métailié).

Lehrer, A. (1983) *Wine and Conversation* (Bloomington: Indiana University Press).

MacNeil, K. (2001) *The Wine Bible* (New York: Workman Publishing Company).

Melcher, J. M. and Schooler, J. W. (1996) 'The misrembrance of wine past: verbal and perceptual expertise differentially mediate verbal overshadowing of taste memory', *Journal of Memory and Language*, 35: 231–45.

Miller, W. I. (1997) *The Anatomy of Disgust* (Cambridge, MA: Harvard University Press).

Navarini, G. (2015) *I mondi del vino. Enografia dentro e fuori il bicchiere* [*Wine Worlds: An Oenography Inside and Outside the Glass*] (Bologna: Il Mulino).

North, A. C. (2011) 'The effect of background music on the taste of wine', *British Journal of Psychology*, 103/3: 293–301.

Peynaud, É. (1983) *Le goût du vin* (Paris: Dunod).

Rosso, T. (2004) 'Manières de boire. L'apprentissage de la dégustation dans les "bars à vin"', *Socio-anthropologie*, 15: 83–97.

Roubin, R. (1989) *Le Monde des odeurs* (Paris: Méridiens-Klincksieck).

Wittgenstein, L. (1961[1923]) *Tractatus Logico-Philosophicus* (London: Routledge and Kegan Paul).
Wittgenstein, L. (1953) *Philosophical Investigations* (Oxford: Basil Blackwell).

12

Then . . .

Ruth Finnegan
Department of Sociology,
The Open University

What then is this volume about? In other words, what do we mean by the terms plentifully scattered through these chapters, like psychic, sixth sense, the ethereal? What can be meant by the mystical or the infinite dimension(s) of humankind or the transcendental modes in which we live – if we do – beyond time and space?

This volume has scarcely reached a conclusion about these age-old preoccupations of humanity and the terms in which to discuss them. But it is interesting to scrutinise the various ways our authors have approached them. In their chapters we find, dear to the anthropologist's heart, case study informing reflection, reflection curving back to the particular: a productive mix of the empirical and the theoretical. In the realm of the spirit too, *evidence*, not empty speculation, should be to the fore.

What then are we about? If there is no established way of speaking about something how can we approach, let alone investigate or analyse it? If indeed there is an 'it' there at all.

But – the taste of wine exists. There is no standard verbal way of capturing it (many fanciful ways of course, only too likely to undermine the credibility of the real thing). But it is there. Might not that be so of the ethereal, the numinous and similar elusive words too? For sure, there has been fanciful verbiage around such concepts which, again, might seem to undermine their credence. But, any more than for wine or dreams, does nonsense disprove existence – in *some* sense at least?

Furthermore I seem to see that everyone has in this life a tendency to appeal to *something* that transcends his or her daily existence – even if only in trite off-hand phrases like 'think of me on Friday', 'good luck', 'blessings!' or whatever – whether or not it is expressed in metaphorical, abstract words like the infinite, the other, rationality, the subconscious – all words that take us into and beyond ourselves, becoming as well as being. Why would they want to do this if there is *no* basis, however elusive of confused or misunderstood, for their actions?

There is no incontrovertible and universally accepted *evidence* you say (I might do too) for the supra-normal or the spiritual or whatever alternative terms we might prefer. We cannot see it, feel it, hear it – not, at least, in the normal course of things.

The same might be said of many things whose existence we accept on faith: gravity, the unconscious, ethereal dust, black holes, the workings of others' minds.

> Who has seen the wind?
> Neither you nor I;
> But when the trees bow down their heads
> The wind is passing by.
> (Christina Rossetti)

We can speak of their *effects* for sure. But not observe the thing itself (note the parallel). Or again, what of the things that we *know* are there but see only at certain times or from certain perspectives? Think of Lucifer the morning star, unseen once extinguished by the sun's light; the new sap rising in the trees that heralds the spring; landscapes hidden by mist; the yearly orbiting of the earth.

Or again, what of the speculations of scientists before they had the technology to test – to real-ise – their hypotheses? Consider the atoms of Democritus and Lucretius, unseen by them but now known to every schoolchild as an unquestioned part of the material universe? Or the mathematically predicted but unseen planet Neptune, postulated then discovered and now accessible by telescope? Or the once apparently unsupported Copernican theory, now virtually unchallenged, that the earth revolves round the sun

– and so much else that we can now observe for ourselves through the once unknown media of telescope, microscope or scintigraph.

But again – if the evidence of our senses does not give it to us, who are we to presume its reality? We may *wish* to postulate that there must be a something out there beyond ourselves, a something that is not just material. But in what could its here-and-now solidity lie if beyond our five senses? It is too easy just to posit God (or whatever) as the upholder of existence, as the thing that lies behind, and supports, our human senses – as in the celebrated Berkleyan limericks:

> There was a young man who said, 'God
> Must think it exceedingly odd
> > If he finds that this tree
> > Continues to be
> When there's no one about in the Quad.'
> > > (Ronald Knox)

> Dear Sir, Your astonishment's odd,
> I am always about in the Quad;
> > And that's why the tree
> > Will continue to be,
> Since observed by Yours faithfully, God.
> > > (Anon.)

That leads into the maze of epistemology. Though to an extent inescapable (what after all *is* reality? what dream? what the rational?), this is a mire into which, in this volume at least, I have no wish to enter. Better to see how others (serious-minded others, that is) have treated this it – what terms, methods, topics – to see what insight(s) this might bring us. And who better or closer to hand than the experienced and knowledgeable contributors to this volume.

So that is what I will do.

What do our Authors have to Say, and, above All, How do they Say it?

Though none seem to insist on a specific terminology, using their chosen terms mainly in an exploratory rather than definitive-sounding manner, the authors here (and others too) seem content to use a range of what some might regard as dubious or controversial terms.[1] Many of these recur again and again in our chapters.

All, that is, seem happy with dream, dreaming and trance, terms that, with all their difficulties and diversities, they treat seriously and take to refer to something with a definite meaning in human life. There's something more than the everyday here – something outside as it were (here and elsewhere metaphors seem the name of the game). Much the same goes for heightened or altered consciousness, especially though not exclusively through music. So too are references to a sense of wholeness – something more than just the actions of the parts –created and experienced in united action within a group, as in a choir or a jointly performed ritual. Such recurrent terms suggest an agreement, up to a point at least, that there is somehow a reality existent in some dimension that is accessible through such means as prophecy, medimship or, as illustrated earlier, predictive dreaming and at least some kind of a terminology with which to study it.

Another take on it is to consider the *types* of words used. More illuminating than it might at first seem, it is worth giving some attention to the *grammatical* features of the terms used by writers in this general area, including our authors, as they struggle, to convey the qualities of what, for want of another term, I have called 'there'?

Some are clearly nouns (objects), often but not always with spatial connotations: another realm, the far domain, the noosphere, heaven, gateway to the soul, the other world; also transcendental reality, infinity, eternity. Others, probably the commonest form, are adjectives, sometimes adjectives used as nouns, as in 'the spiritual'. Thus, among others, we have psychic, ethereal, sacred, unconscious/ subconscious, transcendental, extrasensory, liminal, enchanted, supe/ supra-natural, extra-ordinary, super-normal, noetic, mesmerising, prophetic, dreamlike, shamanistic, numinous. Some are verbs – I like these best: prophesy, speak/feel/act as a medium/speak in tongues, be possessed, see into eternity/the ether/the future. Some nouns – I like these too – ending in –ation, -ence/-ance have a verbal processual feel to them as well: transcendence, renaissance, incarnation, repentance . . . (we have a lot, it seems, to learn from language and its etymology).

Often it is words in common parlance modified and in a sense deepened, or in other cases perhaps marginalised, by some qualifying prefix, as in extra-ordinary, extra-sensory, super-normal, super-natural, extra-ordinary, ab-normal, trams-formation, transcendence, para-normal, and para-psychology (this last now a recognised academic disciple).

Such prefixes (*para-*, *extra-*, *non-*, *ab-*) may well be ultimately misleading in their implication that these dimensions are somehow alien to humanity: *ab*-normal. The consensus of the authors in this volume would seem to be that such essentially negative connotations take us in the wrong direction. But as with the term 'paralinguistic' in the study of language to indicate such utterances as sobs or sighs or, more radically, gestures, now by many linguists regarded as regular parts of language itself, so too with the terms here. While, if taken literally, they take us in unhelpful directions, they do serve the useful purpose, as with language, of directing attention to aspects that have less often been considered and so can, ultimately, be a way of bringing these aspects into the mainstream. I have not hesitated therefore to make use of such terms from time to time.

The referents these terms lead us to vary. Some are personally experienced *states* – meditation, prayer, awe, being possessed or hypnotised (whether unexpectedly or deliberately), acting – as Guy Hayward describes – as a member of a crowd or a swarm (are we so different from other animals?), being in another realm/dream/ heightened consciousness, entranced, using intuition, drawing on some 'sixth' sense, seeing things *sub specie aeternitatis*. Others refer to *people* endowed either involuntarily or by training with special insight such as priests, saints, angels (Stockhausen's inspiration), poets, shamans, mediums, ghosts, the dead; others again to *process,* often overlapping into a particular *dimension or mode of experiencing*: such as being or feeling psychic, insightful, prophetic, imaginative, intuitive, blown away (a nice metaphor), feeling the vibes, beyond time and space, telepathic, engaged in extra-sensory perception (now enough recognised to have its own acronym: ESP), immersed in the absolute, spooky (Einstein's term – and my mother's), mystic(al), dreaming/dreamlike, entranced.

Somehow readers are expected to use these (seldom defined) words to in some way get it – and perhaps they do. For myself while I think it useful in trying to envisage and identify the many dimensions of there-ness by differentiating these varying aspects, I find I want to conglomerate the different dimensions so that in some way I can see them all – *all* the phases of the verb, of voice, of person, tense, location. They cast different lights, but for appreciating the subject explored here they surely must ultimately, for a *full* awareness of the whole wholeness, be taken together.

Do these varied approaches have anything in common that might together in any way add up to this whole?

Amidst the diversities, what does come through loud and clear, to me at least, is a shared belief in the importance and, yes, the *reality* (in some sense at the very least) of this puzzle-dimension of human living and knowing. It is interesting too that so often the term is less 'knowledge' than '*experience*' (no longer it seems, an excluded term in social science), or rather experienc*ing*, the verb.

The most consistent and, to me, most illuminating set of concepts, even if lacking a consistent succinct terminology, that seems to branch over them all is the idea of *in-betweenness*: in-between not in the sense of an empty hiatus but of simultaneous both-ness, a bridge, a way, a translation/transformation, a complex whole: both a *state-of-being* and a *path*: a ladder to travel up.

So it is both waking and dreaming in Tedlock's double language, the self *and* the other, nature and humanity, here and not-here. All through the volume we have this 'double voicing' as Tedlock well puts it: heaven and earth together, science and spirituality, here and there, up over and down under, this life, this consciousness and another. We continutally meet the idea, if not always the word, of a kind of dual awareness – of reading not so much *in* but, as Tim Ingold well puts it, *between* the lines, a step along a way to a greater insight into our reality, in which it may be as important to travel (with our wits about us) as to arrive .

Here the *trans-* prefix rightly holds sway. Let us recall tran(s)-scendence, trans-lation, trans-it (a going across) and the etymologically cognate trance. We may be reminded too, in echoed musical memory, of the beautiful Latin *transire* expressing the deeply set journey of the dead into their eternal rest in many a Requiem Mass: a trans-formation, a passage from one state to another, a liminal passage across the threshold or, as one funeral service memorably had it, 'he has moved from time to eternity'.

Not that that totally solves the problem of terminology. But perhaps it is in the very lack of terminological standardisation that in a sense the strength lies. For why, in the absence of a publicly accredited terminology (a shocking contrast to the accepted vocabulary and tenets of both established religion and conventional science), have so many people through the world and throughout the ages struggled, sometimes in face of active hostility and worse, to devise all these ways to express themselves if there was *no* reason or them to do so, *no* foundation for their endeavours?

Dreaming

Let us take another strategy for furthering our understanding. A long-tried route for attemting to grasp the meaning of some elusive concept, indeed a method much honed by philosophers, is to turn not to abstract verbal definition but to *ostensive* clarification. In other words, one way to explore the bundle of related meanings that might be in play is to examine concrete examples.

Here then let us look back at the cases considered in this volume. They fall (principally) within the experiences of dreaming, of musicking and of being in some way conscious.

So, using this strategy, let us again essay.

Dreaming would seem the most obvious. It is a taken-for-granted part of everyday life. Even those who think they don't dream or forget their dreams or do not talk about them or believe that dreams don't matter, do not doubt their existence. Most people seem to feel that dreams 'must mean something'. Dreams are accepted as part of normal living.

In many indigenous societies dreaming and waking reality are not separate domains but overlapped experiences: an arena where human beings can come into contact with worlds that are at once natural, social and spiritual. Dreaming can also be used as a way to to gain access to their past and control their future. As Barbara Tedlock and Phyllis Ghim-Lian Chew show, experienced dreamers and mediums can move beyond perceiving dreams as static entities or even mythic texts into a process of sharing and becoming within what could be called 'the poetic landscape of the soul'.

Dreams were taken seriously in the past too, and, as will have emerged from the accounts here, in many cultures of our world. It is true that the subject, much studied in antiquity and the Middle Ages, has in the West (it has always been a focus in eastern philosophy) lost something of its scholarly appeal in more recent centuries with the exception of the late nineteenth-century insights of Freud and Jung. By now however the subject of dreaming is again receiving attention from scholars (there have always been popular manuals – often, but far from invariably, uncritical), and is studied, sometimes under the title of oneirology, in a variety of humanistic and social sciences.

The result is that anthropologists, psychologists, writers of literature, neuro-scientists and historians (among others) have much to say about dreaming and its communicative and thinking power, some of them represented here.[2] They mostly take it that we are here dealing with an experience not to be fully explained just by the dreamer's individual conscious or unconscious experience, but by some mode of tappng into something 'outside' and beyond this, even while they may disagree about what this 'something' can be.

In any case there are now, as in the past, multiple accounts of particular instances of literature, music, scientific theory, and political and military policy having originated in dreams, and of the associations of dreaming with both literature and music, those great, linked, arts of humankind. Who brought up in in a western tradition could forget the dreamlike, mystic

> In Xanadu did Kublai Khan
> A stately pleasure dome decree . . .

and the ever-cursed 'person from Porlock' who interrupted Coleridge's dream-memory of the full poem?

Not so many know, however, that Montezuma was said to have been led by dreams and divination, while the great war leader Winston Churchill insisted, no doubt to his aides' despair, on getting undressed and into bed every afternoon, and it was his dreams that guided his war policies. The same dream-lead was apparently true of both Joan of Arc and Abraham Lincoln. Or again, writers from medieval saints and scholars to Milton in his *Paradise Lost* or, more recently, Mark Twain or, indeed, myself for my *Black Inked Pearl*, have been have been inspired by dreams. So too has some at least of the music of Brahms, Schumann and Paul McCartney. Add to this Tartini's 'Devils Trills' (said to have originated in the devil playing this near-impossible work to him in a dream) and Grant's account, above, of Stockhausen's view of the origin of his compositions. Einstein's celebrated theory of relativity, it is said, and perhaps Newton and Descartes too, were influenced by dreams as much as by this-world everyday science. The image inspiring the revelation of the double helix (the DNA foundation of life), and, at a more mundane level, the invention of the sewing machine is said to have lain in dream.

Classical and medieval authors as well as eastern sages took dreams seriously, if also noting that dreams can be false as well as 'true' (through 'the gates of horn' as against those by 'the ivory gates'). For them, as for many modern scholars, dreams are not so much misleading falsehood as another kind of reality, albeit in a different mode of experience.

For we never totally leave dreams and dreaming. For many people dreaming is the start accepted even by those who are in other respects sceptics as representing *some* kind of entry into another domain of consciousness or being. Dreaming, whether congenial or nightmarish, whether consciously recalled or not, is arguably the nearest and most common approach to 'there', to an entry into another world. For those who have looked closer it proves to be fundamental in the understanding and experience of death, of music and of both shared and individual being. Here indeed is one road to a special mode of consciousness.

So what then is dreaming? We cannot do better than to quote Barbara Tedlock, who brings out the liminal there-not-there nature of this experience:

> The imaginal world of dreaming is located halfway between the external reality of sensual knowing and the interior reality of intuitive understanding . . . The images in this enchanted land, like those reflected in a mirror, are both there and not there. Rather than 'mirroring' the everyday face of ego-consciousness, dreams reflect the shadowy face of the Other within the self.

In practice many people, aware of it or not, make their first steps into the extra-normal realm through dreaming. As I too have learned, late in life, both in my own experience and from my reading, far from mere night-time fantasies to put behind you once the reality of the day dawns, dreams can have repercussions far beyond ordinary expectation. They make up a rich resource in our consciousness with significance beyond the concerns of mundane living in this world. Though not explicitly in the titles of some of the chapters of this volume, dreaming permeates the discussions throughout.

It is the in-betweenness that is so striking: sleeping but not sleeping (I know it well), dreaming but not dreaming, often just as fragments taking the dreamer into the unsayable deep within the self. In a similar way Sufi thinkers have described dreams as not their own but messages from the *barzakh*, that intermediate imaginal realm located between spiritual and bodily existence, the unconscious and conscious, self and other, male and female, the living and the dead: a doorway as in Zuni dreams and many others, into another dimension.

In dreaming above all then it seems, often with even greater immediacy than the experience of death, extra-sensory perception or even music, we humans have long, no doubt forever, had a recognised entry to the entrancing experience and consciousness of the other.

Which brings us to music – or rather to *experiencing* in some way that great art of humanind.

Musicking

Music of some kind or another is a constant theme in human living – a human universal if anything is – so music must, equally, be here. How could it not be so, that experiential dimension of human living that can lift us from the mundane into some dimension of – we know not what? It can be a means of mediating and communicating between our own and other realms, bringing us into conjunction with others as well as leading us out of ourselves into deeper experiencing. Less often considered in conjunction with dreams, conscious experience or telepathy, it necessarily comes to attention here as one of the crucial modes through and in which human beings experience altered, but real, states of consciousness.

Along perhaps with the vibes from ancient or sacred places, the heightened or altered state of human consciousness seems especially associated with the transformative experience of music, whether making, hearing or composing (note the (by now established) verbal form rather than noun of this section's heading). This is an aspect to which musicologistics are nowadays paying more attention, increasingly aware of the association of music with dream, trance and altered consciousness. Music, as the cases in Ruth Herbert's chapter so clearly illustrate, can be an alternative space, taking the listener to somewhere else.

For many people, including myself, music is also critical for a knowledge of self-identity and experiential spirituality, a moving out of oneself into the beyonding ethereal dimensions of life. This seems to apply whether the music favoured is labelled as 'classical', 'folk', 'ethnic' or 'popular'. The related experience of 'trance', a surprisingly under-studied topic,[3] clearly related to music, is, in diverse forms, another worldwide phenomenon – think of medieval saints, 'speaking with tongues', poetic composition, possession, the Fijian spiritual experience of composing sacred dance-songs, the Italian frenzied *tarantella* dancing – playing a significant role in the human creation of 'the other'. As 'entrancement' it also of course recurs as an element in the title and the discussion here.

For composers and some practitioners of music, furthermore, the origin of their music, of their sonic poetry (so closely linked to music) or of their talent, is often felt to come from some supranormal source. Coleridge's dream experience is far from unique, for we hear of countless poems and music created in some variant of trance by their composers. The artist-priest Ernesto Lozada-Uzuriaga's 'epiphany moment' led him suddenly to find, in a biblical text often before read but now for the first time standing out as a 'divine revelation', permission to integrate his *dual* mission of both painting and ministry, while the contemporary poet Daphne Gloag recalls the origin of her cosmic poem *Beginnings*.

> One morning when as an undergraduate I was listening to a lecture on Lucretius' great poem *De rerum natura* ('On the Nature of Things') a crazy idea came to me and didn't go away, and I said later to my friends, 'One day I'm going to write a modern *De rerum natura!*' Last year this was published as a long poem sequence in my third poetry collection (Gloag 2013).[4]

We know too of poetry/song such as Milton's *Paradise Lost* coming from some kind of trance or altered consciousness (overlapping into dream) rather than workaday routines. Siberian epic poets were endowed with a 'mysterious gift bestowed on the person of the singer by a prophetic call from on high' (Chadwick and Zhirmunsky 1969: 332), the lone sailor was tranced in the ether's 'Song's End' before his death (Heaney 2007), St Paul and others experienced their enchanted (as it were) 'Damascene moments' of revelation in some 'somewhere' beyond this world's ways on the road to a revolutionary turn in lives. Inspiration and 'creativity', nowadays topics of much interest,[5] seem often to be the fruit of some kind of other experience rather than from the everyday world we know.

Poetry, close kin to music, can be the same. My *Black-Inked Pearl* (prose-poetry interspersed with song) arrived from somewhere outside me, without conscious thought or planning, downloading itself unbeknown to my conscious self in the trance-like liminal state between sleeping and waking. Though few wish to comment publicly on their experience, I know that I am not the only novelist to experience this. As for the London poet Denise Saul (2012, 2015) poems too arrive from somewhere beyond, ready-made in their appropriate genres, rhythms and sonic assonances. Doubtless this was equally so for Homer's famous sung epics and perhaps the sung-danced lyrics of ancient drama.

The importance of music is well exemplified in the chapters above. Morag Grant digs into the mystical side of a major con-temporary composer whose interests in this area have too often been seen as marginal or irrelevant. For Stockhausen the aim is 'to connect you, the player, to the currents that flow through me, to which I am connected . . . a heightened state of awareness' (Stockhausen 1968, 1969b: 125). Guy Hayward shows how not only flocking birds and schooling fishes – even robots – but human singers too are brought together in a shared, integrated, moment, as one not many organisms. Ruth Herbert's discussion too, based on both wide reading and vivid first-hand statements from active participants in music-listening, brings together the topics of music, entrancement and consciousness. It puts us into first-hand touch with what is, I would argue, the deepest consciousness of all: the shared experience of music.

Dreams play their part here too – we never, it seems, get away from that experiential mode– inspiring composers of the present and past: how could the origin of such heavenly beauty be purely mundane? For the baroque violin virtuoso Tartini, mentioned earlier but so often forgotten, one experience in particular was crucial. His near-unplayable 'Devil's Trills', so the story goes, originated in a pact with the devil who came in a dream to play them to Tartini overnight – and hard enough they were, a movement full of trills ad double stoppings that, forgetting the rest, he still remembered when he awoke. Until Yehudi Menuhin, it is said, Tartini alone could play it – with his six fingered devil-endowed left hand.[6]

It is scarcely surprising then that music has entered as a crucial if puzzling element in the discussion of entrancement and altered consciousness. We often forget Albert Einstein who, asked about the origin of his theory of relativity – the start of modern science – is said to have replied (it may be apocryphal, but is not un-believable: he certainly was, himself, a musician)

> The theory of relativity occurred to me by intuition, and music is the driving force behind that intuition. My parents had me study the violin from the time I was six. My new discovery is the result of musical perception . . . I often think in music. I live my daydreams in music . . . Imagination is more important than knowledge.[7]

With some impressive exceptions,[8] music, as it happens, is less noticed than other dimensions in the context of studies of consciousness; yet there is serious research that well justifies the inclusion of this topic. This treats, among other things, the relation of music to dream-revelation, to healing, to psychic energy, the emotions, our sense of structure and rhythm – outcome of the deepest and most enduring of the human senses, touch-audition. Like dreaming, meditation and the experience-and-return from death, music enables the re-creation of mind and supports the enhanced and altered states of consciousness we term entrance-ment.[9] Chanting too is accepted as carrying deep meaning, widely utilised in healiang, in meditation, in hypnosis, in shamanic trancing. And can we picture any kind of heaven without its trumpets and its choirs of angels?

There is much still to be investigated and understood, but even thus far it becomes clear that music is central if we wish to delineate and integrate new approaches to and dimensions of entrance-ment and the conscious. Music is an aspect rather seldom taken seriously within the burgeoning scientific literature on human consciousness, but is rightly pursued, at least a little, in this volume.

Being Conscious

The term consciousness, though of course not absent, has not been particularly prominent in this volume. Rather, authors have tended to use such words as awareness, knowledge or ways of knowing/ experiencing/perceiving. Yet the concept of consciousness underlies and unites the discussion here. Dreaming, musicking, and altered or heightened awareness are indeed three widespread and over- lapping areas of human consciousness. They have much in common too. Thus the 'entrancing' of consciousness while listening to music (as in Herbert and Hayward), or in memories of the dead (in Pahl and in Jarvinen and Timmonen) share significant features with dreaming and with the synaesthetic, telepathic and dream occur- rences explored here, above all in that property which can be summed up as 'liminality' – doubleness, here-and-not-here, together-separate, outside what we think the everyday experience of time and space.

So then to consciousness.

This is nowadays a keen object of study. There is a plethora of works building on, while at the same time challenging, the insights that have shaped our awareness since the time of Plato and, doubt- less, before: the pre-Socratic philosopher-scientists too had much to say, under one term or another, on this, not least on the impossi- bility of stepping into the same river twice, a concept ('fluidity', 'unpredictability') that is returning in recent scientific and epistemo- logical writing. In the West there has also been a growing awareness of eastern philosophies and their insights into ways of knowing and being. In physical science too there has been a surge of new, sometimes revolutionary, ideas, new ways of appreciating the nature of consciousness.

This last category – innovative scientific theory – is of particular relevance. As I understand it (I am no physical scientist) a number or interrelated developments have taken place over the last century, principally initiated by Einstein's insights into the relativity – the interconnection – of space and time. The linked idea of the *in*- determinacy of matter has been further supported by work in quantum physics and the essentially unpredictable nature of the universe and its elements.[10]

This dealt a blow to the confidence of the twentieth-century science in which it could be assumed that all was already known, or at least in principle knowable and predictable: it was fixed in a material and conquerable universe. The real was what was accessible to our senses, 'data' that could be *measured* – that was what, essentially, gave it existence.

The corollary for the content of this volume is far-reaching. In the first place the universe is no longer seen by all scientists as purely material: measurable, predictable, physical, in the tradition of 'rationality' well delineated in Tim Ingold's chapter above. On the contrary, for many, and not necessarily just those 'religiously' inclined, there is also room for what has come to be referred to as the spiritual, the noetic. Indeed many books now emphasise, often with a slight air of surprise, the convergence of 'science with spirituality'.[11]

Further, consciousness or, perhaps better as suggesting its dynamic quality, *being* conscious or being aware is no longer seen as identical with or reducible to the mind in the sense of a material organ that now, with modern technologies, can be analysed and mapped in exact physical terms. The two may indeed be related, but they are not the same: they exist as equally natural modes of being, equally real but manifest in differing realms of existence.

And if consciousness is a dimension or modality rather than a materially identified entity, why, especially in view of the increasingly prevalent wholeness and 'becoming' concepts – the convergence of all things in nature – should we expect it to be confined just to humans or just to those we normally (in the West) think of as living creatures? Why not also the flowers that the Prince of Wales (ahead of the game) is known to talk to, trees and their roots, the sea, the earth, the universe, all by some contemporary scientists deemed in some way conscious. In fact a series of research works now concur that consciousness runs through all things – animals (little surprise there), plants, the sea, the earth.[12]

This brings us to telepathy (not a perfect term with its implication of discrete messages transmitted across space, but now in common usage), a species of somehow shared experience irrespective of not only space (the usual implication) but sometimes also time. This extended view of consciousness is in keeping with the recent developments in scientific understanding about directing attention to the noetic as much as the material universe: by now there is starting to be a serious, not just a hippy or weirdo, literature on the subject, much of it by psychologists and, more recently, by scientific theorists.[13]

Many people of course do not believe that non-verbal, non-local, non-sentory communicating between people separated by time or space can ever be possible – or at any rate, when asked in public to affirm this position (they may at the same believe or, as many people do, *partially* believe in the efficacy of prayer – which is not so different); certainly everything I and most others have been formally taught since a child would seem to rule it out. And yet we accept, even expect, non-verbal communication between twins, even when apart: not so much 'messages' as a shared awareness and feeling. Is that so different? And if between twins – co-members with us of the human species, after all – why not for others? We know if someone is surreptitiously reading over our shoulder in the underground, or when someone, unseen, is fixing their eyes on us. And is it not claimed that those in dementia may indeed have lost their power to recognise even their nearest and dearest with their conscious minds while their emotional memories (a dimension of consciousness surely) may still be intact? Hence the comfort given by visits from those once – and in that sense still – close to them.

Further, it is well accepted – and proven – that dogs and other close pets know when their owners are coming home or are in danger. Hunting herds, whether of animals or scattered desert bands keep in touch, somehow, non-verbally. And if among them, must it be ruled out elsewhere? Is all this yet another case of shared inter-human consciousness even at a distance? There is something to be said after all, it seems, for the existence of Jung's collective unconscious, Teilhard de Chardin's noosphere, Larry Dossey's one mind, concepts that must now be taken seriously.

A further, related, outcome is that once firm notions of causality are breaking up. It is no longer seen as predominantly one-way or driven by somehow inescapable physical causes, but more a matter, perhaps, of an as yet dimly glimpsed reality already existent 'out there' irrespective of time and space and yet, somehow in ways we cannot understand, reconcilable with free will and changeability – something like a video or a computer programme that has been constructed by human intention and free choice, but now runs the same time after time after time. This seems to raise the possibility that in some profound psychic or spiritual sense there are somehow states existent in some dimension and, accessible through such means as prophecy, mediumship or, as illustrated earlier, predictive dreaming. The curtain that – mostly – conceals them from us is more, or less, thin at different points in our lives: witness our experiences in trance, in dream, music, traces of our inner, conscious-unconscious feeling selves.

And do we not – even psychotherapists and councillors seem to admit the possibility, no the *reality* of this – accept some continuing deep connection between living and dead? It is a relationship that is *different* from that in life but nevertheless, as exemplified in several of the chapters above, continuing and manifested in many people's experience, if only at times of dire crisis, by a recourse to prayer. Have we not all known of at least one such enduring, mutually loving, relationship: between mother and dead child, born or unborn; husband and wife; passionate lovers? Why do we automatically exclude a comparable measure of shared awareness of feeling between the living?

Dreams too – do they not, lead us into come kind of empathetic consciousess of *spiritual* phenomena located neither in the natural or social worlds nor totally within our bodies or minds, nor outside either. As Barbara Tedlock suggests they locate us in a kind of mystic space between the tangible and the intangible; the visible and the invisible; the audible and the inaudible, created in the process of living in and dialoguing with the world.

Here then – and not just in deams – is the experience we have perhaps all had of what is often called heightened or altered consciousness: that particular feeling that comes in the vibes from an ancient or sacred place or building, or on seeing a great work of art; the shivers down the spine from a moving performance; the deep mindfulness of prayer or meditation, specially if shared with others; or the emotional reaction to music where *feeling* rather than intellectual apperception is at a premium. All these are aspects of consciousness, no longer necessarily to be explained only in terms of pathology or medical needs (though they indeed have their place), but also through the insights of both humanist and social scientific scholars – and of 'ordinary people'.

So Who Cares?

A lot of people it seems.

The existence and, at least for the participants, the *reality* of the sacred, shamanistic, supernatural (and suchlik*e* descriptions) has long been assumed as an expected and natural feature of those cultures once called primitive: the far-away and long-ago, non-western spocieties, together with ancient cultures before the European scientific revolution described so perspicaciously by Tim Ingold earlier. Then – and there – scholars found the idea of *wholeness,* pervaded with the sacred, of the spiritual inextricably interlocked with the material, dream with waking, insight and participation with wisdom. There are many examples in this volume. Innumerable humans throughout the ages and across the globe, it seems, have been convinced that there is *something* – a dimension a place, a future – outside and beyond the here and now of everyday life, a something immortal about the human soul. Whence could such a notion, realised in centuries of human experiencing, have come from if with *no* foundation?[14]

But what of here and now? Have we lost that ancient wisdom that in some moods (not all) we yearn for? Or, from another view-point, rightly grown beyond it?

If we look around us, it become obvious that suh a perspective is indeed still common at present, and not just as a subliminal kind of yearning for the unattainable. We can see – if we look – a proliferation of paranormal healers, dream and zodiac interpreters, therapists outside the medical fraternity, 'shamans', religious leaders, prophets, prayer groups – not just quietly continuing but actively offering workshops, courses and retreats for which people are prepared to pay good money. Others turn to the ancient science of astrology in its various forms: the serious study of the stars and zodiac signs, that is – there are also many counterfeit, superficial and perhaps fraudulent, copies in popular magazines and on the web. But in the modern world serious astrology has now graduated as an academic discipline with its own courses, centres of education, scholarly research and professional qualifications.

'Heaven', 'the other world', 'dreaming' and all their puzzles are of widespread interest in the contemporary world both east and west. How should it not be so, with those conundrums and yearnings of the human world? We know that people have been concerned with it, often deeply, both throughout the centuries and, notably, in the present era. In the current generation there is a spectacular involvement with spirituality and religious commitment, a pressing need, it would seem, for today's youth, and the inspiration behind the extremist movements, both 'good', and 'bad' that characterise the modern world. It is an age of searching – for charismatic and Pentecostal experience and for truths and experiences beyond the everyday round. The answers may not be sought in the established religions, rich as, for many people, they are, but in spirituality and emotion and the musical effervescence that often goes alngside. This in turn is often strongly connected to the quest to understand the nature of heaven and, yes, of human consciousness.

Here the contributions to this volume come into their own, for they touch on the here and now of the modern West. And lo and behold, under some terminology or other, the ideas of wholeness, 'becoming', 'the spiritual' and 'shared consciousness' in a realm beyond normal time and place are all there.

So it is scarcely surprising that, even in sceptical Britain, there are now an increasing number of scientific centres devoted to psychic research and allied subjects. There are many more around the world, above all in the United States. Any military force worth its salt is interested in remotely controlled minds. The British army has been researching this for at least fifty years (I know from a friend who was involved but not allowed to tell). The Soviet army spent many roubles on this hush-hush subject, and today – and no doubt for many years – the American military is pouring thousands of dollars into telepathy research and, by now, openly advertising on the internet for researchers.[15]

Senior figures in science and the arts propound its interest, readers flock to their ideas, journals abound with names like *Neuro*-whatever, *Cognitive* this or that, *Parapsychology*, or *Consciousness*. Books and speculations about dreams, reliable and not, throng the internet, books on telepathy and returning from the dead rush into the best-seller lists, studies of telephone telepathy ('I was just thinking of you when the phone went . . .', 'I *knew* it was you phoning before I lifted the receiver, and so did my dog . . .') are recognised in university psychology departments, experiments are conducted with all the greater rigour because of the controversies,[16] and even among the top research fund-givers 'consciousness' has become a fashionable topic for scientific projects.

The fact is that, starting with a few (brave) treatments in the late 1970s, expanding in the 1990s and by now a flood, there are now plentiful detailed studies, anthropological and other, of such topics – all this despite the disapproval of such topics in so many conventional circles and their cold-shouldering by most official fund-givers. In hard-copy books, in communications on the web, in journals and newspapers we can read of the nature and images of dream-carriers; of twin communication; of near-death experiences; of up-to-the-minute research in neuroscience, parapsychology and cognitive studies; of new and, to some, iconoclastic challenges to the long-accepted materialist view of the universe in scientific theory. Naturally there is a fair share of money-grabbers, charlatans and sloppy thinkers too (was it not always so?), but well balanced by the weight of substantive and rigorous research.

And in the interest of each and everyone too. For I would surmise that, explicitly aware of it or not (for many years, student of thinking as I was, I myself was not), *everyone* has in this life some reason to appeal to *something* that transcends his or her daily existence. It may be expressed in (necessarily metaphorical, abstract) words like love, the infinite, the other, the subconscious, God, even 'rationality' – all words that take us into and beyond ourselves – but the ideas and the faith are there. We *all* care.

There are puzzles too, of course, quickly evident as soon as serious discussion arises (often it does not – these ideas and feelings are often just part of the given). Where do dreams and inspiration come from – in-*spir*-ation, that breath, *spiritus*, of life? Or the magic of discovery? What, crucially, might be the answer to the question that Larry Dossey so deliberately poses (2013a, 2013b): seven billion minds – or one? On all these questions innumerable blogs and inquiries testify to the continuing interest: ubiquitous offers, genuine and other, horoscope readings on the web and in weekly magazines, and, nowadays, findings validated by higher-level degrees and quality control. Are the many biographies and autobiographies detailing heavenly contact, hallucinations, or, even, time travel to be taken seriously? Or the insights of non-western religions? What is madness, what sanity?

We care about these issues too.

The terms and concepts built up in the chapters of this volume, complementing the substantive studies now surrounding this area, between them build a powerful case for taking the topic seriously. It is something *worth* caring about. In the face of such studies it is hard to avoid the conclusion that the propensity for what might be called short psychic communication – at any rate participating in dimensions other than the ordinary mundane routines of overtly perceived life – would seem to be, if not, perhaps, directly found among *all* individuals, at the very least a potential in all cultures. And not just in cultures far away or long ago, but activated here and now. This is what not only the field and documentary evidence but also the new wave of scientific thinking would now seem to show us

I would like to think that these many concepts and approaches to some extent conflate into giving us a greater feel for the 'there' in human life, for the mysteries of the universe, becoming not just being, togetherness as well as separation, sensual as well as cognitive – and for Tim Ingold's faceable dragon. A 'dual citizenship'.

Notes

[1] The multiplicity and overlap of terms has even become a kind of topic in its own right. The *Inner Camino* (Hollwey 2014) mentions a round dozen – and that is in English only – while Schwartz 2007 has a full appendix discussing the pros and cons of (some of) the many extant terms (he himself opts for 'nonlocal awareness').

[2] See, among other works, Barrett 2001; Basso 1992; Bulkeley 2009; Burke 1997; Edgar 1999; Ehn and Löfgren 2010 (on daydreaming); Harris 2009; Tedlock1987; Vedfelt 1999; Zangrilli 2012.

[3] Notable exceptions are Rouget 1985 and Clement 2014.

[4] It is not just hindsight on her part: I was sitting beside her in that 1950s Oxford lecture and clearly recall her comment (at the time I didn't believe her, but nonetheless remembered).

[5] For example Csikszetnmihaly 2013; Petit 2014.

[6] Further details and references in Finnegan, forthcoming.

[7] Anon. (2016).

[8] For some notable exceptions, often in unexpected places and thus little noticed elsewhere, see Aldridge 2005; Becker 2011; Berger 2010; Clarke and Clarke 2011; Feld 1992; Finnegan 2016; Janis 2010; Rouget 1985; Sacks 2011; Storr 1997; Stewart 1999; Turner and Bruner 1986; also Barker 1984–9 for the classical Greek theorists.

[9] All nowadays emerging as popular topics of research. See among many other popular and/or academic works Baker 2011; Becker 2004; Clayton and Dueck 2013; Dolan 2013; Douglas 1999; Feld 1992.

[10] Amidst the growing literature, sometimes deliberately cast in popular terms but no less scientifically grounded for that, I have found the following especially helpful: Anon. 2011; Blackmore 2008; Brown and Stenner 2009; Dossey 2013; Edelman and Tononi 2001; Harman 1994; Hemingway 2008; Hoy 2012; Humphrey 1993 Radin 1997; Schwartz 2007; Sheldrake 2010; Targ 2012; Wilber 2000.

[11] See most directly Hoy 2012; also (among others) Beauregard and O'Leary 2007; Carter 2012; Goswami 2001; Harman 1994; Radin 1997, 2006; Targ 2012; Tart 2009.

[12] Buhner 2014; Pollan 2013.

[13] For example Anon. 2012c; Butler 1998, 2012; Goswami 2001; Howes 2011; Playfair 2002; Ullman et al. 1989; Zangrilli 2012. Even the US Defense Department (Anon. 2014a) has become interested and is pouring millions into researching the subject.

[14] Strict evolutionists have indeed produced various contortions about 'survival benefits' and so account for its emergence. But even if there

is something in this (I for one find it such speculations to give no more evidence than the lack they attribute to explanations for religion) and a belief in the numinous (or whatever), seems a very clunky way to ensure survival whether of the fittest or, equally in question, of the unfittest (there must surely, *à l'*Ockham, be simpler mechanisms).

[15] Anon. 2014bs; Drummond and Shachtman 2015.

[16] It is worth noting that the most rigorous form of admired hard-science experimentation systems – double blind tests, statistical analyses – had their origins in the study of psychic phenomena. So too did the admirable science of neurology.

References

Aldridge, David and Fachner, Jorg (2009) *Music and Altered States: Consciousness, Transcendence, Therapy and Addiction* (London: Jessica Kingsley).

Anon. (2009) 'Musicians' dreams', *Music, Mind and Medicine*, June, *http://bigpictureeducation.com/musicians%E2%80%99-dreams/*

Anon. (2011) 'What is consciousness?', *http://gnosticteachings.org/faqs/psychology/1720-what-is-consciousness.html*

Anon. (2012a) 'Telepathy', *en.wikipedia.org/wiki/Telepathy/* (referenced 9 May 2012)

Anon. (2016) 'Einstein's musical practice', *www.quora.com/How-did-Ensteins-musical-practice-inform-his-scientific-work?*

Baker, Felicity (2011) *Voicework in Music Therapy. Research and Practice* (London: Jessica Kingsley).

Barker, Andrew (ed.) (1984–9) *Greek Musical Writings*, 2 vols (Cambridge: Cambridge University Press).

Barrett, Deirdre (2001) *The Committee of Sleep: How Artist, Scientists, and Athletes Use Dreams for Creative Problem-Solving* (Warsaw: Oneiroi Press).

Basso, Ellen et al. (1992) *Dreaming: Anthropological and Psychological Interpretations* (Santa Fe: School of American Research Press).

Beauregard, Marie and O'Leary, Denyse (2007) *The Spiritual Brain* (New York: HarperOne).

Becker, J. (2004) *Deep Listeners: Music, Emotion, and Trancing* (Bloomington: Indiana University Press).

Blackmore, Susan (2008) *Consciousness: A Very Short Introduction* (Oxford: Oxford University Press).

Bland, Eric (2008) 'Army developing "synthetic telepathy"', *www. mindcontrol.se/?page_id=967/*

Brown, Steve D. and Stenner, Paul (eds) (2009) *Psychology without Foundations* (London: Sage).

Buhner, Stephen Harrod (2014) *Plant Intellience and the Imaginal Ream/ Beyod the Doors of Perception into the Dreaming of Earth* (Rochester, VT: Bear and Company).

Bulkeley, Kelly (ed.) (2001) *Dreams: A Reader in the Religious, Cultural, and Psychological Dimensions of Dreaming* (New York: Palgrave).

Bulkeley, Kelly and Adams, Kate (2009) *Dreaming in Christianity and Islam* (New Brunswick: Rutgers University Press).

Bulkeley, Kelly and Bulkley, Patricia (2005) *Dreaming beyond Death: A Guide to Pre-Death Dreams and Visions* (Boston: Beacon Press).

Burke, Peter (1997) 'The cultural history of dreams', in Peter Burke, *Varieties of Cultural History* (New York: Cornell University Press).

Butler, D. E. Z. (2012) *Telepathy Will Change Your Life* (North Charleston, SC: CreateSpace).

Butler, W. E. (1998) *How to Read the Aura and Practice Psychometry, Telepathy and Clairvoyance* (Merrimac, MA: Destiny).

Carter, Chris (2012) *Science and the Afterlife Experience: Evidence for the Immortality of Consciousness* (Rochester, VT: Inner Traditions).

Clarke, David and Clarke, Eric (eds) (2011) *Music and Consciousness: Philosophical, Psychological and Cultural Perspectives* (Oxford: Oxford University Press).

Clayton, Martin and Dueck, Byron (2013) *Experience and Meaning in Music Performance* (Oxford: Oxford University Press).

Clement, Catherine (2014) *The Call of the Trance* (London: Seagull).

Csikszetnmihaly, Mihaly (2013) *Creativity. The Psychology of Discovery and Invention* (New York: Harper Perennial).

Dolan, Eric W. (2013) 'Music and children: the raw story', *Schwartz Report*, 28 July.

Dossey, Larry (2013a) '7 billion minds or one?', *Huffington Post*, 24 October.

Dossey, Larry (2013b) *One Mind: How Our Individual Mind is Part of a Greater Consciousness and Why It Matters* (Carlsbad, CA: Hay House).

Douglas R. (ed.) (1999) *Godel, Escher, Bach: An Eternal Golden* Braid (London: Penguin).

Drummond, Katie and Shachtman, Noah (2015) 'Army preps soldier telepathy push', *www.wired.com/2009/05/pentagon-preps-soldier-telepathy-push/*

Edelman, Gerald M. and Tononi, Giulio (2001) *Consciousness: How Matter Becomes Imagination* (London: Penguin).

Edgar, Iain (1999) 'Dream fact and real fiction: the realisation of the imagined self', *Anthropology of Consciousness*, 10/1: 28–42.

Ehn, Billy and Löfgren, Orvar (2010) *The Secret World of Doing Nothing* (Berkeley: University of California Press).

Feld, Steven (1992) *Sound and Sentiment: Birds, Weeping, Poetics and Song in Kaluli Experience* (Philadelphia: University of Pennsylvania Press).

Finnegan, Ruth (forthcoming) 'Heightened awareness', *International Encyclopaedia of Anthropology*, online.

Goswami, A. (2001) *Physics of the Soul* (Charlottesville, VA: Hampton Roads).

Harman, Willis, with Clark, Jane (eds) (1994) *The New Metaphysical Foundations of Modern Science* (Petaluma, CA: Institute if Noetic Sciences).

Harris, William (2009) *Dreaming and Experience in Classical Antiquity* (Cambridge, MA: Harvard University Press).

Hemingway, Annamaria (2008) *Practising Conscious Living and Dying: Stories of the Eternal Continuum of Consciousness* (Ropley: O Books).

Janis, Byron (2010) *Chopin and Beyond: My Extraordinary Life in Music and the Paranormal* (New York: Wiley).

Moss, Robert (1998) *Dreamgates* (Novato, CA: New World Library).

Moss, Robert (2009) *The Secret History of Dreaming* (Novato, CA: New World Library).

Petit, Philippe (2014) *Creativity* (New York: Riverhead).

Playfair, Guy Lyon (2002) *Twin Telepathy: The Psychic Connection* (London: Vega).

Pollan, Michael (2013) 'The intelligent plant', *New Yorker*, 23 December.

Radin, Dean (1997) *The Noetic Universe: The Scientific Evidence for Psychic Phenomena* (London: Transworld).

Radin, Dean (2006) *Entangled Minds: Extrasensory Experiences in a Quantum Reality* (New York: Paraview).

Rouget, G. (1985) *Music and Trance: A Theory of the Relations between Music and Possession* (Chicago: University of Chicago Press).

Sacks, Oliver (2011) *Musicophilia: Tales of Music and the Brain* (London: Picador).

Sacks, Oliver (2012) *Hallucinations* (London: Picador).

Schwartz, Stephan A. (2007) *Opening to the Infinite: The Art and Science of Nonlocal Awareness* (Buda, TX: Nemoseen).

Schwartz, Stephan A. (2012) 'Nonlocality, near-death experiences, and the challenge of consciousness', *Explore*, 8/6: 326–30.

Schwartz, T., White, G. M. and Lutz, C. A. (eds) (1992) *New Directions in Psychological Anthropology* (Cambridge: Cambridge University Press).

Sheldrake, Rupert (2000) *Dogs that Know when Their Owners are Coming Home and other Unexplained Powers of Animals* (London: Arrow).

Spencer, P. (ed.) (1985) *Society and the Dance: The Social Anthropology of Process and Performance* (Cambridge: Cambridge University Press).

Stake, Robert E. (2005) 'Qualitative case studies', in Denzin and Lincoln.

Stanard, Russell (2003) *Science and the Renewal of Belief* (Radnor, PA: Templeton).

Stewart, R. J. (1999) *The Spiritual Dimension of Music: Altering Consciousness for Inner Development* (Rochester, VT: Destiny Books).

Storr, Anthony (1997) *Music and the Mind* (London: Heinemann).

Synnott, A. (1991) 'Puzzling over the senses: from Plato to Marx', in Howes.

Targ, Russell (2004) *Limitless Mind: A Guide to Remote Viewing and Transformation of Consciousness* (Novato, CA: New World Library).

Targ, Russell (2012) *The Reality of ESP: A Physicist's Proof of Psychic Abilities* (Wheaton, IL: Theosophical Publishing House).

Tart, Charles T. (2009) *The End of Materiality* (Oakland, CA: Harbinger Books).

Tedlock, Barbara (ed.) (1987) *Dreaming: Anthropological and Psychological Interpretations* (Santa Fe: School of American Research Press).

Turner, V. W. and Bruner, E. M. (eds) (1986) *The Anthropology of Experience* (Urbana and Chicago: University of Illinois Press).

Ullman, M., Krippner, S. and Vaughan, A. (1989) *Dream Telepathy* (Jefferson, NC: McFarland).

Vedfelt, Ole (ed.) (1999) *The Dimensions of Dreams from Freud and Jung to Boss, PERLS, and R.E.M.: A Comprehensive Sourcebook* (New York: Fromm International).

Wilbur, Ken (2000) *Integral Psychology: Consciousness, Spirit, Psychology, Therapy* (Boston: Shambhala).

Wilkins, Hubert and Sherman, Harold M. (1951) *Thoughts Through Space: A Remarkable Adventure in the Realm of Mind* (Charlottesville, VA: Hampton Roads).

Williams, David (2012) *The Trickster Brain: Neuroscience, Evolution, and Narrative* (Plymouth: Bucknell University Press).

Williams, S. (2000) *Emotion and Social Theory: Corporeal Reflections on the (Ir)Rational* (London: Sage).

Wilson, E. O. (1975) *Sociobiology: The New Synthesis* (Cambridge, MA: Harvard University Press).

Yates, F. A. (1966) *The Art of Memory* (London: Routledge and Kegan Paul).

Zangrilli, Quirino (2012) 'iDream and telepathy', *Science and Psychoanalysis*, online, *www.psicoanalisi.it/psicoanalisi/psicosomatica/articoli/psomaing1117.htm*

13

Coda

The Jesuit musician-poet Robert Murray once reminded us that we know the origin of all things but three: 'poems and dreams and tears' (Murray n.d.).

And so indeed it seems. In dreaming, in feeling and suffering, in music – what else, as the ancient term *musica* implied, is poetry but sung words? – the veil between ourselves and the world of the spirit is at its thinnest. We glimpse the rising star of dawn fleetingly as it fades, while still knowing fully that beyond our vision of the day, it is still there and will return to our sight. Just so that other world, however we try to describe it, is always with us: seen, unseen, glimpsed only at the periphery but, apprehended or not, a dimension where our dual citizenhip is in constant, real existence.

And so we come back, again, to consciousness, the concept that our present vocabulary has such difficulty in capturing. Perhaps 'heightened sense of awareness or of experience' is the closest, for it is not exactly a state consciously, deliberately undertaken. Elusive as ever, it is perhaps better captured as verb or adverb than as noun: thinking mindfully, sensitively, profoundly, hearing the sound of heaven in one's ears, scenting its aroma in the air, feeling the eternity of the cosmos interlaced in ourselves. It is to live in the domain of the sacred, the psychic, the beyond, becoming as well as being.

The message of this volume must be that of our many modes of being aware of the world of the eternal, the there (or whatever label feels best) is no less real that that of what we call the everyday. It is merely that, as those of the ancient and medieval world knew well, its mode of existence – the in-betweenness of dreaming and feeling – is a different one: parallel and sometimes overlapping or interacting, but different and no less in existence.

The veil between the two is thin for essentially they permeate. By various means in our human existence, many of them discussed in this volume, it is sometimes drawn aside – for an instant, a lifetime, a perpetuity. Among these means most notable is surely our capacity to dream, to encounter the experience and rituals of contact with the dead and the living in that other world that is constantly with us; and, perhaps above all, the human gift, most entrancingly given us, to make and to hear music. Here, it seems, the veil is not only drawn back: it dissolves.

Further Reading

General

Sacred Texts of the World's Religions

Anthropology of Consciousness [journal]

Journal of Consciousness Studies

Blackmore, Susan (2008) *Consciousness: A Very Short Introduction* (Oxford: Oxford University Press).

Humphrey, Nicholas (1995) *Soul Searching: Human Nature and Super-natural Belief* (London: Chatto and Windus).

Radin, Dean (1997) *The Noetic Universe: The Scientific Evidence for Psychic Phenomena* (London: Transworld).

Dreams

Barrett, Deirdre (2001) *The Committee of Sleep: How Artists, Scientists, and Athletes Use Dreams for Creative Problem-Solving* (Warsaw: Oneiroi Press).

Bulkeley, Kelly and Adams, Kate (2009) *Dreaming in Christianity and Islam* (NewBrunswick: Rutgers University Press).

Mavromatis, Andreas (2010) *Hypnagogia: The Unique State of Consciousness Between Wakefulness and Sleep* (London: Thyrsos).

Moss, Robert (2009) *The Secret History of Dreaming* (Novato, CA: New World Library).

Newcomb, Jacky and Richardson, Madeline (2011) *Call Me when You Get to Heaven* (London: Piatkus).

Tedlock, Barbara (ed.) (1987) *Dreaming: Anthropological and Psychological Interpretations* (Cambridge: Cambridge University Press).

Vedfelt, Ole (ed.) (1999) *The Dimensions of Dreams from Freud and Jung to Boss, PERLS, and R.E.M. – A Comprehensive Sourcebook* (New York: Fromm International).

Further Reading

Death/after death

Alexander, Eben (2012) *Proof of Heaven: A Neurosurgeon's Journey into the Afterlife* (London: Piatkus).

Carter, Chris (2010) *Science and the Near-Death Experience: How Consciousness Survives Death* (Rochester, VT: Inner Traditions).

Facco, E. and Agrillo, C. (2012) 'Near-death experiences between science and prejudice', *Frontiers in Human Neuroscience*, 6: 1–32.

Guggenheim, Bill and Guggenheim, Judy (1995) *Hello from Heaven* (New York: Bantam).

Music

Becker, Judith (2004) *Deep Listeners. Music, Emotion and Trancing* (Bloomington: Indiana University Press).

Clayton, Martin and Dueck, Byron (2013) *Experience and Meaning in Music Performance* (Oxford: Oxford University Press).

Clément, Catherine (2014) *The Call of the Trance* (London: Seagull).

Feld, S. (1990) *Sound and Sentiment: Birds, Weeping, Poetics and Song in Kaluli Experience* (Philadelphia: University of Pennsylvania Press).

Rouget, G. (1985) *Music and Trance: A Theory of the Relations between Music and Possession* (Chicago: University of Chicago Press).

Stewart, R. J. (1999) *The Spiritual Dimension of Music: Altering Consciousness for Inner Development* (Rochester, VT: Destiny Books).

Storr, Anthony (1997) *Music and the Mind* (London: Heinemann).

Consciousness and New Scientific Theory

Buhner, Stephen Harrod (2014) *Plant Intelligence and the Imaginal Ream: Beyond the Doors of Perception into the Dreaming of Earth* (Rochester, VT: Bear and Co.).

Dossey, Larry (2013) *One Mind: How Our Individual Mind is Part of a Greater Consciousness and Why It Matters* (Carlsbad, CA: Hay House).

Playfair, Guy Lyon (2012) *Twin Telepathy: The Psychic Connection* (London: Vega).

Pollan, Michael (2013) 'The intelligent plant', *New Yorker*, 23 December, *www.newyorker.com/magazine/2013/12/23/the-intelligent-plant/*

Radin, Dean (2006) *Entangled Minds: Extrasensory Experiences in a Quantum Reality* (New York: Paraview).

Schwartz, Stephan A. (2007) *Opening to the Infinite: The Art and Science of Nonlocal Awareness,* Buda, TX: Nemoseen.

Schwartz, Stephan A. (2012) 'Nonlocality, near-death experiences, and the challenge of consciousness', *Explore*, 8/6: 326–30.

Sheldrake, Rupert (2000) *Dogs that Know when Their Owners are Coming Home and Other Unexplained Powers of Animals* (London: Arrow).

Sheldrake, Rupert (2003) *The Sense of Being Stared At and Other Aspects of the Extended Mind* (London: Hutchinson).

Targ, Russell (2012). *The Reality of ESP: A Physicists Proof of Psychic Abilities* (Wheaton, IL: Theosophical Publishing House).

Van Lommel, Pim (2011) *Consciousness Beyond Life. The Science of the Near-death Experience* (New York: HarperOne).

Wagner, Stephen (2012) 'Twin telepathy: the best evidence', *www.paranormal.about.com/od/espandtelepathy/a/Twin-Telepathy-Best-Evidence.html*

Bibliography

The list of works that I have found most illuminating is naturally a personal and somewhat serendipitous list. But though it is only a selection from a large and daily increasing field it may at least provide a start while at the same time demonstrating that this is no offhand, unresearched and unresearchable field, but one as solid, and with as substantial a literature and research tradition, as any other (it can of course be supplemented by the specialised references at the end of each substantive chapter).

Aldridge, David and Fachner, Jorg (eds) (2009) *Music and Altered States: Consciousness, Transcendence, Therapy and Addiction* (London: Jessica Kingsley).

Alexander, Eben (2012a) *Proof of Heaven: A Neurosurgeon's Journey into the Afterlife* (London: Piatkus).

Alexander, Eben (2012b) 'Proof of heaven, a doctor's experience with the afterlife', *Newsweek*, 10 October.

Allenby, Brad (2013) '"What will " mean in the future?', *Slate*, February.

Anon. (2001) 'Extra sensory perception', *The Economist*, 6 January, 76–7.

Anon. (2009) 'Musicians' dreams', *Music, Mind and Medicine*, June, *http://bigpictureeducation.com/musicians%E2%80%99-dreams/*

Anon. (2011) 'What is consciousness?', *http://gnosticteachings.org/faqs/psychology/1720-what-is-consciousness.html*

Anon. (2012a) 'Magnetic Resonance Imaging', *http://en.wikipedia.org/wiki/Magnetic_resonance* (referenced 7 May 2012).

Anon. (2012b) 'A cloud of dust listens . . .', *www.synthetictelepathy.net/brain-computer-interface/defence-research-nanotechnology-a-cloud-of-dust-listens-to-you/*

Anon. (2012c) 'Telepathy', *en.wikipedia.org/wiki/Telepathy/* (referenced 9 May 2012).

Anon. (2012d) 'Telepathic love therapy', *http://www.vibrational-alchemy.com/telepathic/intro.htm* (referenced 18 May 2012).

Anon. (2013) 'Beans' talk', *Economist*, 6 July.

Anon. (2014a) 'Army developing "synthetic telepathy"'.

Anon. (2014b) 'Pentagon plans for telepathic soldiers', *http://www.dailymail.co.uk/news/article-2127115/Pentagon-plans-telepathic-troops-read-minds-field-years.html*

Atkinson, Paul, Coffey, Amanda and Delamont, Sara (2003) *Key Themes in Qualitative Research: Continuities and Changes* (Walnut Creek, CA: Altamira Press).

Atwater, P. M. H. (2011) *Near-death Esperienes: The Rest of the Story* (Charlottesville, VA: Hampton Roads).

Avramides, Anita (2014) 'The minds of others', *Oxford Philosophy*, 6: 12–13.

Baker, Felicity (2011) *Voicework in Music Therapy: Research and Practice* (London: Jessica Kingsley).

Balda, R. P., Pepperberg, I. M., Kamil, A. C. et al. (eds) (1998) *Animal Cognition in Nature: The Convergence of Psychology and Biology in Laboratory and Field* (San Diego and London: Academic Press).

Barker, Andrew (ed.) (1984–9) *Greek Musical Writings*, 2 vols (Cambridge: Cambridge University Press).

Barker, Andrew (2008) *Greek musical writing* (Cambridge: Cambridge University Press).

Barnouw, E. et al. (eds) (1989) *International Encyclopedia of Communications,* 4 vols (New York and Oxford: Oxford University Press).

Barrett, Deirdre (2001) *The Committee of Sleep: How Artists, Scientists, and Athletes Use Dreams for Creative Problem-Solving* (Warsaw: Oneiroi Press).

Basso, B. (1985) *A Musical View of the Universe: Kalapalo Myth and Ritual Performance* (Philadelphia: University of Pennsylvania Press).

Basso, Ellen et al. (1992) *Dreaming: Anthropological and Psychological Interpretation,* (Santa Fe: School of American Research Press).

Baumann, Gerd (2012) Personal communications.

Beauregard, Marie and O'Leary, Denyse (2007) *The Spiritual Brain* (New York: HarperOne).

Becker, J. (2004) *Deep Listeners: Music, Emotion, and Trancing* (Bloomington: Indiana University Press).

Bekoff, M. and Jamieson, D. (eds) (1996) *Readings in Animal Cognition* (Cambridge, MA: MIT Press).

Berger, Harris (2010) *Stance: Ideas about Emotion, Style, and Meaning for the Study of Expressive Culture* (Middletown, CT: Wesleyan University Press).

Birdwhistell, R. L. (1968) 'Communication', in Sills, vol. 3: pp. 24–9.

Blacking, J. (1976) *How Musical is Man?* (London: Faber and Faber).

Blackmore, Susan (2008) *Consciousness: A Very Short Introduction* (Oxford: Oxford University Press).

Bland, Eric (2008) 'Army developing "synthetic telepathy"', *www. mindcontrol.se/?page_id=967/*

Bland, Kristen (2015) 'A guided tour of MRI, Tallahassie', National High Magnetic Field Laboratory.

Blavatsky, Helena (1888) *The Secret Doctrine* (London: Theosophical Publ. Co.)

Bloch, M. (1998) *How We Think They Think: Anthropological Approaches to Cognition, Memory, and Literacy* (Boulder, CO: Westview).

Bloch, M.(1991) 'Language, anthropology and cognitive science', *Man*, 26: 183–98.

Booker, Christopher (2005) *The Seven Greatest Plots: Why We Tell Stories* (London: Continuum).

Brown, Chip (1999) *A Thousand Miles in the Rain: A Four-Year Journey into Telepathy, Energy, Faith-Healing and Consciousness* (London: Thorsons).

Brown, Steve D. and Stenner, Paul (eds) (2009*) Psychology without Foundations* (London: Sage).

Bryman, Alan (2008) *Social Research Methods*, third edn (Oxford: Oxford University Press).

Buhner, Stephen Harrod (2014) *Plant Intelligence and the Imaginal Ream/Beyod the Doors of Perception into the Dreaming of Earth* (Rochester, VT: Bear and Company).

Bulkeley, Kelly (ed.) (2001) *Dreams: A Reader in the Religious, Cultural, and Psychological Dimensions of Dreaming* (New York: Palgrave).

Bulkeley, Kelly and Bulkley, Patricia (2005) *Dreaming beyond Death. A Guide to Pre-Death Dreams and Visions* (Boston: Beacon Press).

Bulkeley, Kelly et al. (2009) *Dreaming in Christianity and Islam* (New Brunswick: Rutgers University Press).

Burgoon, J. K., Buller, D. B. and Woodall, D. (1996) *Nonverbal Communication: The Unspoken Dialogue*, second edn (New York: McGraw-Hill).

Burgoyne, Thomas (2013 [1888]) *The Science of the Soul and the Stars* (Milton Keynes: Callender Press).

Burke, Peter (1997) 'The cultural history of dreams', in Peter Burke, *Varieties of Cultural History* (Ithaca, NY: Cornell University Press).

Buss, D. (1999) *Evolutionary Psychology: The New Science of Mind* (Boston: Allyn and Bacon).

Butler, D. E. Z. (2012) *Telepathy Will Change Your Life* (North Charleston, SC: CreateSpace).

Butler, W. E. (1998) *How to Read the Aura and Practice Psychometry, Telepathy and Clairvoyance* (Merrimac, MA: Destiny).

Campbell, Joseph (2012 [1968]) *The Hero with a Thousand Faces* (Novato, CA: New World Library).

Camporesi, P. (1989) *Bread of Dreams: Food and Fantasy in Early Modern Europe* (Cambridge: Polity).

Carpenter, E. and McLuhan, M. (eds) (1960) *Explorations in Communication* (Boston: Beacon Press).

Carruthers, M. J. (1990) *The Book of Memory: A Study of Memory in Medieval Culture* (Cambridge: Cambridge University Press).

Carter, Chris (2012) *Science and the Afterlife Experience: Evidence for the Immortality of Consciousness* (Rochester, VT: Inner Traditions).

Chamberlayne, Prue, Bornat, Joanna and Wengraf, Tom (eds) (2000) *The Turn to Biographical Methods in Social Science: Comparative Issues and Examples* (London: Routledge).

Clarke, David and Clarke, Eric (eds) (2011) *Music and Consciousness: Philosophical, Psychological and Cultural Perspectives* (Oxford: Oxford University Press).

Classen, C. (1993) *Worlds of Sense: Exploring the Senses in History and across Cultures* (London: Routledge).

Clayton, Martin and Dueck, Byron (2013) *Experience and Meaning in Music Performance* (Oxford: Oxford University Press).

Clement, Catherine (2014) *The Call of the Trance* (London: Seagull).

Coffey, Amanda Jane (1999) *The Ethnographic Self: Fieldwork and the Representation of Identity* (London: Sage).

Collins, Peter and Gallinat, Anselma (eds) (2010) *The Ethnographic Self as Resource: Writing Memory and Experience into Ethnography* (Oxford: Berghahn).

Connerton, P. (1989) *How Societies Remember* (Cambridge: Cambridge University Press).

Coote, J. and Shelton, A. (eds) (1992) *Anthropology, Art and Aesthetics* (Oxford: Clarendon Press).

Cosgrove, D. and Daniels, S. (eds) (1985) *The Iconography of Landscape* (Cambridge: Cambridge University Press).

Craig, J. C. and Rollman, G. B. (1999) 'Somesthesis', *Annual Review of Psychology*, 50: 305–31.

Crapanzano, V. (1994) 'Réflexions sur une anthropologie des émotions', *Terrain: carnets du patrimoine ethnologique*, 22: 109–17.

Csikszetnmihaly, Mihaly (2013) *Creativity: The Psychology of Discovery and Invention* (New York: Harper Perennial).

Csordas, T. J. (ed.) (1994) *Embodiment and Experience: The Existential Ground of Culture and Self* (Cambridge: Cambridge University Press).

Darwin, C. R. (1872) *The Expression of the Emotions in Man and Animals* (London: John Murray).

Davies, Charlotte (2008) *Reflexive Ethnography: A Guide to Researching Selves and Others*, second edn (London: Routledge).

de Hennezel, Marie (2012) *Seize the Day: How the Dying Teach us to Live* (London: Macmillan).

Denzin, Norman K. and Lincoln, Yvonne S. (eds) (2005) *The Sage Handbook of Qualitative Research*, third edn (London: Sage).

Dewey, J. (1958) *Art as Experience* (New York: Putnam).

Dolan, Eric W. (2013) 'Music and children: the raw story', *Schwartz Report*, 28 July.

Dossey, Larry (2012) 'Savants: what they can teach us', *Explore* (August).

Dossey, Larry (2013a) '7 billion minds or one?', *Huffington Post*, 24 October.

Dossey, Larry (2013b) *One Mind: How Our Individual Mind is Part of a Greater Consciousness and Why It Matters* (Carlsbad, CA: Hay House).

Douglas, M. (1973) *Natural Symbols* (Harmondsworth: Penguin).

Douglas R. (ed.) (1999) *Gödel, Escher, Bach: An Eternal Golden Braid* (London: Penguin).

Dreyfus, Georges and Thompson, Evan (2007) 'Asian perspectives: Indian theories of mind', in Philip David Zelaza and Morris Moscovitch (eds), *Cambridge Handbook of Consciousness* (Cambridge: Cambridge University Press).

Drummond, Katie and Shachtman, Noah (2015) 'Army preps soldier telepathy push', *www.wired.com/2009/05/pentagon-preps-soldier-telepathy-push/*

Edelman, Gerald M. and Tononi, Giulio (2001) *Consciousness: How Matter Becomes Imagination* (London: Penguin).

Edgar, Iain (1995) *Dreamwork, Anthropology and the Caring Professions: A Cultural Approach to Dreamwork* (Aldershot: Avebury).

Edgar, Iain (1999) 'Dream fact and real fiction: the realisation of the imagined self', *Anthropology of Consciousness*, 10/1: 28–42.

Bibliography

Edgar, Iain (2009) 'A comparison of Islamic and Western psychological dream theories', in K. Bulkeley, K. Adam and P. Davis, *Dreaming in Christianity and Islam: Culture, Conflict, and Creativity* (New Brunswick: Rutgers University Press).

Ehn, Billy and Löfgren, Orvar (2010) *The Secret World of Doing Nothing* (Berkeley: University of California Press).

Eliade, M. (ed.) (1987) *Encyclopedia of Religion* (New York: Macmillan).

Fabian, J. (1983) *Time and the Other: How Anthropology Makes its Object* (New York: Columbia University Press).

Facco, Enrico and Agrillo, Christian (2012) 'Near-death experiences between science and prejudice', *Frontiers in Human Neuroscience*, 6: 1–32.

Farrar, Catherine [Ruth Finnegan] (2012a) *The Little Angel and the Three Wisdoms* (Houston: SBPRA).

Farrar, Catherine [Ruth Finnegan] (2012b) *The Wild Thorn Rose* (Milton Keynes: Callender Press).

Farrar, Catherine [Ruth Finnegan] (2012c) 'Dreams and communication revolutions: a personal exploration', *Compaso: Journal of Comparative Research in Anthropology and Sociology*, 3/1: 1–12.

Feld, Steven (1986) 'Orality and consciousness', in Tokumaru and Yamaguti.

Feld, Steven (1989) 'Sound', in Barnouw et al., 4: 101–7.

Feld, Steven (1990) *Sound and Sentiment: Birds, Weeping, Poetics and Song in Kaluli Experience* (Philadelphia: University of Pennsylvania Press).

Finnegan, Ruth (2011) 'Creativity looks at language', in Joan Swann, Rob Pope and Ronald Carter (eds), *Creativity in Language: The State of the Art* (New York: Palgrave Macmillan).

Finnegan, Ruth (2012a) 'Language as talisman: a story of dreaming and waking', *Applied Linguistics*, 101: 16–39.

Finnegan, Ruth (2012b) 'Performance and competence: a fresh look at an old contrast', in Sandra Bornand and Cécile Leguy (eds), *Compétence et performance* (Paris: Karthala).

Finnegan, Ruth (2013) *Communicating*, second edn (London: Routledge).

Finnegan, Ruth (2015) *The Black-Inked Pearl: A Novel* (New York: Garn Press).

Finnegan, Ruth (forthcoming) 'Heightened awareness', *International Encyclopaedia of Anthropology*, online.

Finnegan, Ruth (forthcoming) *The Shared Mind*.

Fodor, G. (1983) *The Modularity of Mind: An Essay on Faculty Psychology* (Cambridge MA: MIT Press).

Fox, Mark (2002) *Religion, Spirituality and the Near-Death Experience* (London: Routledge).

Frey, L. R. (ed.) (1999) *The Handbook of Group Communication Theory and Research* (Thousand Oaks, CA: Sage).

Gans, Eric (1981) *The Origin of Language* (Berkeley: University of California Press).

Gardner, H. (1983) *Frames of Mind: The Theory of Multiple Intelligences* (New York: Basic Books).

Gell, A. (1992) 'The technology of enchantment . . .', in J. Coote and A. Shelton (eds), *Anthropology, Art and Aesthetics* (Oxford: Clarendon Press).

Gillespie, Marie (2012/13) Personal communications.

Gloag, Daphne (2013) *Beginnings and Other Poems* (Blaenau Ffestiniog: Cinammon Press).

Glowczewski, B. (1999) 'Dynamic cosmologies and Aboriginal heritage', *Anthropology Today*, 15/1: 3–9.

Goodale, Melvyn and Milner, David (2005) *Sight Unseen* (Oxford: Oxford University Press).

Goodman, N. (1978) *Ways of Worldmaking* (Hassocks: Harvester Press).

Goswami, A (2001) *Physics of the Soul* (Charlottesville, VA: Hampton Roads).

Gray, P. M., Krause, B., Atema, J., Payne, R., Krumhansl, C. and Baptista, L. (2001) 'The music of nature and the nature of music', *Science*, 291: 52–4.

Greenwood, Susan (2009) *The Anthropology of Magic* (Oxford; Berg).

Griffin, D. A. (1984) *Animal Thinking* (Cambridge, MA: Harvard University Press).

Guggenheim, Bill and Guggenheim, Judy (1995) *Hello from Heaven* (New York: Bantam).

Hammersley, Martyn and Atkinson, Paul (2007) *Ethnography: Principles in Practice* (London: Routledge).

Hanna, J. L. (1979) *To Dance is Human: A Theory of Nonverbal Communication* (Austin: University of Texas Press).

Harman, Willis, with Clark, Jane (eds) (1994) *The New Metaphysical Foundations of Modern Science* (Petaluma, CA: Institute of Noetic Sciences).

Harré, R. (ed.) (1986) *The Social Construction of Emotions* (Oxford: Blackwell).

Harris, William (2009) *Dreaming and Experience in Classical Antiquity* (Cambridge, MA: Harvard University Press).

Heiney, Nicholas (2007) *The Silence at the Song's End* (n.p.: Songsend Books).

Hemingway, Annamaria (2008) *Practicing Conscious Living and Dying: Stories of the Eternal Continuum of Consciousness* (Ropley: O Books).

Henecy, Diane (2008) *The ESP Enigma: The Scientific Case for Psychic Phenomena* (London: Walker & Company).

Hewitt, William (1996) *Psychic Development for Beginners: An Easy Guide to Releasing and Developing Your Psychic Abilities* (Woodbury MN: Llewellyn).

Hirschfeld, L. A. and Gelman, S. A. (eds) (1994) *Mapping the Mind: Domain Specificity in Cognition and Culture* (Cambridge: Cambridge University Press).

Hollwey, Sara and Brierley, Jill (2014) *Inner Camino: A Path of Awakening* (Forres: Findhorn Press).

Horton, Robin and Finnegan, Ruth (eds) (1973) *Modes of Thought: Essays on Thinking in Western and Non-Western Societies* (London: Faber).

Howes, David (ed.) (1991) *The Varieties of Sensory Experience: A Sourcebook in the Anthropology of the Senses* (Toronto: University of Toronto Press).

Howes, David (ed.) (2011) *The Sixth Sense Reader* (Oxford: Berg).

Hull, J. (1997) *On Sight and Insight: A Journey into the World of Blindness* (Oxford: Oneworld).

Humphrey, Nicholas (1993) *Soul Searching: Human Nature and Supernatural Belief* (London: Random House).

Hymes, Dell H. (1964) 'Introduction: toward ethnographies of communication', *American Anthropologist*, 66/6, part 2: 1–34.

Janis, Byron (2010) *Chopin and Beyond: My Extraordinary Life in Music and the Paranormal* (New York: Wiley).

Jaworski, A. (1993) *The Power of Silence: Social and Pragmatic Perspectives* (Newbury Park, CA: Sage).

Jedrej, M. and Shaw, R.(eds) (1992) *Dreaming, Religion and Society in Africa* (Leiden: Brill).

Jones, S., Martin, R. and Pilbeam, D. (eds) (1992) *The Cambridge Encyclopedia of Human Evolution* (Cambridge: Cambridge University Press).

Keane, Webb (2013) 'On spirit writing: materialities of language and the religious work of transduction', *Journal of the Royal Anthropological Institute*, 19: 1–17.

Keil, C. and Feld, S. (1994) *Music Groove* (Chicago: University of Chicago Press).

Keller, Helen (1933) *The World I Live In* (London: Methuen).

Krippner, Stanley and Fracasso, Cheryl (2011) 'Dreams, telepathy and various states of consciousness', *NeuroQuantology*, 9/1: 1–4.

Laderman, C. and Roseman, M. (eds) (1996) *The Performance of Healing* (London: Routledge).

Lang, Andrew (2012 [1898]) 'Anthropology and hallucination', in Andrew Lang, *The Making of Religion* (London: Longmans & Co.).

Layton, R. (1991) *The Anthropology of Art* (Cambridge: Cambridge University Press).

Lock, A. and Peters, C. R. (eds) (1996) *Handbook of Human Symbolic Evolution* (Oxford: Clarendon Press).

Lohmann, Roger Ivar (ed.) (2003) *Dream Travelers: Sleep Experiences and Culture in the Western Pacific* (New York: Palgrave Macmillan).

Lozarianga, Ernesto (2014) Personal communication.

Lutz, C. A. and White, G. (1986) 'The anthropology of emotions', *Annual Review of Anthropology*, 15 :405–36.

Madden, Raymond (2010) *Being Ethnographic: A Guide to the Theory and Practice of Ethnography* (London: Sage).

Mannheim, Bruce and Tedlock, Dennis (1995) (eds) *The Dialogic Emergence of Culture* (Urbana: University of Illinois Press).

Martin, Joel (190908) *Love beyond Life: The Healing Power of After-death Communications* (New York: Dell Publishing Company).

Mavromatis, Andreas (2010) *Hypnagogia: The Unique State of Consciousness Between Wakefulness and Sleep* (London: Thyrsos).

McAdams, S. and Bigand, E. (eds) (1993) *Thinking in Sound: The Cognitive Psychology of Human Audition* (Oxford: Clarendon Press).

Mellor, D. H. (ed.) (1990) *Ways of Communicating* (Cambridge: Cambridge University Press).

Milner, A. David (1998) *The Visual Brain in Action* (Oxford: Oxford UniversityPress).

Mitchell, W. J. T. (1986) *Iconology: Image, Text, Ideology* (Chicago: University of Chicago Press).

Moss, Robert (1998) *Dreamgates* (Novato, CA: New World Library).

Moss, Robert (2009) *The Secret History of Dreaming* (Novato, CA: New World Library).

Murray, Robert (n.d.) *Poems*, unpublished.

Newcomb, Jacky and Richardson, Madeline (2011) *Call Me When You Get to Heaven* (London: Piatkus).

Pepperberg, I. M. (1999) *The Alex Studies: Cognitive and Communicative Abilities of Grey Parrots* (Cambridge, MA: Harvard University Press).

Petit, Philippe (2014) *Creativity* (New York: Riverhead).

Playfair, Guy Lyon (2002) *Twin Telepathy: The Psychic Connection* (London: Vega).

Polanyi, M. (1958) *Personal Knowledge* (Chicago: University of Chicago Press).

Pollan, Michael (2013) 'The intelligent plant', *New Yorker*, 23 December.

Radin, Dean (1997) *The Noetic Universe: The Scientific Evidence for Psychic Phenomena* (London: Transworld).

Radin, Dean (2006) *Entangled Minds: Extrasensory Experiences in a Quantum Reality* (New York: Paraview).

Rée, J. (1999) *I See a Voice: A Philosophical History of Language, Deafness and the Senses* (London: HarperCollins).

Ristau, C. A. (ed.) (1991) *Cognitive Ethology: The Minds of Other Animals* (Hillsdale, NJ: Erlbaum).

Roseman, M. (1988) 'The pragmatics of aesthetics: the performance of healing among the Senoi Temiar', *Social Science and Medicine*, 27: 811–18.

Roseman, M. (1991) *Healing Sounds from the Malaysian Rainforest: Temiar Music and Medicine* (Berkeley: University of California Press).

Rouget, G. (1985) *Music and Trance: A Theory of the Relations between Music and Possession* (Chicago: University of Chicago Press).

Sacks, O. (1991) *Seeing Voices: A Journey into the World of the Deaf* (London: Pan).

Sacks, Oliver (2011) *Musicophilia: Tales of Music and the Brain* (London: Picador).

Sacks, Oliver (2012) *Hallucinations* (London: Picador).

Schiller, F. (1982) *On the Aesthetic Education of Man* (Oxford: Clarendon Press).

Schutz, A. (1951) 'Making music together: a study in social relationship', *Social Research*, 18: 76–97.

Schwartz, Stephan A. (1979) *The Secret Vaults of Time* (New York: Grosset and Dunlap).

Schwartz, Stephan A. (2007) *Opening to the Infinite. The Art and Science of Nonlocal Awareness* (Buda, TX: Nemoseen).

Schwartz, Stephan A. (2012) 'Nonlocality, near-death experiences, and the challenge of consciousness', *Explore*, 8/6: 326–30.

Schwartz, T., White, G. M. and Lutz, C. A. (eds) (1992) *New Directions in Psychological Anthropology* (Cambridge, Cambridge University Press).

Searle, J. R. (1984) *Minds, Brains and Science* (London: BBC Publications).

Sheldrake, Rupert (2000) *Dogs that Know when Their Owners are Coming Home, and other Unexplained Powers of Animals* (London: Arrow).

Sheldrake, Rupert (2003) *The Sense of Being Stared at and Other Aspects of the Extended Mind* (London: Hutchinson).

Sheldrake, Rupert (2010) 'Nonlocality, near-death experiences, and the challenge of consciousness', *Explore*, 8/6: 326–30

Sheridan, Dorothy (2005), 'Researching ourselves? The Mass Observation project', in Ruth Finnegan (ed.), *Participating in the Knowledge Society: Researchers beyond the University Walls* (Basingstoke: Palgrave Macmillan).

Sills, D. L. (ed.) (1968) *International Encyclopedia of the Social Sciences*, 17 vols (New York: Macmillan and Free Press).

Simmel, G. (1924 [1908]) 'Sociology of the senses; visual interaction', in R. E. Park and E. W. Burgess (eds) (1924), *Introduction to the Science of Sociology* (Chicago: University of Chicago Press).

Spencer, P. (ed.) (1985) *Society and the Dance: The Social Anthropology of Process and Performance* (Cambridge: Cambridge University Press).

Stake, Robert E. (2005) 'Qualitative case studies', in Denzin and Lincoln.

Stanard, Russell (2003) *Science and the Renewal of Belief* (Radnor, PA: Templeton).

Stewart, R. J. (1999) *The Spiritual Dimension of Music: Altering Consciousness for Inner Development* (Rochester, VT: Destiny Books).

Storr, Anthony (1997) *Music and the Mind* (London: Heinemann).

Synnott, A. (1991) 'Puzzling over the senses: from Plato to Marx', in Howes.

Targ, Russell (2004) *Limitless Mind: A Guide to Remote Viewing and Transformation of Consciousness* (Novato, CA: New World Library).

Targ, Russell (2012) *The Reality of ESP: A Physicist's Proof of Psychic Abilities* (Wheaton, IL: Theosophical Publishing House).

Tart, Charles T. (2001) *States of Consciousness* (Bloomington, IN: iUniverse).

Tart, Charles T. (2009) *The End of Materiality* (Oakland, CA: Harbinger Books).

Tedlock, Barbara (ed.) (1987) *Dreaming: Anthropological and Psychological Interpretations* (Santa Fe: School of American Research Press).

Tokumaru, Yosihiko and Yamaguti, Osamu (eds) (1986) *The Oral and the Literate in Music* (Tokyo: Academia Music).

Tuan, Yi-Fu (1993) *Passing and Wonderful: Aesthetics, Nature, and Culture* (Washington, DC: Island Press).

Turner, Bob (2012) Personal communication.

Turner, V. W. and Bruner, E. M. (eds) (1986) *The Anthropology of Experience* (Urbana and Chicago: University of Illinois Press).

Ullman, M., Krippner, S. and Vaughan, A. (1989) *Dream Telepathy* (Jefferson, NC: McFarland).

Van Leeuwen, T. (1999) *Speech, Music, Sound* (Basingstoke: Macmillan).

Van Lommel, Pim (2011) *Consciousness Beyond Life: The Science of the Near-death Experience* (New York: HarperOne).

Van Lommel, Pim, van Wees, R., Meyers V. and Elfferich, I. (2001) 'Near-death experience in survivors of cardiac arrest: a prospective study in the Netherlands', *Lancet*, 358: 2039–45.

Vedfelt, Ole (ed.) (1999) *The Dimensions of Dreams from Freud and Jung to Boss, PERLS, and R.E.M.: A Comprehensive Sourcebook* (New York: Fromm International).

Wagner, Stephen (2012) 'Twin telepathy: the best evidence', *http://paranormal.about.com/od/espandtelepathy/a/Twin-Telepathy-Best-Evidence.htm* (referenced 28 May 2012).

Warren, Jeff (2013) 'Enlightenment: is science ready to take it seriously?', *www.jeffwarren.org/column/inscapes3/*

Wentworth, W. W. and Ryan, J. (eds) (1994) *Social Perspectives on Emotion*, vol. 2 (Greenwich, CT: JAI Press).

Wier, Dennis R. (2009) *The Way of Trance* (New York: Strategic Books).

Wilbur, Ken (2000) *Integral Psychology: Consciousness, Spirit, Psychology, Therapy* (Boston: Shambhala).

Wilkins, Hubert and Sherman, Harold M. (1951) *Thoughts Through Space: A Remarkable Adventure in the Realm of Mind* (Charlottesville, VA: Hampton Roads).

Williams, David (2012) T*he Trickster Brain: Neuroscience, Evolution, and Narrative* (Plymouth: Bucknell University Press).

Williams, S. (2000) *Emotion and Social Theory: Corporeal Reflections on the (Ir) Rational* (London: Sage).

Wilson, E. O. (1975) *Sociobiology: The New Synthesis* (Cambridge, MA: Harvard University Press).

Yates, F. A. (1966) *The Art of Memory* (London: Routledge and Kegan Paul).

Zangrilli, Quirino (2012) 'iDream and telepathy', *Science and Psychoanalysis*, online, *www.psicoanalisi.it/psicoanalisi/ psicosomatica/articoli/psomaing1117.htm*

Zeman, A. (2001) 'Consciousness,' *Brain*, 124: 1263–89.

Zukerkandl, V. (1958) *Sound and Symbol: Music and the External World*, tr. Willard R. Trask (Princeton: Princeton University Press).

Index

Center

Index

Milton Kohn 245, 248
mind *see* consciousness; rationality
mindfulness *see* meditation
Misch, Imka 186
Mitchell, S. P. 190–2
modes *see* dreams, paths, senses
Montezuma 245
Moore 190
Morocco 71–5
mental map 131
Mexican wave 198
Mitchell S. D. 194
modern, modernity
modern, modernity 37–60, 250; *see also* science
Moss, Robert 267
Mozart. W. A. 27
Murray, Robert 264
music, musicking 27, 33, 134, 137–9, 163–86, 187–214, 247–50, 268; and daydreams 149–62; and trance 149–62
mystic, mysticism *see* consciousness

Nagy, M. 197
Native American Church 68–9
Nature, book of 46–54
Navajo 68–9
Navarini, Gianmarco 215–35
Nenola, Aili 89
Nettl, Bruno 150–1
New Mexico 75–7
New Zealand 4–6, 17, 18–19, 194
Newton 245
Niwa, H. S. 212
North, A. C. 220

O'Leary, Denyse 159
O'Shaunessy, Arthur 179
objects 2, 24, 33, 91–106 *and passim*
Odin 129
odour 19, 27, 220–2; *see also* senses
Ojibwa 43–5, 52–3, 56–8, 67
Olson, David R. 48, 49

Olst, Van 201
Other, the 69, 74–7 *and passim*; *see also* dream, liminal

Pahl, Kate 91–106
Pahl, Ray 91–2
Pandolfo, Stefania 73–4
Paradise Lost 245, 248
Parker, Robert 217
Partridge, B. 202
paths, to 'there' 21–2; *see also* dream, medium, place, telepathy
Paynaud, E. 234
Pearce, P. 162
Pentekäinen, J. 131
people with special insight 241, 248, 255–6; *see also* medium, prophecy
perfume *see* odour
Peru 67–8
Peters, R. G. 169, 178
Pine, B. J. 162
place, vibes of 26–7; *see also* liminal
Playfair, Guy Lyon 259, 268
poetry, poetic 2, 29, 244, 248, 249; *see also* dream, music, language
Poewe, Karla 69
Pollan, Michael 259, 268
Pollard, A. 106
Potts, W. 198–202, 209, 210
pre-dreams 107–24
presence, of another 24; *see also* telepathy
prophecy 17–24, 49
Purcell 27

Quaker 22
Quiller-Couch, A. 36

Rabinov, R. 104, 267
Radin, Dean 259, 268
radio 27, 181
Rafael, V. L. 143
rationality 37–64; *see also* science
Rawmarsh, Rotherham 99–103

Index